Critical Theory and Pedagogy

⟨COVNTERPOINTS▶⟩

Studies in Criticality

Shirley R. Steinberg
General Editor

Vol. 534

The Counterpoints series is part of the Peter Lang Education list.
Every volume is peer reviewed and meets
the highest quality standards for content and production.

PETER LANG
New York • Berlin • Brussels • Lausanne • Oxford

Douglas Kellner

Critical Theory and Pedagogy

Towards the Reconstruction of Education

PETER LANG

New York • Berlin • Brussels • Lausanne • Oxford

Library of Congress Cataloging-in-Publication Control Number: 2022006788

Bibliographic information published by **Die Deutsche Nationalbibliothek.**
Die Deutsche Nationalbibliothek lists this publication in the "Deutsche
Nationalbibliografie"; detailed bibliographic data are available
on the Internet at http://dnb.d-nb.de/.

ISSN 1058-1634
ISBN 978-1-4331-9460-3 (hardcover)
ISBN 978-1-4331-9459-7 (paperback)
ISBN 978-1-4331-9457-3 (ebook pdf)
ISBN 978-1-4331-9458-0 (epub)
DOI 10.3726/b19638

© 2023 Peter Lang Publishing, Inc., New York
80 Broad Street, 5th floor, New York, NY 10004
www.peterlang.com

Table of Contents

Foreword

STEVE GENNARO AND JEFF SHARE

For more than half a century Douglas Kellner has helped shape the critical consciousness of academics, students, media critics, and activists. His writings have called for critical engagement with media, information, and technology, what he has termed "critical media literacy" (CML). He asserts the need to redesign public education to include CML with critical analysis and production, taught through dialogical Freirean pedagogy that engages students as co-constructors in the learning process. In the same way that Kellner himself once occupied John Dewey's desk while a graduate student at Columbia University in New York in the 1960s, he has always believed in the Deweyian notion of the democratic potential of education and the responsibility of the education system to serve the people as centers for civic engagement and social justice, and not ideological indoctrination that perpetuates inequality, injustice, and oppression.

After earning his PhD at Columbia, Kellner spent several years studying in Europe with many of the academic giants of the time, from Ernest Bloch to Jacques Derrida. In 1969, he met Herbert Marcuse, a moment that changed his life, leading him to write numerous articles and books about Marcuse and upon his death, Kellner became the executor of Marcuse's archives. In the early 1970s Kellner began teaching at the University of Texas at Austin (UTA) where he created one of the longest running public access TV shows called *Alternative Views*. With his co-host, Frank Morrow, they interviewed many of the leading intellectuals and progressives who were ignored by the commercial media. The popularity of this community television show made Kellner a celebrity of the left, as he was often recognized, even on the streets of New York.

During this period while teaching at UTA, Kellner received grants to travel throughout Texas and the Mississippi Delta giving workshops on critical media literacy to high school teachers. It was not enough to teach and produce media, Kellner has also been a prolific author writing almost fifty books and hundreds of articles. After twenty-five years in Texas, Kellner moved to California where he held the George F. Kneller Chair in the Philosophy of Education at the University of California, Los Angeles (UCLA) until his retirement in 2019.

At the time of the publishing of this book, many of the same concerns from Kellner's time as a graduate student in Philosophy at Columbia remain. Capitalism reigns and the divide between the world's richest 2 % and the remaining 98 % widens as digital media mammoths like Google, Amazon, Apple, Facebook, and Microsoft have taken a stronghold on the digital commons and reap the massive economic benefits of globalization, digitization, and yes, even pandemics. According to separate reports by Oxfam and the Institute for Policy Studies, during the first year of COVID 19's global pandemic, the number of people of living in poverty doubled to more than 500 million at the very same time as the world's richest, a mere 2,365 billionaires, witnessed an increase of more than $4 trillion dollars to their wealth. Adding more than 50 % to their global monetary dominance. Of the ten wealthiest people in the world, more than half own media or technology empires: Amazon, Google, Facebook, Microsoft, Oracle and more. Kellner has always recognized the significant power of media and of technology and has spent a lifetime encouraging others to speak to the truth, to challenge the ideology of capitalism and the inequity it produces, and to recognize the liberatory potential of democratic pedagogy.

For more than half a century, Douglas Kellner has continued to write about the importance of political economy and remind us that as technology changes, the need to understand and question the means of production in media, and now digital media, remains of utmost importance. Kellner's writings invite us to connect our understanding of current media and technology to a public pedagogy and civic engagement that at its core equals and underpins participatory democracy. Critical Media Literacy is social justice. It is pedagogy as lived out and experienced by many and not just by few. It is a necessity for understanding our past and a fundamental requirement to our democratic future. Critical Media Literacy and the reconstruction of Education are an important part of Douglas Kellner's legacy, and this collection of essays stands as a reminder for us all—that our struggle is far from over and we have the tools at our disposal to name the word and the world that surrounds us.

Steve Gennaro is a Lecturer in the Department of Humanities, York University, Toronto. He is the co-editor of *Selling Youth* (2010) and co-editor of *Youth and Social Media* (2021). He regularly publishes in areas relating to the philosophy of technology and critical media studies of youth, identity and politics.

Jeff Share teaches in the School of Education and Information Studies at the University of California, Los Angeles and co-authored with Douglas Kellner (2019), *The Critical Media Literacy Guide: Engaging Media and Transforming Education.*

CHAPTER ONE

Toward a Critical Theory of Education

It is surely not difficult to see that our time is a time of birth and transition to a new period. The spirit has broken with what was hitherto the world of its existence and imagination and is about to submerge all this in the past; it is at work giving itself a new form. To be sure, the spirit is never at rest but always engaged in ever progressing motion …. the spirit that educates itself matures slowly and quietly toward the new form, dissolving one particle of the edifice of its previous world after the other, …. This gradual crumbling … is interrupted by the break of day that, like lightning, all at once reveals the edifice of the new world. Hegel, *The Phenomenology of Spirit*, (1965 [1807])

As the second decade of the second millennium unfolds, against the backdrop of COVID-19, the human species is undergoing one of the most dramatic technological revolutions in history, one that is changing everything from the ways that people work to the ways that they communicate with each other and spend their leisure time. The technological revolution centers on a removal of time and space as the precedents for education and bears witness to online, blended, hybrid, virtual, AI, and even gamified synchronous and asynchronous options for teaching and learning no longer occupying the periphery of education, but instead now holding steady as normalized educational options. This Great Transformation poses tremendous challenges to educators to rethink their basic tenets, to deploy the emergent technologies in creative and productive ways, and to restructure education to respond constructively and progressively to the technological and social changes now encompassing the globe.[1]

At the same time technological revolution is underway, important demographic and socio-political changes are taking place throughout the world. COVID-19 has left no corner of the world untouched and has altered all forms of daily living on a global scale. The global explosion of COVID-19 provides a reminder of how earlier conceptualizations and critiques of globalization may not have gone far enough to note the true interconnectedness of all peoples on this globe. Early colonization by imperial European nations brought pandemic and death to large segments of the colonized world, as Europeans imported deadly diseases throughout the colonized world. Ironically, this time the pandemic came from a former colonized part of the globe, so that the COVID-19 pandemic can be seen as revenge of the colonized world, just as the pandemic can be seen as the revenge of nature for slaughtering animals in monstrous conditions of mass production and mechanized killing to feed hungry humans.[2]

In this context, as Gennaro noted in 2010, our definition of globalization needs to be expanded to account for "the movement, interaction, sharing, co-option, and even imposition of economic goods and services, cultures, ideas, ideologies, people's lives and lived experiences, food, plants, animals, labor, medicine, disease, learning, play, practices, and knowledge(s) across time and space(s) previously thought to be impossible or at the very least improbable."[3] Furthermore, the Black Lives Matter and other liberation movements brought into perspective the very real challenge of providing equitable access to people from diverse races, classes, and backgrounds to the tools and competencies to succeed and participate in an ever more complex and changing digital world despite institutions that have institutionalized and normalized their very oppression.[4]

In this chapter, I propose developing a critical theory of education for democratizing and reconstructing education to meet the challenges of a global and technological society. This involves articulating a metatheory for the philosophy of education and providing a historical genealogy and grounding of key themes of a democratic reconstruction of education which indicates what traditional aspects of education should be overcome and what alternative pedagogies and principles should reconstruct education in the present age. Education has always involved colonization of children, youth, the underclasses, immigrants, and members of the society at large into the values, behavior, labor skills, competitiveness, and submission to authority to serve the needs of white, patriarchal capitalism and to transmit the ideologies that Marx and Engels saw as the "ruling ideas of the ruling class" (1978), and which bell hooks (1994) reminds us also includes the ruling ideas of white men and colonization of the subjects of education into White, Patriarchal Capitalism.

The decolonization of education thus necessarily involves critique of dominant ideologies, pedagogies, and the current organization of education, to be replaced by what Freire calls "the pedagogy of the oppressed" (1970). This project includes developing multiple critical literacies as a response to digital technologies and developing critical pedagogies to meet the challenges of globalization, multiculturalism, and institutionalized racism, classism, and sexism, while promoting radical democratization to counter the trend toward the imposition of a neo-liberal business model on education. In addition, a democratic and intersectional reconstruction of education needs to build on and synthesize perspectives of classical philosophy of education, Deweyean radical pragmatism, Freirean critical pedagogy, poststructuralism, and various critical theories of gender, race, class, sexuality, ethnicity, disability, indigeneity, and more, while criticizing obsolete idealist, elitist, and antidemocratic aspects of traditional concepts of education.

While in much of the world hunger, shelter, and basic literacy are necessary requirements for survival, in a globalized world it is important to project normative visions for education and social transformation that could be used to criticize and reconstruct education and society in a variety of contexts. Great strides have been made towards basic global education since the introduction of the United Nations Convention on the Rights of the Child in 1989, where UNICEFs millennium goals of extending education to all witnessed a rise in global schooling by across the first twenty-five years of the UNCRC.[5]

The last decade has witnessed a push from UNCIEF to extend rights of the child to high school access globally, and more recently to push for global access to STEM (Science technology, engineering, and mathematics) programming and job opportunities for girls and girls of color.[6] Our project requires critical awareness that we are reflecting positions of theorists in the overdeveloped world, and that in different parts of the world education will be reconstructed in various ways depending on the exigencies of the system and possibilities for democratic transformation of education and society.[7] Nonetheless, now is the time to reflect on the philosophy of education, to consider what might be constructed as a critical theory of education and radical pedagogy, and to articulate a vision of how education could be reconstructed and democratized in the present age to serve as an instrument of democratic social transformation.

Critical Theory, Critique, and the Search for the Good Life

In using the term "critical theory," I am building on the Frankfurt School (Kellner, 1989), but the critical theory anticipated and aimed at is broader than the version developed by the German-American exiles from World War II. In the context of theorizing and reconstructing education for the contemporary era, a contemporary critical theory of education would include the tradition of Freirean critical pedagogy, Deweyean pragmatism, British cultural studies, feminism, critical race theory, and other intersectional theories of oppression and resistance, as well as poststructuralism. Our appropriation of the latter would encompass both the critiques of the subject, reason, and liberal democracy in especially French versions of "post" theory (see Best and Kellner, 1991). Yet a critical theory of education would engage and emphasize the critical theories of gender, race, sexuality (i.e., GLBTQ+ theories), and constructions of subjectivity that have developed from a broad range of theoretical formations over the past years. These themes can enrich critical theory and pedagogy and help with the Deweyean project of democratizing and reconstructing education so that aims of social justice and progressive transformation can inform pedagogy and practice.

I thus use the metatheoretical concept of "critical theory" as a cover concept for this project to signify the critical dimension, the theoretical aspirations, and the political dynamics that will strive to link theory and practice. This conception of "critical" is synoptic and wide-ranging encompassing of "critical" in the Greek sense of the verb *krinein*, which signifies to discern, reflect, and judge, and "theory," in the sense of the Greek noun *theoria* which refers to a way of seeing and contemplation. Greek critique is rooted in everyday life and exemplified in the Socratic practice of examining social life, its institutions, values, and dominant ideas, as well as one's own thought and action.

Critique became central to the Enlightenment project of criticizing authority and legitimating one's intellectual and political positions. The Kantian sense of critique, for example, required putting in question all the ideas of reason, morality, religion, aesthetics, and other dominant ideas to see if they could be well-grounded and legitimated. Kantian critique aims at autonomy from prejudice and ill-grounded ideas and requires rigorous reflection on one's presuppositions and basic positions and argumentation to support one's views.

Critical theory also builds on a Hegelian concept of critique (1965 [1807]), as well by criticizing one-sided positions (such as technophobia vs. technophilia) and developing more complex dialectical perspectives that reject and neglect

oppressive or false features of a position, while appropriating positive and emancipatory aspects (see Kellner 2021). Critical theory adopts a Hegelian concept of
theory by developing holistic theories that attempt to conceptualize the totality of
a given field, but that importantly make connections and articulate contradictions,
overcoming idealist or reductive theories of society, nature, humanity, or the world.

A critical theory of education also draws on Marxian critique, stressing the
importance of critique of ideology and situating analysis of a topic like education within the dominant social relations and system of political economy and
society (Marx and Engels, 1978). The Marxian project systematically criticized the
assumptions of an established hegemonic discipline, as in Marx's critique of political economy, and constructed an alternative theory and practice to overcome the
limitations and oppressive features of established institutions and systems of production. Marxian critique involves radical examination of existing ideologies and
practices of education and the need for pedagogical and social transformation to
free individuals from the fetters of consumer capitalism and to help make possible
a free, more democratic and human culture and society.

Marxian theorists like Gramsci (1971) criticized the ways that Italian education and culture reproduced ideologies of the bourgeoisie and fascism and
called for a counterhegemonic cultural project that would encompass alternative institutions from schooling to theater to journalism to help construct a socialist and democratic society. Further, as Charles Reitz has demonstrated (2000),
Herbert Marcuse carried out sustained criticisms of the existing system of education as a mode of reproducing the existing system of domination and oppression
and called for counter-institutions and pedagogies to promote democratic social
transformation and the full development of individuals.[8]

Critical theory must also be intersectional, drawing on Patricia Hill Collins
and Sirma Bilge (2016) who argue that intersectionality is not a theory, but is
also an analytical tool that exposes and makes visible multiple domains of power
and oppression and inequality. Hill Collins and Bilge argue that human rights,
academia, and technology are sites where intersectionality of critical praxis and
critical inquiry occur. Intersectional approaches, like critical theory, are multilay-
ered, multi-perspectival, multidimensional, and include not only what we see/
touch/smell (what our senses reveal), but also what we don't see or cannot see
(implicit ideological structures of power). Intersectional approaches require both
critical inquiry and critical praxis to better understand power in our society and
in our lives. Intersectionality is an approach to exploring social conditions across
multiple layers and converging spaces, beginning with the unique experiences of
the individual and expanding to include how social variables and markers of difference (such as race, class, gender, age, etc.) multiply an individual's privilege or

marginalization, and continuing to note how forms of oppression and discrimination (from racism, sexism, homophobia, etc.) impact individual experiences as they exist inside larger structural forces of history, capitalism, colonialism, misogyny and more. Hence, the concept indicates that the social conditions of each individual are not experienced equally.

Building on this tradition, I am arguing in a critical Hegelian spirit that classical philosophies of education can aid in the project of reconstructing and democratizing education and society, but that certain idealist, elitist, and oppressive elements of classical and contemporary pedagogy must be rejected and re-visited with an intersectional approach. A critical theory of education has a normative and even utopian dimension, attempting to theorize how education and life construct alternatives to the existing society and way of life. Developing a model of education that promotes the good life and the good society could be aided by normative reflection on classical philosophy of education from the Greeks through John Dewey and critics of classical Western education like Ivan Illich and Paulo Freire.

During the epoch of classical Greek culture, philosophy signified love of wisdom (*philo-sophia*) and the practice of philosophy involved *Paideia*, the shaping, formation, and development of human beings and citizens (Jaeger, 1965). In classical Greek culture, it was language and communication that created human beings and philosophical dialogue involved the search for wisdom and the good life. Using the light of reason, the philosopher was to discover concepts for human life and society that would enable the educator to create more fully developed human beings and citizens able to participate in their society.

Thus, for the classical Greek philosophy of education, proper education involved the search for the good life and the good society. Of course, Greek society was built on slavery so only the upper class, and mostly men, could dedicate themselves to education and becoming citizens. In later appropriations of Greek notions of *Paideia*, such as are evident in Werner Jaeger's classical study (1965), the Greek notion of education was idealized and essentialized, leading to idealist notions of culture from the Romantics to those of current conservative elitists who fetishize idealized aspects of culture, elevate the mind over the body, the superior individual over the masses, and thus undermine democracy, citizenship, and the project of developing an egalitarian and just society.[9]

While the Greeks developed a primarily aristocratic conception of education, for the Romans education was shaped to meet the needs of Empire and to expand a universalized conception of culture and citizenship grounded in Roman ideals that provided the basis for the Western conception of *Humanitas*. For classical Roman civilization, education involved transmission of basic skills and literacy training for the plebs, more advanced schooling for the administrative class of the imperial society, and a form of ruling class-oriented tutoring for the patrician class in the codes and manners of Roman aristocracy. Education, then, for the Romans involved *educatio* and *instructio*, in which the teacher was to train children much as the horticulturist cultivated plants and the animal trainer molded animals, even as it aspired to mimic Platonic notions of education within its highest ranks.

Following the Latin roots, the early English conceptions of education involved bringing up and rearing young people from childhood to teach them good manners, habits, and to cultivate the qualities of personality and thought. Curiously, the Latin roots of the English term *education* and *educate* were used to signify the training and discipline of both animals and humans, connotations that lasted into the 19th century when more idealized notions of culture gained currency and the word "education" was restricted to human beings. By the late 19th century, both classicist educational conservatives and progressives like Dewey harked back to the Latin term *eductio*, to enrich and legitimate their pedagogical projects. However, as E.D. Hirsch (1988) and Ivan Illich (1981) have both noted, modern progressives made an unfortunate conflation of the term *eductio* (signifying a moving out, leading, or stretching forth) with the Roman pedagogical term *educo*, which meant either nourishment or training. The result was an idealized version of Western education in which the teachers were to draw out or educe innate human potentials, a tradition pointing back towards Plato and the Greeks and Roman classics.

The classical ideals of education remain important insofar as they aim at the forming of more developed human beings and what Cicero conceived of as the citizen and "political philosopher." The latter embodied and disseminated humane values and tolerance, and whose wide-ranging knowledge was directed towards the regulation and construction of a public space that accorded with civic values and not towards the ivory tower of theoretical abstraction. To the degree that classical ideals of education articulated a vision of humanity as being capable of transcending itself and reshaping itself and its world is a positive heritage, as is the emphasis on the cultivation of unrealized human potentials, a utopian dimension later brought out by the philosopher Ernst Bloch (1986).

The classical ideals also speak to the ethical duty that any citizen has toward its community and notions of political virtue that would later influence Rousseau and Enlightenment figures. Hence, to the extent that classical education develops pedagogic practices that allow for the greatest release of human potential and cultivation of citizens who will produce a just society, the project counters education contrived to fit students into the existing social system and which reduce schooling to an instrument of social reproduction.

Yet we should recall the elitist and idealist roots of classical education and that *Paideia* and *Humanitas* were used to legitimate slave societies and in the case of the

Romans to promote Empire. Indeed, a study of the classical ideals also underlines for us the ways in which previous models of education have been produced within and as discourses of power and domination. Hence, a radically historicist approach to the philosophy of education does not superficially (or mistakenly) draw upon and reproduce theoretical positions that would otherwise prove problematical, but in the spirit of Ernst Bloch and Walter Benjamin's "redemptive criticism" appropriates and reconstructs ideas from the past to produce critical theories of the present and visions of a better future.

Public Education, Democracy, and Pedagogies of the Oppressed

A similar dialectical approach is relevant for reflection on the idealist notion of education encoded in the German *Bildung* tradition, itself connected to an idealized version of Greek *Paideia*, which intended education to shape and form more fully realize human beings. Both Hegel and Marx shared this tradition, with Hegel stressing the formation and development of spirit as a historical and educational process that properly formed students to work through and appropriate tradition as one's own, while criticizing and moving beyond it. Marx, however, was inspired by a vision of socialism as producing more realized many-sided human beings and envisaged in his early writings, a la Schiller, the education of all the senses as an important dimension of becoming a human being (Marx and Engels, 1978: 88 ff.)—a theoretical position taken up by Marxists like Marcuse.

In their 1848 "Communist Manifesto," Marx and Engels made liberation of the working class from bourgeois education and expanded public education for the working class one of their major demands, offering as a key measure to constructing socialism: "Public education of all children free of charge. Elimination of children's factory labor in its present form. Combination of education with material production, etc. etc." (Marx and Engels, 1978: 490). Of course, the infamous "etc. etc." signals the Marxist philosophy of education that was never fully developed, although one could argue that free public education was a key demand of Marxian socialism. Crucially, Marx and Engels wanted to "rescue education from the influence of the ruling class" (1978: 487), arguing that education currently reproduces capitalist-bourgeois societies and must be completely reconfigured to produce alternative ones. In the key text "Theses on Feuerbach," the young Marx wrote: "The materialist doctrine that humans are products of circumstances and upbringing, and that, therefore changed humans are products of other circumstances and changed upbringing, forgets that it is humans who change circumstances and that it is essential to educate the educator" (1978: 144).

As the 20th century unfolded, it was John Dewey (1995) who developed the most sustained reflections on progressive education, linking education and democracy. Dewey insisted that one could not have a democratic society without education, that everyone should have access to education for democracy to work, and that education was the key to democracy and thus to the good life and good society. Dewey was a proponent of strong democracy, of an egalitarian and participatory democracy, where everyone takes part in social and political life. For Dewey, education was the key to making democracy work, and argued that to intelligently participate in social and political life, one had to be informed and educated to be able to be a good citizen and competent actor in democratic life.

Dewey, like Rousseau, and even more so, was experimental, pragmatic, and saw education as an evolving and experiential process in which one would learn by doing. The term "pragmatism" is associated with Dewey, and in one of its meanings signifies that theory should emerge from practice, that education should be practical, aimed at improving everyday life and society, and that by using the method of trial and error, one could learn important life skills, and gradually improve democratic society and education.

From similar pedagogical perspectives yet from a different historical location of Brazil in the 1960s and following, often in exile, Paulo Freire argued that the oppressed, the underclasses, have not equally shared or received the benefits of education and they should not expect it as a gift from the ruling classes, but should educate themselves, developing a "pedagogy of the oppressed" (1970; 1978;). For Freire, emancipatory education involves subverting the Hegelian master/slave dialectic, in which oppressed individuals undertake a transformation from object to subject, and thus properly become a subject and more fully developed human beings. Responding to the situation of colonization and oppression, Freire's pedagogy of the oppressed involved a type of decolonization, a consciousness-raising (*conscientizacao*), and allowed the educated the right to thematize issues of study, to engage in dialogue with teachers, and to fully participate in the educational process (Freire and Shore 1987).

Developing a "pedagogy of the oppressed" requires the creation of learning-processes that will help individuals improve themselves and create a better life through social transformation and empowerment, rather than conforming to dominant views and values. Freire is famous for his critique of "banking" education and creation of a dialogical pedagogy. Freire perceived that education is often a form of indoctrination, of enforcing conformity to dominant values, and of social reproduction in which one is tutored into submission and acceptance of an oppressed and subordinate status. Therefore, pedagogy of the oppressed must oppose dominant conceptions of education and schooling and construct more critical and emancipatory pedagogies aiming at radical social transformation.

It is interesting that all the classical philosophers of education that we have discussed, as well as Marx and Freire, assume that education is of central importance to creating better, and more fully-realized individuals, as well as a good society, and therefore that philosophy of education is a key aspect of social critique and transformation. Critical philosophies of education provide radical critique of the existing models of education in the so-called Western democracies and provide progressive alternative models, still relevant to our contemporary situation. Many of these philosophies of education, however, work with questionable conceptions of reason, subjectivity, and democracy, and neglect the importance of the body, gender, race, sexuality, the natural environment, and other dimensions of human life that some modern theories failed to adequately address.[10] Consequently, the poststructuralist critique of modern theory provides important tools for a critical theory of education in the present age.

Poststructuralist theories emphasize the importance of difference, marginality, heterogeneity, and multiculturalism (see Giroux 1991 and Freire 1998), calling attention to dimensions of experiences, groups and voices that have been suppressed in the modern tradition. They develop new critical theories of multicultural otherness and difference, which includes engagement with class, gender, race, sexuality, and other important components of identity and life that many modern pedagogies neglect or ignore. Poststructuralists also call for situated reason and knowledges, stressing the importance of context and the social construction of reality that allows constant reconstruction. A critical poststructuralism also radicalizes the reflexive turn found in some critical modern thinkers, requiring individuals involved in education and politics to reflect upon their own subject-position and biases, privileges, and limitations, forcing theorists to constantly criticize and rethink their own assumptions, positions, subject-positions, and practices, in a constant process of reflection and self-criticism (Best and Kellner, 1991, 1997).

Poststructuralist theories have empowered women, people of color, people identifying as GLBTQ+, and others excluded from modern theory and educational institutions. Yet feminist theories of education can also draw upon classical feminism, as well as poststructuralist critique. Mary Wollstonecraft (1988), for example, rethought education after the French revolution to realize the program of the Enlightenment and to make individual freedom, equality, and democracy a reality for men and women. Education in Wollstonecraft's conception involved the restructuring of society, enabling women to participate in business, politics, and cultural life, extending the privileges of education to women (although she tended to neglect the need to educate and uplift working-class men and women). Radicalizing Enlightenment positions, Wollstonecraft argued that women, like men, are human beings who have reason, and are thus capable of education. Moreover, she argued that education is the only way for women to better themselves, that if women do not pursue education they cannot be emancipated, they cannot be participants in society, they cannot be equal to men, and thus the Enlightenment project cannot be realized.

More recent feminists, influenced by poststructuralism and multiculturalism, like bell hooks (1994), have stressed the importance of gaining agency and voice for oppressed groups and individuals who have traditionally been marginalized in educational practice and social life. Giving a voice within education and society to individuals in oppressed groups marked by race and ethnicity, sexuality, or class articulates well with the perspectives of Paulo Freire, although he himself did not bring in these domains until his later work. Freire's eventual turn toward more inclusive and articulated gender and multicultural perspectives was in part a response to critique from feminists, critical race theory, people identifying as GLBTQ+, and other oppressed groups, and in part the evolution of Freire's thinking marked a development of his theory as he interacted with more groups and individuals.

Reflecting on the term "intersectionality" in a 2020 *Time Magazine* Feature, scholar and activist Kimberlé Crenshaw, who is credited with introducing the term into our collective lexicon three decades ago, defined intersectionality as "a lens, a prism, for seeing the way in which various forms of inequality often operate together and exacerbate each other. We tend to talk about race inequality as separate from inequality based on gender, class, sexuality or immigrant status. What's often missing is how some people are subject to all of these, and the experience is not just the sum of its parts."[11] Crenshaw noted how the main argument inside of academia and in mainstream media positions intersectionality as identity politics. However, for Patricia Hill Collins and Sirma Bilge (2016), limiting intersectionality to a theory of identity is reductionist and largely used to discredit and devalue the components of intersectionality that are most pressing; namely the component of critical praxis in the need to make social inequality visible for all. There is more than just one "intersectionality," as there are multiple politicized localities which individuals occupy—that is they sit in, they rest in, they lay in, they live in, they stay inside of. These localities are occupied however, in unequal terms and with unequal access which creates the possibilities for alliances of the oppressed across different fields, spaces, identities, and social groupings. Some individuals and groups have more power than others in educational, cultural, and political spaces and so an intersectional alliance of the oppressed can fight for equality and justice across racial, gender, class, and regional lines.

Indeed, the issue of privilege and the life-and-death necessity for access to the fundamentals of health, welfare, education and housing have come to the forefront of discussions in light of the COVID-19 pandemic and Black Lives Matter and other social movements that have created new awareness of oppression and inequality which should inform our struggles for equality, social justice, and the reconstruction of education for the future.

Thus, intersectionality provides a language for inhabitants of multiple localities of oppression and struggle to make visible the politicization of space and the real, lived, and material conditions of the moment. To use intersectionality to explore identity without reducing it to a theory of identity requires locating intersectional dynamics and struggles inside larger philosophical dichotomies of objectivity and subjectivity. Paulo Freire in *Pedagogy of the Oppressed* (1970) argued that one cannot conceive of objectivity without a subjectivity, and that when we talk about oppression, we are speaking about marginalization and the ways in which a society works to provide access to some and deny access to others to the basic necessities of life like education and healthcare. Some of us, like the authors of this piece, based on our privilege, get to be subjects, while others, because of a lack of access and privilege are subjected to being objectified.

It is indeed this unjust world that we seek to change and that drives education to be an instrument of social transformation and justice. Returning to Freire, an objectified person cannot see the oppression they're living in until they see themselves first as an individual who is living inside of oppression. Once an individual sees themselves as a subject, that they embody subjectivity and the possibility of resistance and struggle, an individual can perceive him or herself as a person of worth and value and seek to actualize their potentialities for a better life. Only then can they see the structures around them, which are actively oppressing them, to which they were previously oblivious. So, one should not conceive of objectivity without first acknowledging their own individual subjectivity and the possibilities of collective subjectivities that provide the possibilities for radical action, and that can bring about social justice and democratic and emancipatory social change.

Building on these perspectives enables a philosophy of education to develop more inclusive philosophical vision and to connect education directly to democratization and the changing of social relations in the direction of equality and social justice. Since social conditions and life are constantly changing, a critical theory of education must be radically historicist, attempting to reconstruct education as social conditions evolve and to create pedagogical alternatives in terms of the needs, problems, and possibilities of specific groups of people in concrete situations. Yet philosophical and normative insight and critique is also needed, driving efforts at reconstructing education and society by visions of what education and human life could be and what are their specific limitations in existing societies.

Hence, a critical theory of education involves conceiving a vision of the democratic transformation of education, and in how radicalizing education could help democratize and create a more just and inclusive society. In this section, we have proposed a comprehensive metatheory that draws on both classical and contemporary philosophies of education to comprehend and reconstruct education. The classical critical theory of the Frankfurt School while rigorously engaging in the critique of ideology always drew on the more progressive elements of the most advanced theories of the day, developing dialectical appropriations, for instance, of Nietzsche, Freud, and Weber (Kellner, 1989). Many other Marxian theorists or groups, by contrast, would just be dismissive and rejecting of these "bourgeois ideologies." In the same spirit, we would argue that a critical theory of education should draw on the radical democratic tradition of John Dewey's pragmatism, Freirean critical pedagogy, and intersectional contemporary critical theories of race, gender, class, and sexuality.

Yet a critical theory of education must be rooted in a critical theory of society that conceptualizes the specific features of existing capitalist societies, and their relations of domination and subordination, contradictions and openings for progressive social change, and transformative practices that will create what the theory projects as a better life and society. A critical theory signifies a way of seeing and conceptualizing, a constructing of categories, making connections, mapping, and engaging in the practice of theory-construction, and relating theory to practice.

In the next section, I accordingly deploy a critical theory framework to suggest some transformations in the situation of youth today and the need to reconstruct education and promote multiple critical literacies appropriate to the novel material conditions, transformations, and subjectivities emerging in the contemporary era. Theorizing important changes in the contemporary moment requires broad-ranging and robust reconstructive theories to grasp the changing social and psychological conditions of life in a globalized, high-tech, digitized, multicultural, and highly conflicted world with its intense challenges, problems, and potential (Kellner and Best 2001). Indeed, in this situation of dramatic change in the 21st millennium, radical transformations of education are necessary to create subjects and practices appropriate to an expanding global society, digitized culture, and world of novel identities, social relations, cultural forms, and social movements and struggles.

Changing Life Conditions, Subjectivities, and Identities

Allan and Carmen Luke (2000) have argued that current educational systems, curricula, and pedagogies were designed to produce a laboring subject in the modern era who has become an "endangered species" in the current economic, social, and cultural system. Modern education was constructed to develop a compliant work force which would gain skills of print literacy and discipline that would enable them to function in modern corporations and a corporate economy based on rational accounting, commercial organization, and discursive communicative practices, supported by manual labor and service jobs (Braverman 1974). The life trajectory for a laboring modern subject was assumed to be stable and predictable, progressing through K-12 schooling, universities and perhaps, onto professional schools or higher degrees, to well-paying jobs that would themselves offer lifetime employment, a stable career, and solid identities.

All of this has changed in a global economy marked by constant restructuring, flux and rapid change, and novel material conditions and subjectivities. Students coming into schools have been shaped by years of computer and video games, television, a variety of music technologies and forms, and new spheres of multimedia and interactive cyberculture. Moreover, the steady jobs that were waiting for well-disciplined and performing students of the previous generation are disappearing, while new jobs are appearing in the high-tech sector, itself subject to frenzied booms, busts, and restructuring that is now known as a "gig economy" (Woodcock, 2020). Events such as the September 11, 2001 terrorist attacks on the U.S., ongoing climate crisis, and the current global COVID-19 pandemic, and accompany economic recession, have demonstrated, life in a high-tech and global society is much more complicated, fragile, and subject to dramatic disruptions and transformations than was previously perceived.

There is a fundamental misfit between youth life-experience and schooling, the expectations of an older generation concerning labor and new work conditions, and the previous print-based and organizational economy and culture in contrast to the new digital and multimedia based culture and hybridized global economy. Postmodern theorists have amassed cultural capital theorizing such breaks and ruptures, but have had few positive recommendations on how to restructure institutions like schooling (although there are stacks of books, generally of little worth, on how to succeed in the new economy).[12] Indeed, in the current conjuncture, advocates of neo-liberal business models for education have used the obviously transformative technological revolution to legitimate technology as the panacea and magic cure for problems of education today and to sell corporate technologies and business models as the solution to educational problems (see Kellner 2021).

One of the major challenges for democratizing education today is thus to draw the consequences for restructuring education and democratizing society from reflection on changing life conditions, experiences, and subjectivities in the context of technological revolution and globalization that envisages using technology to democratically reconstruct education and promote progressive social and political change without promoting neo-liberal and capitalist agendas. This task is advanced, I believe, by drawing on the radical critique of schooling and proposals for transforming education and learning found in the work of the late Ivan Illich, who was one of the chief educational gurus of the 1970s and most radical critic of schooling whose work has fallen from view but is still important and should be re-engaged in the present situation.[13]

Ivan Illich's postindustrial model of education contains a radical critique of existing schooling and alternative notions like webs of learning, tools for conviviality, and radically reconstructing education to promote learning, democracy, and social and communal life, thus providing salient alternatives to modern systems (1971, 1973). Illich analyses in detail how modern schooling prepares students for the modern industrial system and how its "hidden curriculum" promotes conformity, bureaucracy, instrumental rationality, hierarchy, competition, and other features of existing social organization. For Illich, modern systems of schooling are no longer appropriate for postindustrial conditions and require radical restructuring of education and rethinking pedagogy. But unlike many of his contemporaries, Illich had a powerful, explicit and prescient analysis of the limits and possibilities of technologies and those strange institutions called "schools".

Illich's "learning webs" (1971) and "tools for conviviality" (1973) anticipate the Internet and how it might provide resources, interactivity, and communities that could help revolutionize education. For Illich, science and technology can either serve as instruments of domination or progressive ends. Hence, whereas big systems of computers promote modern bureaucracy and industry, personalized computers made accessible to the public might be constructed to provide tools that can be used to enhance learning. Thus, Illich was aware of how technologies like computers could either enhance or distort education depending on how they were fit into a well-balanced ecology of learning.

"Tools of conviviality" for Illich are appropriate, congenial, and promote learning, sociality, and community (1973). They are tools in which ends dictate means and individuals are not overpowered or controlled by their technologies (as say, with assembly lines, nuclear power plants, or giant computer systems).

Convivial tools produce a democratic and convivial society in which individuals communicate, debate, participate in social and political life, and help make decisions. Convivial tools free individuals from dependency and cultivate autonomy and sociality. They provide individuals and society with the challenge of producing convivial tools and pedagogies that will create better modes of learning and social life.

Conviviality for Illich involves "autonomous and creative intercourse among persons, and the intercourse of persons with their environment" (1973: 27). Illich proposes a normative dimension to critique existing systems and construct alternative ones using values of "survival, justice, and self-defined work" as positive norms (1973: 13). These criteria could guide a reconstruction of education to serve the needs of varied communities, to promote democracy and social justice, and to redefine learning and work to promote creativity, community, and an ecological balance between people and the Earth. Indeed, Illich was one of the few critics working within radical pedagogy in his period who took seriously ecological issues and critically appraised institutions like schooling, medicine, transportation, and other key elements of industrial society within a broad social, political, economic, and ecological framework. His goal was nothing less than a critique of industrial civilization and a project of envisaging postindustrial institutions of learning, democratization, and social justice.

At a time when many were enamoured of the autonomous power and emancipatory potential of the school, Illich insisted on seeing schools as part and parcel of industrial society and one of the major instruments of its social reproduction. One of Illich's enduring contributions is to see relationships between modern industrial institutions like schooling, production, medicine, transportation and other major sectors of industrial society. To engage with how what goes on in educational institutions we must have far better and more critical self-understandings of what a specific institutions like schooling do in their institutional structure within the broader society, their hidden curriculum and how they engage in social reproduction. Understanding schooling beyond its institutional sites also requires grasping its dialectical relationships to the public pedagogies of media and the street, and the networked civic and social space of the Internet, as well as how schooling relates to the oppressions and operations of workplaces, government institutions, and corporations.

Illich thus provides concrete analyses and a critique of how schooling reproduces the existing social order and is flawed and debased by the defects and horrors of the industrial system. Illich also recognizes that postindustrial society requires certain competencies and that a major challenge is to construct convivial technologies that will improve both education and social life. While he resolutely opposed neo-liberal agendas and was critical of encroaching corporate domination of the Internet and information technologies, Illich's notion of "webs of learning" and "tools of conviviality" can be appropriated for projects of the radical reconstruction of education and learning in the contemporary era. Within this framework, let us consider how the expanding social roles of information and communication technologies require multiple critical literacies and how focusing on the current technological revolution can lead us to rethink learning and reconstruct educational theory and practice.

Expanding Technologies/Multiple Critical Literacies

Prior to COVID 19, schooling in the modern era has been largely organized around the transmission of print literacies and segregated academic knowledges based on a modern division of disciplines into such things as social science, literature, or physical education. The immediate change from classroom learning or school (as a physical entity) to digital spaces around the globe to enforce social distancing and to help combat the spread of COVID-19 in the spring of 2020 though until the editing of this text in summer 2022 has dramatically exposed how the rapidly expanding technologies of information and communication, mutating subjectivities and cultural forms, and the demands of a networked society culture indeed require multiple critical literacies, more flexible subjects, and inventive skills and capabilities. Theorists such as Allan Luke and Carmen Luke and Kellner suggested solutions to these emerging issues almost two decades ago. For the Lukes (2000) and for Kellner (2000, 2002a, 2002b), the solution was to cultivate in the sphere of education multiple literacies, such as media, computer, and information critical literacies that will respond to emergent technologies and cultural conditions and empower students to participate in the expanding high-tech culture and networked society.[14]

Hence, the constant development and mutation of information and communication technologies and new forms of culture, economy, and everyday life require a careful rethinking of education and literacy in response to novel challenges that will involve an era of Deweyean experimental education, trial and error, and research and discovery. Yet a critical theory of education will reject pedagogies and literacies that merely aim at the reproduction of existing capitalist societies and creating capabilities aimed primarily at providing cultural capital put in the service of the reproduction of global capitalism. A critical theory of education with a critical intersectional approach could draw on the reconstruction of neo-Marxian, Deweyean, Freirean, and intersectional critical pedagogies of race, gender, and class to attempt to develop Illichian tools and communities of conviviality and genuine learning that would promote democracy, social justice, and cultivate conceptions of the good life and society for all.

This requires teaching traditional literacies as well as multiple forms of computer, information, and communication literacies that will empower students to develop their potentials, create communities of learning, and work toward democratizing society. As Gennaro argued in 2015, in the same fashion that we teach reading, writing, and arithmetic to our kindergarten aged students, we must actively seek to introduce coding with the same importance, enshrined in curriculum, to children as soon as they enter the school system.[15] If young people are to write themselves into existence, they must be literate in the language of the digital culture, which presides over modern subjectivity in current moment. To be sure, digital literacies are necessary, but they need to be articulated with print literacy, in which multiple critical literacies enable students and citizens to negotiate word, image, graphics, video, and multimedia digitized culture.

In the Hegelian concept of *Geist*, the subject develops through mediations of culture and society in specific historical ways, but encounters contradictions and blockages which are overcome by sublation or *Aufhebung*, i.e., overcoming obsolete or oppressive conditions that are transcended. In a contemporary version of the Hegelian dialectic, the emergent technologies and conditions of postmodern life are producing novel experiences and subjectivities that come into conflict with schooling, itself based on earlier historical subjectivities and congealed institutions, discourses, and practices, modeled on the industrial factory system (i.e., time-parceled segments, staying immobile at a specific site to perform labor, submitting to the discipline of bosses, etc.).

The optimistic Hegelian scenario is that this conflict can be overcome through an *Aufhebung* that sublates (i.e., negates, preserves, takes to higher stage) the positivities in the conflict and negates the obsolete aspects. Put more concretely: when there are contradictions between, say, a print-based curriculum and evolving subjectivities mediated by multimedia, then resolving the contradiction requires going to a higher level; e.g., restructuring schooling to preserve, for instance, the importance of print-based culture and literacy, while developing evolving multiple critical digital literacies.

Hence, restructuring schooling to meet challenges of expanding technologies and emergent social and cultural conditions requires cultivation of multiple critical literacies, tools, and pedagogies to respond to, mediate, and develop in pedagogically progressive ways the technologies and global conditions that help make possible democratized transformative modes of education and culture. Further, following the calls of Marshall McLuhan (1964) and the digerati, education must be transformed to meet the challenges of technological revolution, yet we must also recognize that a globalized world is fraught with growing inequalities, conflicts and dangers, so to make education relevant to the contemporary situation it must address these problems.

Indeed, globalization has been creating growing divisions between haves and have nots, and to economic inequality there now emerge growing information inequalities and gaps in cultural and social capital as well as a growing divide between rich and poor. A transformed democratic education must address these challenges and make education for social justice part of a radical pedagogy, as envisaged by theorists like Marcuse, Illich and Freire, as well as developing eco-pedagogy to address the environmental crises which accompanied the COVID-19 pandemic as I worked on these essays in 2020 and 2021.

Further, decolonizing education (Smith 1999) requires constantly questioning biases of class, race, gender, region, and social positioning to create education appropriate for all individuals in one's society. A radical and decolonizing pedagogy must also engage the difficult issue of overcoming differences, understanding cultures very dissimilar from one's own, and developing a more inclusive democracy that will incorporate marginalized groups and resolve conflicts between diverse groups and cultures. This requires the three dimensionality of intersectionality articulating the differences between a radical pedagogy that employs an intersectional approach and one that does not in terms of depth, with a multi-layered and multi-perspective mode of seeing that grasps alternatives for emancipation and democratization beyond what is immediately visible to us.

This problem of democratizing and decolonizing education is also part of the issue we're having right now in trying to have social discussions around race relations, white privilege, gender and sexual oppression and the structural inequality that exists in the current social moment as we move into a multicultural and diverse future contested by rightwing reactionaries. A lack of multiple perspectives serves as a significant roadblock to those with privilege acknowledging the systemic injustice experienced by marginalized individuals and groups. Life is experienced simultaneously in multiple dimensions, and within multiple relationships of power simultaneously that involve economic, politics, culture, and society, all of which are experienced simultaneously in socially constructing our identities that are constantly reconstructed in social interactions and experiences. This is to say that we are simultaneously gendered, racialized, sexualized, abilitized, culturized, and class-positioned in our social interactions and experience. Further, this process is intensified by new technologies, like iPhones, multiple digital devices, and social media, at a pace faster than any moment previous in human history. So how do we engage with this? How do we take this on?

Critical pedagogy is not just about theory or critical inquiry, but it is also about the real lived experiences of the people. Critical pedagogy must examine the material conditions and changes, as informed by theory and, as reflected upon by individuals as change happens, and across many different venues and dimensions. Crucially, a critical theory seeks to reconstruct education not to fulfill the agenda of capital and the high-tech industries, but to radically democratize education to advance the goals of progressive educators like Dewey, Marcuse, Freire, and Illich in cultivating learning that will promote the development of individuality, citizenship and community, social justice, and the strengthening of democratic participation in all modes of life.

Over the past decades, there has been sustained efforts to impose a neoliberal agenda on education, reorganizing schools on a business model, imposing standardized curriculum, and making testing the goal of pedagogy. This agenda is disastrously wrong, a critical theory of education needs to both critique the neo-liberal restructuring of education and to propose alternatives conceptions and practices. Globalization and technological revolution have been used to legitimate a radical restructuring of schooling and provide radical educators with openings to propose their own models of pedagogy and reconstruction of education to serve democracy and progressive social change. Technological revolution is destabilizing traditional education and creating openings for change. Although one needs to fiercely criticize the neo-liberal model, it is also important to propose alternatives. Thus, one needs to accompany demands for new literacies and a restructuring of education with a program of the democratization of education, as we suggest in our concluding remarks to this chapter.

Toward a Radical Reconstruction and Democratization of Education

In calling for the democratic reconstruction of education to promote multiple critical literacies as a response to emergent technologies and globalization, one encounters the problem of the "digital divide." It has been well documented that some communities, or individuals in privileged groups, are exposed to more advanced technologies and given access to more high-tech skills and cultural capital than those in less privileged communities. One way to overcome the divide, and thus a whole new set of inequalities that mirror or supplement modern divides of class, gender, race, and education, is to restructure education so that all students have access to evolving technologies which they can engage with multiple critical literacies, so that education is democratized, and the very learning process and re-lation between student and teacher is rethought.

The Hegelian Master/Slave dialectic can help characterize relations between students and teachers today in which teachers force their curricula and agendas onto students in a situation in which there may be a mismatch between genera-tional cultural and social experiences and subjectivities. Educators, students, and citizens must recognize this generational divide and work to overcome conflicts and make differences more productive. That is, many students may be more tech-nologically skilled than teachers and can themselves be important pedagogical re-sources. We acknowledge now that much of what we've learned about how to use computers we've absorbed from students and continue to draw upon them both in and out of class to help navigate the new high-tech culture and to devise produc-tive pedagogies and practices for the contemporary era. Democratizing education can be enhanced by more interactive and participatory forms of education and the move to Google Classroom, Microsoft Teams, Zoom, and other technologies in diverse parts of the world for schooling during lockdown and isolations periods in response to the COVID-19 pandemic has illuminated the opportunities for co-constructed learning spaces that technology makes possible—although it also creates problems of access and meeting multiple technological challenges with diverse students and different environments who have differential access to tech-nology, often creating new "digital divides." Building on previous examples such as developing convivial discussion boards on platforms like Moodle, the collective building of websites, on-line discussion, and collaborative computer-based research projects, in the current environment we can use Wikis and shared documents, like Google Docs, to co-create in real time. Blogs and YouTube videos can allow for asynchronous engagement that transcends time and space barriers but still allows for communities of practice. And the aforementioned video conferencing tech-nology has presented the world of online, text- based discussions, with a synchro-nous alternative where "breakout rooms" can place individuals around the globe into small groups for dialogue instantaneously—providing new opportunities for intercultural communication and for global networks of activism—although dif-ferent forms of technology and models of pedagogy will be used in different parts of the world.

In addition, a critical theory of education would envisage merging classroom-based Socratic discussion with computer research and projects that would combine oral, written, and multimedia cultural forms in the process of education without privileging one or the other. Some educators still insist that face-to-face dialogue in the classroom is the alpha and omega of good education and while there are times that classroom dialogue is extremely productive, it is a mistake to fetishize face-to-face conversation, books and print media, or new multimedia. We must be careful not to view the educational process through the same lens of nostalgia with which we often view childhood and youth, since nostalgia as a process of memory can act to depoliticize the inhabitants of memory more than it does to liberate the self of future oppression. Rather, the challenge is to draw upon, in an experimental and supplemental way, all of the dimensions of the traditional educational process into a dialectical conversations with emerging technologies to restructure and democratize education.

Since concrete reconstructions of education will take place in specific local and national contexts, the mix between classroom pedagogy, books and reading print-material, and multimedia and Internet-based education will vary according to locale, age, access to digital technologies, and the needs and interests of students and teachers. The idea behind multiple critical literacies is that diverse and multimodal forms of culture blend in lived experience to form new subjectivities, and the challenge for radical pedagogy is to cultivate subjectivities that seek justice, more harmonious social relations, and ecologically-informed relations with the natural world. Ivan Illich called for education to take ecological problems into account (1971, 1973), and as Richard Kahn argues (2010), the extent of current ecological crisis is such that environmental collapse and disaster faces the current generation if ecological issues are not addressed. These ecological issues ring true to heart of the UN sustainable development goals, and should be embraced by a transformative pedagogy.[16]

A glaring problem with contemporary educational institutions is that they become fixed in monomodal instruction with homogenized lesson plans, curricula, and pedagogy, and neglect to address challenging political, cultural, or ecological problems. As Paulo Freire notes: "One cannot expect positive results from an educational or political action program which fails to respect the particular view of the world held by the people. Such a program constitutes cultural invasion … The starting point for organizing the program content of education or political action must be the present, existential, concrete situation, reflecting the aspirations of the people" (1970, p. 85). A *Pedagogy of the Oppressed* is about simultaneous individual and social awakening through action and reflection to seeing the structural domination in our lives, and then working through theory and reflection towards action and praxis, to overcome oppression and to change the structure and the structural powers at play in our everyday lives.

The development of tools of conviviality and radical pedagogies thus enable teachers and students to break with colonizing and limited models and to engage in Deweyean experimental education. A reconstruction of education could help create subjects better able to negotiate the complexities of emergent forms of everyday life, labor, and culture, as contemporary life becomes more multifaceted and dangerous. More supportive, dialogical, and interactive social relations in learning situations can promote cooperation, democracy, and positive social values, as well as fulfill needs for communication, esteem, and learning.

Whereas modern mass education tended to see life in a linear fashion based on print models and developed pedagogies which broke experience into discrete moments and behavioral bits, critical pedagogies could produce skills that enable individuals to better navigate the multiple realms and challenges of contemporary life. Deweyean education focused on problem solving, goal-seeking projects, and the courage to be experimental, while Freire developed alternative pedagogies and Marcuse and Illich produced oppositional conceptions of education and learning and critiques of schooling. It is this sort of critical spirit and vision to reconstruct education and society that can help produce new pedagogies, tools for learning, and social justice for the present age.[17]

Democratizing education can be enhanced by more interactive and participatory forms of education such as developing convivial list-serves and discussion forums, the collective building of websites with relevant course material, and collaborative computer-based research projects. Yet the restructuring of education also requires cultivating literacy concerning limitations of Internet-based knowledge and the need for library inquiry and accessing books as important pedagogical resources. For learning and teaching, books and print-based materials and multimedia Web—based materials should be seen as supplementary and not as oppositional, in which one is uncritically favored over the other, as some traditionalists privilege print literacy and book culture, while some of our contemporaries excessively celebrate the Internet and cyberculture.

Likewise, critical digital literacies involve understanding the political economy of digital technology and how giant corporations control access to information and structure computer world as described in the work of Robert McChesney (2004, 2013) and Scott Galloway's (2018) *The Four*. In addition, students should know there are biases, including racial, class, and gender biases in the algorithms of search engines as documented by Safiya Umoja Noble (2018) in *Algorithms of oppression: how search engines reinforce racism.*

The development of tools of conviviality and radical pedagogies enable teachers and students to break with problematical and outmoded forms of education and to engage in Deweyean experimental education. A reconstruction of education could help create subjects better able to negotiate the complexities of emergent forms of everyday life, labor, and culture, as contemporary life becomes more multifaceted and dangerous. More supportive, dialogical, and interactive social relations in learning situations can promote cooperation, democracy, and positive social values, as well as fulfill needs for communication, esteem, and learning. Whereas modern mass education tended to see life in a linear fashion based on print models and developed pedagogies which broke experience into discrete moments and behavioral bits, critical pedagogies could produce skills that enable individuals to better navigate the multiple realms and challenges of contemporary life. Deweyean education focused on problem solving, goal-seeking projects, and the courage to be experimental, while Freire developed alternative pedagogies and Illich and Marcuse developed oppositional conceptions of education and learning and critiques of schooling. It is this sort of critical spirit and vision to reconstruct education and society that can help produce new pedagogies, tools for learning, and social justice for the present age.

In This Book

This opening chapter on "Critical Theory and Education" has provided an introduction to the "Historical and Metatheoretical Perspectives" which will inform the studies of this book. The following chapters will, first, provide more detailed presentation of critical pedagogical theories and practices that I find relevant for a democratic and social justice-oriented transformative philosophy of education. Since many critical pedagogies developed by Freire and fellow critical pedagogues and neo-Marxist critical educators throughout the world are influenced by Marxist perspectives, in Chapter 2, I provide a discussion of Marx and Engels on education. By chance, I was hired to teach a yearly course on Marxist philosophy at the University of Texas-Austin in 1973 which I taught for twenty-five years, and during the past twenty-five-plus years that I've been teaching Philosophy of Education at UCLA, I always put Marxian theorists in my seminars, so I felt it was necessary to do a genealogical and historical study of the writings of Marx and Engels on education in the next chapter on "Marxian Perspectives on Educational Philosophy: From Classical Marxism to Critical Pedagogy."

In Chapter Three, I present my perspectives on "Evolving Critical Media Literacy" through discussion of my own encounters with media literacy debates and developments of the past decade and the "Multiple Grand and (God)Fathers" who influenced my own views and analyses of critical media and digital literacies. I present in this chapter some "Critical Reflections on Herbert Marcuse and Education," since Herbert Marcuse's perspectives on education had rarely been focused on, as I note above in the discussion of Marcuse and critical theory, and he is the theorist that I have engaged most deeply over the past decades, as one of my major academic productions was my 1984 book *Herbert Marcuse and the Crisis of Marxism* and I have also edited six volumes of the *Collected Papers of Herbert Marcuse.*

Since my first introduction to critical pedagogy was through Henry Giroux when I entered the field of education in the mid-1990s, Chapter Four engages "Critical Pedagogy, Cultural Studies, and Radical Democracy at the Turn of the Millennium: Reflections on the Work of Henry Giroux." Giroux has continued to this day to be one of the most productive and prolific critical theorists of education, and we share attempts to merge neo-Marxian critical theory with Freirean critical pedagogy and British Cultural Studies which engages the problematics of race, gender, class, and sexuality, and so I present Giroux's ideas and their continued value and relevance for critical pedagogy today.

During the time I have been teaching Philosophy of Education from the mid-90s to the present, U.S. society has witnessed an explosion of technology, social media, and digital devices which have influenced all domains of life. This technological revolution has influenced how students, citizens, and teachers access information, communicate with each other, present themselves to public, and in general live their lives. Accordingly, in Chapter Five I present a chapter co-authored with Rhonda Hammer "Multimedia Pedagogy and Multicultural Education for the New Millennium." Rhonda has been my partner since the mid-1990s and we have done books, articles, and conference presentations together, as well as having participated in each other's classes. Hammer was one of the first critical pedagogues to teach critical media literacy through having her students produce media texts that engage crucial issues of gender, race, class, politics, or their personal lives when she was teaching at the University of Windsor in Canada in the 1990s, and she has continued this practice up to the present in many of her classes at UCLA. The text was written at the beginning of the new millennium in the early 2000s and we argued that explosion of new technologies and cultural diversities as represented by multiculturalism required a reconstruction of education, a project both of us have pursued over the past decades and that I will articulate in this and following chapters of this book.

Chapter Six on "Reading Images Critically. Toward a Postmodern Pedagogy" focuses on interpreting images, narratives, and spectacles of media texts from multiple perspectives that engage the dimensions of gender, race, class, sexuality, and the socio-political values and ideologies in media texts. Sometimes hidden messages concerning race, gender, class, and sexuality are inscribed in images, scenes, and narratives, as well as discourses of texts. Accordingly, I read media texts as polyvocal and polysemic with multiple layers of meaning and the possibility of multiple readings, sometimes which conflict.

Chapter Seven on "New Technologies/New Literacies: Reconstructing Education, for Democracy and Social Justice" presents the Deweyean and Freirean emphasis on reconstructing education to help create democratic citizens and highlights the importance of the nexus of democracy and education. The chapter also argues that in an era of intense technological transformation with evolving technologies, social media, and digital devices and culture constantly transforming society and everyday life, education needs to engage and transmit the critical media and digital literacies necessary to function in a high-tech economy and society and to participate in social and democratic life. Multiple critical literacies enable citizens to distinguish between fact-based information and disinformation, an increasingly important task in an era marked by political Big Lies, disinformation, and the deployment of false information and propaganda via bots, social media, and even mainstream television channels (Rupert Murdoch and his family know who I am referring to here ....). Yet critical multiple literacies also need to teach students, teachers, and citizens to discern racial, gender, class, sexual, religious, and other forms of bias and discrimination in media and digital culture, a task that is one of the most pressing in the contemporary era.

The text concludes with a study co-authored with Steve Gennaro on "Digital Culture, Media, and the Challenges of Contemporary Cyborg Youth." Building on Donna Haraway's notion of the cyborg in which humans are increasingly merging with their technology, we find an acceleration of the process since Haraway first published her "Cyborg Manifesto" in 1985. The implosion of human beings with their technologies has intensified in the past decades so Haraway's manifesto takes on contemporary relevance. Individuals today are challenged to use their technologies to create desired identities and lives and to resist identities that they find oppressive and constricting. Of course, gender, race, class, and sexuality remain highly contested fields of identity, exclusion, and oppression, and today's cyborg youth face the challenges of using their technologies and creating lives and identities opposed to sexism, racism, classism, homophobia, and the biases of the past. We thus introduce a notion of "fighting cyborg youth" who used their technologies to mobilize and struggle for a better and freer world with oppressions and alienations of the past seen as social conditions and problems to be overcome in a non-racist, non-sexist and homophobic, non-classist, and a freer, happier and more egalitarian future. We find evidence of fighting cyborg youth in the Occupy Movement, Black Lives Matter, Dreamers, #MeToo, Bernie Youth, and gay and lesbian movements, as well as environmental and peace movements and all of the other efforts to create a freer and happier world, with liberty, education, and justice for all in a future full of hope and challenges.

Notes

1 Karl Polanyi saw a "Great Transformation" (1944; 2001; 2nd edition) taking place in Europe with the rise of market economies and modern states which create a change in social conditions and relations and all forms of economy, culture, politics, and society; we see another "great transformation" evolving out of revolutions in digital technologies and culture.

2 On the COVID-19 pandemic as the revenge of nature a la the Frankfurt School, see Douglas Kellner, "Trump, Authoritarian Populism, and Covid-19 From a U.S. Perspective," *Cultural Politics*, March 2021, Vol.17, pp. 28-36. On the background for the COVID-19 pandemic, see "Wildlife Markets and COVID-19," *Humane Society International*, April 19, 2020 at https://www.hsi.org/wp-content/uploads/2020/04/Wildlife-Markets-and-COVID-19-White-Chapter.pdf (accessed on August 11, 2020). For background on pandemics, viruses and human animal markets, see Quammen (2013).

3 Gennaro, Stephen "Globalization, History, Theory, and Writing" *Society for the History of Childhood and Youth Newsletter*. Winter 2010, No. 16 at http://www.history.vt.edu/Jones/SHCY/Newsletter16/Pedagogy-GennaroArticle.html (accessed November 8, 2016).

4 On youth resistance, Black Lives Matter, and other forces of the Trump resistance who have emerged in recent years, see Kellner and Satchel (2020).

5 A 2020 report from UNICEF, Plan International, and UN Women noted "that the number of out-of-school girls has dropped by 79 million in the last two decades" and that "girls became more likely to be in secondary school than boys in just the last decade." https://www.unicef.org/press-releases/25-years-uneven-progress-despite-gains-education-world-still-violent-highly (accessed February 23, 2021).

6 "Towards an equal future: Reimagining girls' education through STEM" UNICEF, October 6, 2020. https://www.unicef.org/media/84046/file/Reimagining-girls-education-through-stem-2020.pdf (accessed February 23, 2021).

7 Studies reveal that women, minorities, and immigrants now constitute roughly 85% of the growth in the labor force, while these groups represent about 60% of all workers; see Duderstadt 1999–2000: 38. In the past decade, the number of Hispanics in the United States increased by 35% and Asians by more than 40%. Since 1991, California has had no single ethnic or racial minority and almost half of the high school students in the state are African-American or Latino. Meanwhile, a "tidal wave" of children of baby boomers are about to enter college; see Atkinson 1999–2000: 49–50. Obviously, I am writing this study from a North American perspective, but would suggest that the arguments have broader reference in an increasingly globalized society marked by a networked economy, increasing migration and multiculturalism, and a proliferating Internet-based cyberculture.

8 On Marcuse and education, see Kellner, Lewis, and Pierce (2008) and Kellner, Cho, Lewis and Pierce (2009).

9 Herbert Marcuse radicalized the Greek concept of *Paedeia* and German concept of *Bildung* to reconstruct education as a form of self-development and social transformation; see the sources on Marcuse and education and analyses in note 8 above and in Reitz (2000).

10 For a critique of modern theories of the subject and reason from postmodern perspectives, see Best and Kellner (1991, 1997); for a critique of modern pedagogy neglecting the body, environment, and cosmos, see Kahn (2010).

11 Katy Steinmetz "She Coined the Term 'Intersectionality' Over 30 Years Ago. Here's What It Means to Her Today," *Time Magazine at* https://time.com/5786710/kimberle-crenshaw-inters ectionality/ (accessed February 19, 2021). Kimberlé Crenshaw's (2022) key chapters will be collected in *On Intersectionality: Essential Writings* (forthcoming).

12 See the critique of how to succeed in the new economy books in Best and Kellner (2001).

13 While reviewing Illich's work for a memorial for him sponsored by the UCLA Paulo Freire Institute, I discovered that much of Illich's work, including his major books, has been preserved on websites; see, for example, http://www.preservenet.com/theory/Illich.html (accessed March 16, 2021).

14 Kellner and Share (2019) introduced the term "critical media literacy" (CML) to distinguish a form of media literacy that engage the problematic of power and domination, and that critically engaged the dimensions of gender, race, class, sexuality, and other domains of oppression and struggle; these perspectives on CML will be applied throughout the following studies.

15 This was the topic of Gennaro's TEDxYork Proposal; see: "Teach Kids to Code" https://youtu. be/SKLgl58GrqY (accessed February 19, 2021).

16 "The 17 Sustainable Development Goals (SDGs), which are an urgent call for action by all countries—developed and developing—in a global partnership. They recognize that ending poverty and other deprivations must go hand-in-hand with strategies that improve health and education, reduce inequality, and spur economic growth—all while tackling climate change and working to preserve our oceans and forests." United Nations Department of Economic and Social Affairs at https://sdgs.un.org/goals (accessed February 23, 2021).

17 For examples of how evolving digital technologies can be used to enhance education, see Kellner and Share (2019) and the Foreward to this book by Gennaro and Share.

References

Best, Steven, and Douglas Kellner (1991) *Postmodern Theory: Critical Interrogations.* London and New York: Macmillan and Guilford Press.

———(1997) *The Postmodern Turn.* London and New York: Routledge and Guilford Press.

——— (2001) *The Postmodern Adventure.* London and New York: Routledge and Guilford Press.

Bloch, Ernst (1986) *The Principle of Hope.* Cambridge, MA: MIT Press.

Braverman, Harry (1974). *Labor and Monopoly Capital: The Degradation of Work in the Twentieth Century.* New York: Monthly Review Press.

Crenshaw, Kimberlé (2022) *On Intersectionality: Essential Writings.* New York: The New Press.

Dewey, John (1995) *Democracy and Education.* New York: The Free Press.

Freire, Paulo (1970). *Pedagogy of the Oppressed.* New York: Continuum Books.

——— (1998). *Pedagogy of Freedom: Ethics, Democracy, and Civic Courage.* Lanham: Rowman & Littlefield Publishers, Inc.

Freire, Paulo and I. Shor (1987) *A Pedagogy for Liberation: Dialogues on Transforming Education.* Westport: Bergin & Garvey.

Gramsci, Antonio (1971) *Prison Notebooks.* New York: International Publishers.

Haraway, Donna (1985) "Manifesto for Cyborgs: Science, Technology, and Socialist Feminism in the 1980s", *Socialist Review*, 80: 65–108.

Hegel, G.H.F. (1965 [1807]) *The Phenomenology of Spirit*. New York: Harper and Row.

Hill Collins, Patricia and Selma Bilge (2016) *Intersectionality*. New York: Flatiron Books.

Hirsch, E.D. (1988) *Cultural Literacy: What Every American Needs to Know*. New York: Vintage.

Hobbs, Renee (editor) (2016) *Exploring the Roots of Digital and Media Literacy through Personal Narrative*. Philadelphia: Temple University Press.

hooks, bell (1994) *Teaching to Transgress: Education as the Practice of Freedom*. New York: Routledge.

Illich, Ivan (1971) *Deschooling Society*. New York: Harper and Row.

——— (1973) *Tools for Conviviality*. New York: Harper and Row.

——— (1981) *Shadow Work*. London: Marion Boyars.

Jaeger, Werner (1965) *Paideia. The Ideals of Greek Culture*. New York: Oxford University Press.

Kahn, Richard (2010) *Critical Pedagogy, Ecoliteracy, and Planetary Crisis: The Ecopedagogy Movement*. New York: Peter Lang.

Kellner, Douglas (1989) *Critical Theory, Marxism, and Modernity*. Cambridge, UK and Baltimore, MD: Polity Press and John Hopkins University Press.

——— (2000) "New Technologies/New Literacies: Reconstructing Education for the New Millennium," *Teaching Education*, 11(3): 245–265.

——— (2002a) "New Life Conditions, Subjectivities and Literacies: Some Comments on the Lukes' Reconstructive Project," *Journal of Early Childhood Literacy*, 2(1): 105–112.

——— (2002b) "Technological Revolution, Multiple Literacies, and the Restructuring of Education," in *Silicon Literacies*, edited by Ilana Snyder. London and New York: Routledge, 154–169.

——— (2021) *Technology and Democracy: Toward A Critical Theory of Digital Technologies, Technopolitics, and Technocapitalism*. Springer Publications.

Marcuse, Herbert (2008) *On Marcuse: Critique, Liberation, and Reschooling in the Radical Pedagogy of Herbert Marcuse*, edited by Douglas Kellner, Tyson E. Lewis and Clayton Pierce. Rotterdam, the Netherlands: Brill Publishers.

——— (2009) *Marcuse's Challenge to Education*, edited by Douglas Kellner, Tyson E. Lewis, Clayton Pierce, and Daniel Cho. Lanham, N.J.: Rowman and Littlefield Publishers.

Kellner, Douglas and Jeff Share (2019) *The Critical Media Literacy Guide: Engaging Media and Transforming Education*. Rotterdam, The Netherlands: Brill-Sense Publishers.

Kellner, Douglas and Roslyn M. Satchel (2020). "Resisting Youth: From Occupy Through Black Lives Matter to the Trump Resistance," in *The SAGE Handbook of Critical Pedagogies*, Chapter 107, edited by Shirley Steinberg and Barry Downs. London: Sage Publications.

Luke, Allan and Carmen Luke (2002) "Adolescence Lost/Childhood Regained: On Early Intervention and the Emergence of the Techno-Subject," *Journal of Early Childhood Literacy*, 1(1): 91–120.

Marx, Karl and Friedrich Engels (1978) *The Marx-Engels Reader*, edited by Robert Tucker. New York: Norton.

McChesney, Robert (2004) *The Problem of the Media: U.S. Communication Politics in the 21st Century*. New York: Monthly Review Press.

_____ (2013) Blowing the Roof Off the Twenty-First Century: Media, Politics, and the Struggle for Post-Capitalist Democracy. New York: NYU Press.

McLuhan, Marshall (1964) *Understanding Media*. New York: Signet.

Noble, Safiya Umoja (2018) in *Algorithms of Oppression: How Search Engines Reinforce Racism*. New York: NYU Press.

Polanyi, Karl (1944; 2001; 2nd edition) *The Great Transformation the Political and Economic Origins of Our Time*. Boston: Beacon Press.

Reitz, Charles (2000) *Art, Alienation, and the Humanities: A Critical Engagement with Herbert Marcuse*. Albany, N.Y.: SUNY Press.

Smith, Linda Tuhiwai (1999) *Decolonizing Methodologies—Research and Indigenous Peoples* (London: Zed Book Ltd, and Dunedin: University of Otago Press.

Wollstonecraft, Mary (1988) *A Vindication of the Rights of Woman*. New York: Norton.

Zuboff, Shoshana (1988) *In the Age of the Smart Machine: The Future of Work and Power*. New York: Basic Books.

——— (2020) *The Age of Surveillance Capitalism: The Fight for a Human Future at the New Frontier of Power*.

CHAPTER TWO

Marxian Perspectives on Educational Philosophy: From Classical Marxism to Critical Pedagogy

Education is free. Freedom of education shall be enjoyed under the condition fixed by law— **Karl Marx, Das Kapital**

The theory associated with Marxism was developed in mid-19th century Europe by Karl Marx and Friedrich Engels. Although Marx and Engels did not write widely about education, they developed theoretical perspectives on modern societies that have been used to highlight the social functions of education, and their concepts and methods have served to both theorize and criticize education in the reproduction of capitalist societies, and to support projects of alternative education. In this study, I will first briefly sketch the classical perspectives of Marx and Engels, highlighting the place of education in their work. Then, I lay out the way that Marxian perspectives on education were developed in the Frankfurt School critical theory, British cultural studies, and other neo-Marxian and post-Marxian approaches grouped under the label of critical pedagogy, that emerged from the work of Paulo Freire and is now global in scope. I argue that Marxism provides influential and robust perspectives on education, still of use, but that classical Marxism has certain omissions and limitations that contemporary theories of society and education need to overcome.

Marx and Engels: The Classical Paradigm

> The materialist doctrine that men are products of circumstances and upbringing, and that, therefore, changed men are products of other circumstances and changed upbringing, forgets that it is men who change circumstances and that it is essential to educate the educator himself. Karl Marx

Both Marx and Engels left comfortable bourgeois families to pursue a life of revolutionary scholarship and struggle (see McLellan, 1973; Carver, 1989; Wheen, 2000). Meeting in Paris with Engels in 1843, Marx began studying economics and associated himself with communist groups, writing: "When communist *artisans* form associations, education and propaganda are their first aims. But the very act of associating creates a new need—the need for society—and what appeared to be a means has become an end. The most striking results of this practical development are to be seen when French socialist workers meet together. Smoking, eating, and drinking are no longer simply means of bringing people together. Company, association, entertainment which also has society as its aim, are sufficient for them; the brotherhood of man is no empty phrase but a reality, and the nobility of man shines forth upon us from their toil-worn bodies" (Marx and Engels, CW4 [1844]: 313).

Marx's collaborator Engels grew up in the German town of Barmen, his family owned factories, and he experienced the industrial revolution and rise of the working class at first hand. In his early writings, Engels describes the lot of the new industrial working class as a miserable one: "Work in low rooms where people breathe in more coal fumes and dust than oxygen—and in the majority of cases beginning already at the age of six—is bound to deprive them of all strength and joy in life. The weavers, who have individual looms in their homes, sit bent over them from morning till night, and desiccate their spinal marrow in front of a hot stove. Those who do not fall prey to mysticism are ruined by drunkenness" (Engels in CW2 [1839], 9). Likewise, the "local-born leather workers are ruined physically and mentally after three years of work: "three out of five die of consumption." In sum, "terrible poverty prevails among the lower classes, particularly the factory workers in Wuppertal; syphilis and lung diseases are so widespread as to be barely credible; in Elberfeld alone, out of 2,500 children of school age 1,200 are deprived of education and grow up in the factories—merely so that the manufacturer need not pay the adults, whose place they take, twice the wage he pays a child" (Engels CW2, 10).

The young Marx and Engels thus perceived that without education the working class was condemned to lives of drudgery and death, but that with education they had a chance to create a better life. In their famous 1848 "Communist Manifesto," Marx and Engels argued that growing economic crises would throw ever more segments of the middle classes, and the older peasant and artisan classes, into the impoverished situation of the proletariat and would thus produce a unified working class, at least one with interests in common. They declared that the bourgeois class is constantly battling against the older feudal powers, among its own segments, and against the foreign bourgeoisie, and thus enlists the proletariat as its ally. Consequently, the proletariat gains education and experience which it can use to fight the ruling class. As bourgeois society dissolves, a section of the bourgeoisie goes over to the proletariat, including a radical intelligentsia "who have raised themselves to the level of comprehending theoretically the historical movement as a whole" (CW6 [1848]: 494).

In the *Manifesto*, expanded public education for the working class was one of the major demands, and henceforth both Marx and Engels saw themselves as providing education and theoretical guidance to the working class and socialist movement. Marx and Engels did not write much on educational institutions in bourgeois society, or develop models of education in socialist societies. Yet their historical materialist theory of history has been used to theorize and critique educational institutions within capitalist society and to develop alternative conceptions of education, which are in accord with Marxian socialist principles. As the "Thesis from Feuerbach" which opens this section suggests, changing social conditions create new forms of education, so that the rise of capitalist-bourgeois societies would produce educational institutions that reproduce dominant social relations, values, and practices. Likewise, transforming capitalist societies and creating socialist ones requires new modes of education and socialization.

The classical Marxian paradigm thus sees education as functioning within the hegemonic social system which is organized by and serves the interest of capital, while calling for alternative modes of education that would prepare students and citizens for a more progressive socialist mode of social organizations. Marx and Engels envisaged education and free time as essential to developing free individuals and creating many-sided human beings. The sketch of socialism in *The German Ideology*—where one would "hunt in the morning, fish in the afternoon, rear cattle in the evening, criticize after dinner, just as I have a mind, without ever becoming hunter, fisherman, shepherd or critic" (CW5: 47)—reflects the ideals of a non-alienated life in which education is a key part of the life process.

Increasing free time under socialism, Marx argued in his 1857–8 notebooks collected under the name of the *Grundrisse*, would allow for more education and development of a social individual who can then enter "in the direct production process as this different subject. This process is then both discipline, as regards the human being in the process of becoming; and, at the same time, practice [*Ausubung*], experimental science, materially creative and objectifying science, as regards the human being who has become, in whose head exists the accumulated knowledge of society" (Marx and Engels, 1978, p. 290). For Marx, transforming social relations would produce the basis for a new society of non-alienated labor in which individuals could utilize their free-time to fully develop their human capacities and labor itself would be a process of experimentation, creativity, and progress. In the vision of a free society sketched out in the *Grundrisse*, the system of automation would produce most of society's goods, and individuals could thus enjoy leisure and the fruits of creative work, whereby education would become an essential part of the life-process.

Such a society would be a completely different social order from that of capitalist society which is organized around work and the production of commodities. Marx acknowledges that the new society would have a totally "changed foundation of production, a new foundation first created by the process of history" (Marx and Engels, 1978, p. 293). In the third volume of *Capital*, Marx described this radically new social order in terms of a "realm of freedom," writing: "Freedom in this field can only consists in socialized man, the associated producers, rationally regulating their interchange with Nature, bringing it under their common control, instead of being ruled by it as by the blind forces of Nature; and achieving this with the least expenditure of energy and under conditions most favorable to, and worthy of, their human nature" (Marx and Engels, 1978, p. 441).

Marx's most distinctive vision of socialism thus envisages socialism as constituting a break in history as dramatic as the rupture between pre-capitalist and capitalist societies that produced modernity. While capitalism is a commodity-producing society organized around work and production, socialism would be a social order aiming at the full development of many-sided individual human beings. Marx formulated this radical vision of a new society in his late text *Critique of the Gotha Program* (1875) as the product of a transition to a higher phase of communism. In the first stage, the "prolonged birth pangs from capitalist society" would limit the level of social and individual development, but:

> In a higher phase of communist society, after the enslaving subordination of the individual to the division of labor, and therewith also the antithesis between mental and physical labour, has vanished; after labour has become not only a means of life but life's prime want; after the productive forces have also increased with the all-round development of the individual, and all the spring of cooperative wealth flow more abundantly -- only then can the narrow horizon of bourgeois right be crossed in its entirety and society inscribe on its banner: From each according to his ability, to each according to his needs! (Marx and Engels, 1978, p. 531).

Thus, in Marx's utopian vision of communism, education would help fully develop socialized individuals, create a cooperative and harmonious society, and unleash creativity in all its forms. In historical retrospect, however, the lack of a more fully articulated theory of education and subjectivity, and of the subjective conditions of revolutionary transformation, in the classical Marxian theory vitiated its theory and practice. Marx seemed to think that class and revolutionary consciousness would develop naturally, as a result of the workers' position in the process of production. Subsequent Marxian theorists, however, engaged in a heated debate concerning whether class consciousness developed spontaneously (as Rosa Luxembourg claimed), or would have to be brought to the workers from outside (as Kautsky and Lenin argued). And later generations of neo-Marxian theorists would develop more sophisticated theories of consciousness, communication, and education, whereby political subjectivities could be formed which would strive for socialist and radical democratic social change.

Succeeding generations of Marxists perceived that the classical paradigm overemphasized the dimension of class, playing down the importance of gender, race, sexuality, and other key constituents of human experience, lacunae filled in by many neo-Marxian theories, as I note in the following sections. Moreover, many of Marx's texts also seem to place too heavy an emphasis on labor as the distinctly human activity, as the key to the development of the human being. Overemphasis on production is accompanied by an inadequate concept of intersubjectivity, lacking a fully developed theory of individual consciousness and its development in communication, symbolic action, and culture. Unlike later social theorists such as Durkheim, Mead, Dewey, and Habermas, Marx failed to perceive the importance of wider communication in the development of new forms of association and solidarity. He thus put too much emphasis on class struggle, on direct action, and not enough on communication and democracy.

Indeed, Marx never grasped the significance of the institutions of liberal democracy as an important heritage of modern societies that should be absorbed into socialism and put too much emphasis on the state (which he and Engels claimed would wither away, although this prophecy is far from being realized in the contemporary world). Although Marx and Engels espoused a model of radical democratic self-government in their writings on the Paris Commune, and while they long championed democracy as an ideal, they never properly appreciated the separation of powers and system of rights, checks and balances, and democratic participation developed within bourgeois society. Thus, Marx had an inadequate theory of education and democracy, and failed to develop an institutional theory of democracy, its constraints under capitalism, and how socialism would make possible fuller and richer democracy. These lacunae in the classical Marxian theory would be filled by later generations of Marxist theorists.

Within the Marxian tradition, a tremendous variety and diversity of different schools, movements, and positions have evolved. In the following narrative, I will trace developments within key contemporary neo-Marxian traditions, including those of the Frankfurt school, British cultural studies, and a diverse grouping of neo- and post-Marxian positions covered by the label of "critical pedagogy." In these traditions, certain positions overlap and there are also divergences based, in part, on responses to different socio-historical conditions in the trajectory from state capitalism in the 1930s to the resurgence of neo-liberalism and return to market capitalism in the 1980s. The dynamics of globalization and a variety of anti-globalization movements in the 1990s to the present have also generated a global proliferation of the various formations of neo-Marxian theory which has produced a dizzying diversity of Marxian discourse.

Other narratives of the trajectory of Marxism and education have traced the development of different positions within education through the prisms of Gramsci, Althusser and structural Marxism, and reproduction theory, as well as the modes of thought that I chart. There have also been studies of the role of Marxian ideas in curriculum and schooling in capitalist societies (see Pinar et al., 1996, pp. 243 ff.), as well as presentations of contemporary debates within Marxian theory on a vast range of topics in the field of education (see Rikowski, 1996, 1997; Hill, 2001, and the articles collected in *Capital Logic* 2001). I, however, will focus on the development of perspectives on education within the tradition of critical social theory and pedagogy developed by critical neo-Marxism. This perspective and presentation is shaped by the work I have done within the traditions I discuss and in the context of teaching Marxism and education at state universities in Texas and California in the U.S. and giving lectures and going to conferences all over the world.

The Frankfurt School, Culture, and Regimes of Capital

Not only within social philosophy in the narrower sense, but likewise in sociological circles as well as those of general philosophy, discussions about society have gradually and ever more clearly crystallized around a question which is not only presently important, but is at the same time the topical version of the oldest and most important philosophical problems: namely, the question of the connection between the economic life of society, the psychic development of individuals, and changes in the cultural domains in the narrower sense. To these belong not only the so-called spiritual contexts of science, art, and religion, but also law, custom fashion, public opinion, sports, leisure pastimes, life style, etc. Max Horkheimer

Frankfurt School theorists have rarely explicitly addressed problems of education and pedagogy, although I will suggest that its critique of the culture industries provides an important model of Marxian cultural studies and pedagogy that anticipates the Birmingham School and that provides important contributions to educational philosophy today. The Frankfurt School stress on consciousness, ideology, culture, and socialization highlights the importance of transforming individuals and societies through change of consciousness, culture, and the institutions of everyday life such as education.

In Weimar Germany in the early 1930s, the Frankfurt School were carrying out research into the family and authority, and were concluding that the family was declining as an agent of authority, giving way to the media, peer groups, schooling, and other institutions. In exile in the United States after 1934, the Frankfurt School focused on the role of the media in educating and socializing individuals. To a large extent, the Frankfurt school inaugurated critical studies of mass communication and culture, and thus produced an early model of media and cultural studies (see Kellner 1989, 1995). In a wide-ranging set of research and texts, the group developed a critical and transdisciplinary approach to cultural and communications studies, combining critique of political economy of the media, analysis of texts, and audience reception studies of the social and ideological effects of mass culture and communications (see the texts collected in Arato and Gebhardt, 1982; Bronner and Kellner, 1989, and the discussions of the Frankfurt school in Jay, 1973; Kellner, 1989; Wiggershaus, 1994).

The Frankfurt School theorists coined the term "culture industries" to signify the process of the industrialization of mass-produced culture and the commercial imperatives which drove the system. The group analyzed all mass-mediated cultural artifacts within the context of industrial production, in which the products of the culture industries exhibited the same features as other goods of mass production: commodification, standardization, and massification.

The culture industries had the specific function, however, of providing ideological legitimation of the existing capitalist societies and of integrating individuals into the framework of its social formation. Adorno's analyses of popular music (1978 [1932], 1941, 1982, and 1989), Lowenthal's studies of popular literature and magazines (1961), Herzog's studies of radio soap operas (1941), and the critiques of mass culture developed in Horkheimer and Adorno's famous study of the culture industries (1972 and Adorno 1991) provide many examples of the value of the critical theory approach. Moreover, in their theories of the culture industries and critiques of mass culture, they were the first to systematically analyze and criticize mass-mediated culture and communications within critical social theory. The critical theorists scrutinized the pedagogical and social functions of the culture industries in the reproduction of contemporary societies. In their optic, mass culture and communications stand at the center of leisure activity, are important agents of socialization and education, mediators of political reality, and should thus be seen as major institutions of contemporary societies with a variety of economic, political, cultural and social effects.

Furthermore, the critical theorists investigated the cultural industries in a political context as a form of the integration of the working class into capitalist societies. The group were among the first neo-Marxian theorists to examine the effects of mass culture and the rise of the consumer society on the working classes which were to be the instrument of revolution in the classical Marxian scenario. They also analyzed the ways that the culture industries and consumer society were performing new kinds of pedagogy and stabilizing contemporary capitalism. Accordingly, they sought novel strategies for political change, agencies of political transformation, and models for political emancipation that could serve as norms of social critique and goals for political struggle. This project required rethinking the Marxian project and produced many important contributions—as well as some problematical positions.

After World War II, the critical theorists examined how the state and public education produced a form of "*Halbbildung*," half-education, and themselves called for education that fully developed individual subjectivities.[1] Their form of "critical theory" emphasized the importance of critique, reflexivity, and gaining emancipatory consciousness, free from indoctrination and socialization. Although the Frankfurt School did not systematically explore the institutions of higher education, Adorno, Horkheimer, Marcuse, and Habermas wrote occasional critiques of the University and intervened frequently in educational debates.

In retrospect, one can see the Frankfurt group's critical theory as articulation of a stage of state and monopoly capitalism which became dominant during the 1930s (see Kellner, 1989). In this era of "organized capitalism," the state and giant corporations managed the economy and individuals submitted to state and corporate control. This period is often described as "Fordism" to designate the system of mass production and the homogenizing regime of capital which wanted to produce mass desires, tastes, and behavior. It was thus an era of mass production and consumption characterized by uniformity and homogeneity of needs, thought, and behavior producing a "mass society" and what the Frankfurt school described as "the end of the individual." No longer was individual thought and action the motor of social and cultural progress; instead giant organizations and institutions overpowered individuals. The era corresponds to the staid, ascetic, conformist, and conservative world of corporate capitalism that was dominant in the 1950s with its organization men and women, its mass consumption, and its mass culture.

During this period, mass culture and communication were instrumental in generating the modes of thought and behavior appropriate to a highly organized and homogenized social order. Likewise, public education was creating standardized education and curricula which was serving as instruments of massification and social control. For instance, Herbert Marcuse's *One-Dimensional Man* (1964) criticized the ways that educational institutions, the media, and other forms of socialization were creating conformist modes of thought and behavior, producing what he called "one-dimensional man."

Thus, the Frankfurt School theory of mass culture articulates a major historical shift to an era in which mass consumption and culture was indispensable to producing a consumer society based on homogeneous needs and desires for mass-produced products. In this context, the media and public education helped generate a mass society based on social organization and homogeneity. It is culturally the period of highly controlled network radio and television, insipid top forty pop music, glossy Hollywood films, national magazines, and standardized public schooling.

Of course, media culture and schooling were never as massified and homogeneous as in the Frankfurt school model. Indeed, one could argue that the model was flawed even during its time of origin and influence and that other models were in some ways preferable, such as those of Walter Benjamin (1969), Siegfried Kracauer (1995), Ernst Bloch (1986) and others of the Weimar generation. Yet the original critical theory model of the culture industry and mass society did articulate the vital social roles of media culture and schooling during a specific regime of capital. It provided a model, still of use, of a highly commercial and technologically advanced culture that serves the needs of dominant corporate interests, plays a major role in ideological reproduction, and in enculturating individuals into the dominant system of needs, thought, and behavior. The Frankfurt school also influenced and helped produce other neo-Marxian approaches to culture, society, and education as we see in the following sections.

The Trajectories of Cultural Studies

Traditionally, mass-communications research has conceptualized the process of communication in terms of a circulation circuit or loop. But it is also possible (and useful) to think of this process in terms of a structure produced and sustained through the articulation of linked but distinctive moments -, production, circulation, distribution/ consumption, reproduction. Stuart Hall

From a historical perspective, British cultural studies emerges in a later era of capital, on the cusp of what became known as "post-Fordism," and is seen as a more variegated and conflicted cultural formation. The forms of culture described by the earliest phase of British cultural studies in the 1950s and early 1960s articulated conditions in an era in which there were still significant tensions in England and much of Europe between an older working class-based culture and the newer mass-produced culture whose models and exemplars were the products of American culture industries. The initial project of cultural studies developed by Richard Hoggart, Raymond Williams, and E.P. Thompson attempted to preserve working class culture against onslaughts of mass culture produced by the culture industries.

Thompson's historical inquiries into the history of British working class institutions and struggles (1963), the defenses of working class culture and education by Hoggart (1957) and Williams (1961, 1962), and their attacks on mass culture were part of a socialist and working class-oriented project that assumed that the industrial working class was a force of progressive social change and that it could be mobilized and organized to struggle against the inequalities of the existing capitalist societies and for a more egalitarian socialist one. Williams and Hoggart were deeply involved in projects of working class education and oriented toward socialist working class politics, seeing their form of cultural studies as an instrument of progressive social change.

The early critiques in the first wave of British cultural studies of Americanism and mass culture, in Hoggart, Williams, and others, thus paralleled to some extent the earlier critique of the Frankfurt school, yet valorized a working class that the critical theorists saw as defeated in Germany and much of Europe during the era of fascism and which they never saw as a strong resource for emancipatory social change. The early work of the Birmingham school, as I will now argue, was continuous with the radicalism of the first wave of British cultural studies (the Hoggart-Thompson-Williams "culture and society" tradition) as well, in important ways, with the Frankfurt school (see Kellner, 2002). Yet the Birmingham project also paved the way, as I suggest below, for a postmodern populist turn in cultural studies, which responds to a later stage of capitalism.

It has not yet been widely recognized that the second stage of the development of British cultural studies—starting with the founding of the University of Birmingham Centre for Contemporary Cultural Studies in 1963/64 by Hoggart and Stuart Hall—shared many key perspectives with the Frankfurt school (Kellner, 1999, 2002). During this period, the Centre developed a variety of critical approaches for the analysis, interpretation, and criticism of cultural artifacts (see the articles collected in Grossberg, Nelson, Triechler, 1992; During, 1993; Durham and Kellner 2001; see also the commentary in Hall 1980b; Johnson 1986/7; McGuigan 1992; Kellner 1995, 2020).

Through a set of internal debates, and responding to social struggles and movements of the 1960s and the 1970s, the Birmingham group came to focus on the interplay of representations and ideologies of class, gender, race, ethnicity, and nationality in cultural texts, including media culture. Like the Frankfurt School, they analyzed critically the pedagogical effects of newspapers, radio, television, film, music, and other popular cultural forms on audiences, as well as to develop critiques of schooling in Britain. They also focused on how various audiences interpreted and used media culture in varied and different ways and contexts, analyzing the factors that made audiences respond in contrasting ways to media texts.

The now classical period of British cultural studies from the early 1960s to the early 1980s continued to adopt Marxian approaches to the study of culture, especially those influenced by Althusser and Gramsci (see Hall, 1980a; Johnson 1986/7). Yet although Hall and his colleagues usually omit the Frankfurt school from their narratives of their history and influences, some of the work done by the Birmingham group replicated certain classical positions of the Frankfurt School, in their social theory and methodological models for doing cultural studies, as well as in their political perspectives and strategies. Like the Frankfurt School, British cultural studies observed the integration of the working class and its decline of revolutionary consciousness and studied the conditions of this catastrophe for the Marxian project of revolution. Like the Frankfurt school, British cultural studies concluded that mass culture was playing an important role in integrating the working class into existing capitalist societies and that a new consumer and media culture was forming a new mode of capitalist hegemony.

Both traditions focused on the intersections of culture and ideology and saw ideology critique as central to a critical cultural studies (CCCS 1980a, 1980b). Both viewed culture as a mode of ideological reproduction and hegemony, in which educational institutions and cultural forms help to shape the modes of thought and behavior that induce individuals to adapt to the social conditions of capitalist societies. Both also interpreted culture as a potential form of resistance to capitalist society and both the earlier forerunners of British cultural studies, especially Raymond Williams, and the theorists of the Frankfurt school perceived high culture as forces of resistance to capitalist modernity. Later, British cultural studies would valorize resistant moments in media culture and audience interpretations and use of media artifacts, while the Frankfurt school tended, with some exceptions, to view mass culture as a homogeneous and potent form of ideological domination—a difference that would seriously divide the two traditions.

From the beginning, British cultural studies was highly political in nature and focused on the potentials for resistance in oppositional subcultures, first, valorizing the capacities for resistance and struggle within working class cultures, and then, focusing on how youth subcultures resist the hegemonic forms of capitalist domination. Unlike the classical Frankfurt school (but similar to Herbert Marcuse), British cultural studies turned to youth cultures as providing potentially new forms of opposition and social change. Through studies of youth subcultures, British cultural studies demonstrated how subcultural formations came to constitute distinct forms of identity and group membership and appraised the oppositional potential of various youth subcultures (see Jefferson 1976; Hebdige 1979).

British cultural studies also investigated how schooling integrates youth into capitalist societies and the ways that working class youth rebel and resist. Paul Willis' now classic *Learning to Labor* (1981) carried out ethnographic and critical studies of how working class youth confront disciplinary schooling that tries to get them to conform to authority and middle class values and mores. Willis documents both modes of disciplinary schooling and resistance, showing how working class youth rebel and construct identities outside of schooling and middle class norms.

Within the University, British cultural studies developed interdisciplinary programs to study the intersection of culture, society, and politics, and developed critiques of academic fragmentation and disciplinarity (i.e. how disciplines like English literature studies cut off literary studies from society, politics, culture, and history at large). British cultural studies—like the Frankfurt school—insists that culture must be studied within the social relations and system through which culture is produced and consumed, and that thus study of culture is intimately bound up with the study of society, politics, economics, and ideology (Centre for Contemporary Cultural Studies 1980a and 1980b).

British cultural studies and the Frankfurt school were thus both founded as fundamentally transdisciplinary enterprises which resisted established academic divisions of labor and implicitly revolutionize University education. Indeed, their boundary-crossing and critiques of the detrimental effects of abstracting culture from its socio-political context elicited hostility among those who are more disciplinary-oriented and who, for example, believe in the autonomy of culture and renounce sociological or political readings. Against such academic formalism and separatism, cultural studies insists that culture must be investigated within the social relations and socio-economic system through which culture is produced and consumed (Hall et al 1980). From this perspective, analysis of culture is intimately bound up with the study of society, politics, and economics. Employing Gramsci's model of hegemony and counterhegemony, it sought to analyze "hegemonic," or ruling, social and cultural forces of domination and to seek "counterhegemonic" forces of resistance and struggle. The project was aimed at social transformation and attempted to specify forces of domination and resistance in order to aid the process of political struggle and emancipation from oppression and domination.

Some earlier authoritative presentations of British cultural studies stressed the importance of a transdisciplinary approach to the study of culture that analyzed its political economy, process of production and distribution, textual products, and reception by the audience—positions remarkably similar to the Frankfurt school. For instance, in his classical programmatic article, "Encoding/Decoding," Stuart Hall began his analysis by using Marx's *Grundrisse* as a model to trace the articulations of "a continuous circuit," encompassing "production—distribution—consumption—production" (1980b: 128 ff.). Hall concretizes this model with focus on how media institutions produce meanings, how they circulate, and how audiences use or decode the texts to produce meaning. Moreover, in a 1983 lecture, published in 1985/1986, Richard Johnson provided a model of cultural studies, similar to Hall's earlier model, based on a diagram of the circuits of production, textuality, and reception, parallel to the circuits of capital stressed by Marx, illustrated by a diagram that stressed the importance of production and distribution. Although Johnson emphasized the importance of analysis of production in cultural studies and criticized the British movie-journal *Screen* for abandoning this perspective in favor of more idealist and textualist approaches (63 ff.), much work in British and North American cultural studies has replicated the neglect of production and political economy.

In some following models of cultural studies, however, there has been a turn—throughout the English-speaking world—to what might be called a "postmodern" problematic which emphasizes pleasure, consumption, and the individual construction of identities in terms of what McGuigan (1992) has called a "cultural populism." Media culture from this perspective produces material for identities, pleasures, and empowerment, and thus audiences constitute the "popular" through their consumption of cultural products. During this phase—roughly from the mid-1980s to the present—cultural studies in Britain, North America, and elsewhere, turned from the socialist and revolutionary politics of the previous stages of cultural studies to postmodern forms of identity politics and less critical perspectives on media and consumer culture. Emphasis was placed more and more on the audience, consumption, and reception, and displaced focus on production and distribution of texts and how texts were produced in media industries and reproduced and disseminated dominant ideologies.

In context, the forms of cultural studies developed from the late 1970s to the present, theorize a shift from the stage of state monopoly capitalism, or Fordism, rooted in mass production and consumption to a new regime of capital and social order, sometimes described as "post-Fordism" (Harvey, 1989), or "postmodernism" (Jameson, 1991), and characterizing a transnational and global capital that valorizes difference, multiplicity, eclecticism, populism, and intensified consumerism in a new information/entertainment society. From this perspective, the proliferating media and digital culture, postmodern architecture, shopping malls, and the culture of the spectacle described by Debord (1968, 1972) became the promoters and palaces of a new stage of technocapitalism, the latest stage of capital, encompassing a postmodern image, digital, and consumer culture (see Best and Kellner, 1991, 1997, 2001 and Zuboff 1988 and 2020).

Consequently, the turn toward a postmodern cultural studies can be interpreted as a response to a new era of global capitalism. What is described as the "new revisionism" (McGuigan, 1992: 61 ff.) severs cultural studies from political economy and critical social theory. Hence, in some forms of cultural studies, there is a widespread tendency to decenter, or even ignore completely, economics, history, and politics in favor of emphasis on individual pleasures, consumption, and the construction of hybrid identities from the material of the popular. This cultural populism replicates the turn in postmodern theory away from Marxism and its alleged reductionism, master narratives of liberation and domination, and historical teleology.

The emphasis in postmodern cultural studies arguably articulates experiences and phenomena within a new mode of social organization. The emphasis on active audiences, resistant readings, oppositional texts, utopian moments, and the like describes an era in which individuals are trained to be more active media consumers, and in which they are given a much wider choice of cultural materials, corresponding to a new global and transnational capitalism with a much broader array of consumer choices, products, and services. In this regime, difference sells, and the diversities, multiplicities, and heterogeneity valorized in postmodern theory describes the proliferation of consumer choices in a new social order predicated on an ever-expanding proliferation of products, desires, and needs.

Critical Pedagogy from Freire to North America and Beyond

The pedagogy of the oppressed is a task for radicals; it cannot be carried out by sectarians. Paulo Freire

Alongside of the proliferation of neo-Marxian theories of culture and society and globalization of cultural studies, forms of an oppositional critical pedagogy emerged that explicitly criticized schooling in capitalist societies while calling for more emancipatory modes of education. In his now classic *The Pedagogy of the Oppressed* (1972), Brazilian educator and activist Paulo Freire criticized the "banking concept of education" while calling for more interactive, dialogical, and participatory forms of pedagogy that are parallel in interesting ways to those of John Dewey. While Dewey wanted education to produce citizens for democracy, however, Freire sought, in the spirit of Marxist revolutionary praxis, to develop a pedagogy of the oppressed that would produce revolutionary subjects, empowered to overthrow oppression and to create a more democratic and just social order.

Freire's pedagogy of the oppressed seeks to transform individuals from being objects of educational processes to subjects of their own autonomy and emancipation. Freire suggests that classical Marxism had not adequately developed the subjective and pedagogical dimension, and that the oppressed must be educated so that they can perform their own self-emancipation. Setting up schools that practiced his critical pedagogy in his native Brazil, Freire was expelled when a military dictatorship took over his country, but continued his work in Chile and throughout the world until his death in 1997.

Freire's work found resonance on a global scale and by the 1980s there were many schools of critical pedagogy. In North America, a series of books on Freire appeared and groups and individuals took up his ideas in a variety of contexts (see McLaren and Leonard, 1993). Theorists such as Henry Giroux, Donaldo Macedo, and Peter McLaren linked Freire's perspectives with those of Frankfurt school critical theory and other neo-Marxian approaches in works from the 1990s to the present.

Cultural theorists and educators developed critical pedagogies of media and representation and articulated neo-Marxian class perspectives with those of gender, race, and multiculturalism (see Luke and Gore, 1992; hooks, 1994; Kellner, 1995, 2020; McLaren, Hammer, Sholle and Reilly, 1995; Steinberg, 2001, Gottesman, 2016) and the journal *Taboo: The Journal of Culture and Education*, founded by Joe L. Kincheloe and Shirley R. Steinberg). Feminists, poststructuralists and others criticized what they saw as biases and limitations of critical pedagogy (see, for example, Lather, 2001), and there were sharp debates over the value or limitations of the continuing role of Marxism within critical pedagogy.

Henry Giroux's early work was frequently linked to Michael Apple's attempts to link neo-Gramsci theories of hegemony to analyses of capitalist schooling as instruments of corporate power and domination, such as were produced by Bowles and Gintis (1976). Apple was more influenced by Althusserian structural Marxism, and Bowles and Gintis' critique of schooling in capitalist society. Both Giroux and Apple, however, saw the need for theories of resistance, transforming education in the interests of radical democracy, and bringing in multiculturalist problematics that would address issues of gender and race, as well as class. These moves led Marxist critics to suggest that they were abandoning Marxism for democratic populism, although one could argue that they are reconstructing Marxism for the present age, in the spirit of a revisionist dialectic.

Giroux urged movement from a language of critique to a language of hope and possibility, combining critique of the dominant mode of schooling with valorization of resistance and alternative conceptions of education. After publishing a series of books that many recognize as major works on contemporary education and critical pedagogy, Giroux turned to cultural studies in the late 1980s to enrich education with expanded conceptions of pedagogy and literacy (see Giroux, 1992; 180 ff.). This cultural turn is animated by the hope to reconstruct schooling with critical perspectives that can help us to better understand and transform contemporary culture and society in the contemporary era. Giroux provides cultural studies with a critical pedagogy missing in many versions and a sustained attempt to link critical pedagogy and cultural studies with developing a more democratic culture and citizenry. The result is an intersection of critical pedagogy and cultural studies that enhances both enterprises, providing a cultural and transformative political dimension to critical pedagogy and a pedagogical dimension to cultural studies (see Giroux, 2000a, 2000b, 2001 and the analysis of Giroux's work in Kellner, 2001).[2]

In an ever-mushrooming profusion of books, Peter McLaren has been advocating a return to classical Marxism as a strategy to transform educational practices within a project of social and cultural transformation. McLaren's *Che Guevara, Paulo Freire, and the Pedagogy of Revolution* (2000) sets out to introduce educators to the life and politics of Che Guevara; to recover the legacy of Paulo Freire from the interpretive efforts of educational humanists who have for the most part depotentiated the revolutionary import of Freire's teachings and have largely domesticated the Marxist trajectory of his politics; and to analyze the philosophical and political writings of these two figures in the context of their pedagogical theories and practices. In McLaren's view, the work of Marxist revolutionaries are too often overlooked in discussions of educational theory and pedagogical practice. Whereas such thinkers often occupy a prominent place in other disciplines such as philosophy and the social sciences, McLaren argues that educational theory is remiss in failing to discuss their important contributions. In setting forth his arguments, McLaren adopted Marxist-Humanist perspectives in his recent work and continues to produce frequent works in critical pedagogy (McLaren 2005 and 2016).[3]

Other noteworthy books in critical pedagogy include a co-edited a book by Nicholas Burbules and Carlos Torres on *Globalization and Education. Critical Perspectives* (1999) that articulates an overview of the challenges to education from globalization. Various contributors address the different components of globalization and offer conflicting perspectives. They argue that the economic restructuring of the global economy suggests both the need to reconstruct education to make it relevant to the needs of a new economy, but also provides challenges to resisting the imposition of a market-based model of education that would impose similar business models and imperatives on educational institutions throughout the world, with problematic results. Indeed, one of the major thrusts of the collection is to present some of the dangers involved in the imposition of neo-liberalism and market models on the institutions of education, while benefiting from potential advances of globalization, such as the Internet and new technologies, new forms of global and cosmopolitan culture, and a globalization of democracy and human rights.

In her 2001 book *Multi/Intercultural Conversations*, Shirley Steinberg introduces the concept of "critical multiculturalism" as a pedagogy focused on the intersection of power, identity and knowledge, engaging race, gender, class, and sexuality, and criticizing liberal versions of multiculturalism that serve as ideologies of "the melting pot" and that occlude forms of oppression. This perspective also informs Joe Kincheloe and Shirley Steinburg's *Changing Multiculturalism* (1997), which introduces concepts of "different ways of seeing" that encourage "learning from difference." In this critical pedagogy, the problematic liberal term "multiculturalism" is reconstructed into a "critical multiculturalism" which explores "the way power shapes consciousness" and that interprets race, gender and class as sites of oppression rooted in social and economic structures. Kincheloe and Steinberg analyze how these forces of oppression play out in the classroom and help construct student understandings, sense of identity and aspirations which can lead students to succumb to dominant ideologies of race, gender, and class and submit to dominant ideologies, thus producing a salient example of how Marxian ideology critique can be focused on themes like education, multiculturalism, and youth which classical Marxists did not address.

Steinberg and Kincheloe also introduce notion of "kinderculture" and explore childhood in *Kinderculture: The Corporate Construction of Childhood* (1997), an edited collection of essays focusing on the social construction of childhood in contemporary America. Steinberg and Kincheloe demonstrate that our society's most influential pedagogues are no longer either parents or classroom teachers, but are large media corporations which use media culture, such as television, films, popular music, and video games to enculturate and socialize consumers of media culture into proper social roles, behavior, attitudes and values, thus establishing that media is a major form of pedagogy, especially for children who are indoctrinated into Kinderculture at an early age, through Disney films, Barbie dolls, horror films, youth novels, multiple other forms of popular culture, and advertising and consumption.

Steinberg, Kincheloe, and their collaborators thus expand critical pedagogy into studies of media culture that transmits dominant ideologies and is a major force of enculturation and socialization, thus articulating critical pedagogy with the Frankfurt school. Steinberg's other major contributions to critical pedagogy include her approach to media, as developed in a book co-edited with Donaldo Macedo: *Media Literacy: A Reader.* The authors argue that social, cultural, and political forces are transmitted through the media that affect all members, groups, and classes of society and thus, to use Noam Chomsky's phrase, serve in helping construct the manufacture of consent" to mainstream society.[4] Teaching critical media literacy thus empowers students and students to question, decode, and critique dominant forms of media culture—a pedagogical project also recently articulated by Kellner and Share (2019).

Thus, critical pedagogy in recent decades has expanded into topics such as globalization, media culture and critical media literacies, and into arenas such as child culture, youth culture, and a variety of debates over education.[5] These works demonstrate the growing productivity of critical pedagogy and the productiveness of its appropriation of Marxian themes, showing that reconstructed versions of Marxism continue to be relevant into the 21st century.

Concluding Comments

Hence, neo-Marxian engagement with globalization, media culture, education, and a transformative pedagogy that links critical pedagogy with transformative social practice aiming at social justice point to the continuing relevance of Marxian perspectives for educational philosophy and practice today. Critical neo-Marxist pedagogues throughout the world have articulated problematics of gender, race, sexuality, and multiculturalism with Marxist concepts of class and domination, thus providing potential expansion and enrichment of Marxist perspectives. The type of structuralist Marxist theories of capital and schooling that began to circulate in the 1970s have been largely replaced by more poststructuralist and intersectional versions of Marxism that articulate together gender, race, class, and other subject positions (see Chapter One below and other chapters in this book). Some Marxist critics have argued, however, that the orthodox Marxist focuses on class and capital are often too decentered in more postmodern theories and have called for a return to class as the basis for a Marxist philosophy of education (see McLaren, 1998).

Indeed, the continuing viability of Marxian perspectives today are bound up with the continuing expansion of capitalism in a global economy and growing importance of the economy in every domain of life. Marxism has historically presented critical perspectives on capitalism and the ways that economic imperatives shape institutions like schooling to correspond to the interests of the ruling class. Neo-Marxist theories have sought to overcome a too-narrow focus on class and economics by stressing the importance of developing theories of agency and resistance and incorporating dimensions of gender, race, sexuality, and other subject positions into an expanded notion of multicultural education, democratization, and social justice. They have also developed a wide range of proposals for the reconstructions of education and development of alternative pedagogies and educational practices. These neo-Marxian positions are fiercely contested by conservative positions, however, and the field of education remains today a contested terrain where neo-Marxian positions are part of the force of opposition.

Notes

1   For a contemporary application of Adorno's theory of *Halbbildung*, see Lucas Lundbye Cone, "Towards a university of *Halbbildung*: How the neoliberal mode of higher education governance in Europe is half-educating students for a misleading future," *Educational Philosophy and Theory*, Volume 50, 2018—Issue 11: Special Issue of Submissions from European Liberal Education Student Conference," June 16, 2017, Pages 1020–1030; Published online at https://www.tandfonline.com/doi/abs/10.1080/00131857.2017.1341828 (accessed March 21, 2021).

2   Giroux has continued to be one of the most productive figures in critical pedagogy and educational theory in the 2000s publishing over forty books in the new millennium as of 2021.

3   McLaren also continued to be one of the most productive figures in critical pedagogy and educational theory in the 2000s with many authored and co-authored books including McLaren

(2005, 2016), McLaren, P., Macrine, S., and Hill, D., (Eds.) (2010) and McLaren and Jandric (2020).

4   Chomsky and Herman's *Manufacture of Consent* (2002) provides important contributions to demonstrating how Marxian political economy help understand the nature and social functions of corporate media in capitalist societies, an argument also made in Douglas Kellner's *Media Culture* (1995, 2020, second edition).

5   Shirley Steinberg and her associates have produced a wealth of books expanding critical pedagogy into child and youth cultures, popular cultures and media literacies, and a wide range of books articulating a tremendous range of topics within education and society in a dazzling array of books, including Steinberg 2018 and Steinberg and Kinchloe 1987; see also Steinberg's Amazon page at https://www.amazon.com/Shirley-R.-Steinberg/e/B00IO29NJK%3Fref=dbs_ a_mng_rwt_scns_share (accessed March 22, 2021).

References

Adorno, T.W. (1941) "On Popular Music," (with G. Simpson), *Studies in Philosophy and Social Science*, 9(1): 17–48.

——(1978 [1932]) "On the Social Situation of Music," *Telos* 35 (Spring): 129–165.

——— (1982) "On the Fetish Character of Music and the Regression of Hearing," in Arato and Gebhardt 1982: 270–299.

——— (1989) "On Jazz," in Bronner and Kellner 1989: 199–209.

——— (1991) *The Culture Industry*. London: Routledge.

Arato, Andrew and Eike Gebhardt (1982) *The Essential Frankfurt School Reader*. New York: Continuum.

Benjamin, Walter (1969) *Illuminations*. New York: Shocken.

Best, Steven and Douglas Kellner (1991) *Postmodern Theory: Critical Interrogations*. London and New York: Macmillan and Guilford Press.

——— (1997) *The Postmodern Turn*. New York: Guilford Press.

——— (2001) *The Postmodern Adventure*. New York: Guilford Press.

Bloch, Ernst (1986) *The Principle of Hope*. Cambridge: MIT Press.

Bowles, Samuel and Herbert Gintis (1976) *Schooling in Capitalist America*. New York: Basic Books.

Bronner, Stephen and Douglas Kellner (1989) *Critical Theory and Society. A Reader*. New York: Routledge.

Carver, Terence (1989) *Friedrich Engels. His Life and Thought*. London: Macmillan.

Centre for Contemporary Cultural Studies (1980a) *On Ideology*. London: Hutchinson.

——— (1980b) *Culture, Media, Language*. London: Hutchinson.

During, Simon (editor) (1993) *The Cultural Studies Reader*. London and New York: Routledge.

Freire, Paulo (1972) *The Pedagogy of the Oppressed*. New York: Herder and Herder.

Giroux, Henry (1992) *Border Crossings. Cultural Workers and the Politics of Education*. New York: Routledge.

———— (2000a) *Stealing Innocence*. New York: St. Martiní's Press.

———— (2000b) *Impure Acts. The Practical Politics of Cultural Studies*. New York and London: Routledge.

———— (2001) *Public Spaces, Private Lives*. Lanham, MD: Rowman and Littlefield.

———— (2019) *The New Henry Giroux Reader: The Role of the Public Intellectual in a Time of Tyranny*. New York: Myers Education Press.

———— (2020) *On Critical Pedagogy, 2nd edition*. London: Bloomsbury Academic.

Gottesman, Isaac (2016) *The Critical Turn in Education: From Marxist Critique to Poststructuralist Feminism to Critical Theories of Race*. New York: Routledge.

Grossberg, Lawrence, Nelson, Cary and Paula Treichler (1992) *Cultural Studies*. New York: Routledge.

Hall, Stuart, et al. (1980) *Culture, Media, Language*. London: Hutchinson.

Hall, Stuart (1980a) "Cultural Studies and the Centre: Some Problematics and Problems," in Hall et al., 1980, 15–47.

———— (1980b) "Encoding/Decoding," in Hall et al., 1980, 128–138.

Harvey, David. *The Condition of Postmodernity*. Cambridge: Blackwell: 1989.

Hebdige, Dick (1979) *Subculture. The Meaning of Style* . London: Methuen.

Herman, Edward and Noam Chomsky (2002) *Manufacture of Consent: The Political Economy of the Mass Media*. New York: Pantheon, reprint edition.

Hill, Dave (2001) "State Theory and the Neo-Liberal Reconstruction of Schooling," *British Journal of Sociology of Education*, 22(1): 135–155.

Hoggart, Richard (1957) *The Uses of Literacy*. New York: Oxford University Press.

hooks, bell (1994) *Teaching to Transgress*. London and New York: Routledge.

Horkheimer, Max and T.W. Adorno (1972) *Dialectic of Enlightenment*. New York: Herder and Herder.

Jameson, Fredric (1991) *Postmodernism, or the Cultural Logic of Late Capitalism*. Durham, N.C.: Duke University Press.

Jay, Martin (1973) *The Dialectical Imagination*. Boston: Little, Brown and Company.

Jefferson, Tony (editor) (1976) *Resistance through Rituals*. London: Hutchinson.

Johnson, Richard (1986/87) "What Is Cultural Studies Anyway?" *Social Text* 16: 38–80.

Kellner, Douglas (1989) *Critical Theory, Marxism, and Modernity*. Cambridge and Baltimore: Polity and John Hopkins University Press.

———— (1995) *Media Culture. Cultural Studies, Identity, and Politics Between the Modern and the Postmodern*. London and New York: Routledge; second revised edition 2020.

———— (2001) "Critical Pedagogy, Cultural Studies, and Radical Democracy at the Turn of the Millennium: Reflections on the Work of Henry Giroux," *Cultural Studies<>Critical Methodologies*, 1(2): 220–239.

———— (2002) "The Frankfurt School and British Cultural Studies: The Missed Articulation," in *Rethinking the Frankfurt School. Alternative Legacies of Cultural Critique*, edited by Jeffrey T. Nealon and Caren Irr. Albany, N.Y.: State University of New York Press, 31–58.

Kincheloe, Joe L. and Shirley R. Steinberg (1997) *Changing Multiculturalism*. Bristol, PA: Open University Pres.

Kracauer, Siegfried (1995) *The Mass Ornament*. Cambridge, MA: Harvard University Press.

Lather, Patti (2001) "Ten Years Later, Yet Again: Critical Pedagogy and its Complicities," in *Feminist Engagements*, edited by Kathleen Weiler. London and New York: Routledge.

Lowenthal, Leo (1961) *Literature, Popular Culture and Society*. Englewood Cliffs, NJ: Prentice-Hall.

Luke, Carmen and Jennifer Gore (1992) *Feminisms and Critical Pedagogy*. London and New York: Routledge.

Marcuse, Herbert (1964) *One-Dimensional Man*. Boston: Beacon Press; second edition, Beacon and Routledge Press, 1999.

Marx, Karl and Frederick Engels (1975–) *Collected Works*. New York and London: International Publishers and Lawrence & Wishart (referred in text as CW with volume number, i.e. CW5).

——— (1978) *The Marx-Engels Reader*, edited by Robert Tucker. New York: Norton.

McGuigan, Jim (1992) *Cultural Populism*. London and New York: Routledge.

McLaren, Peter (1998) "Revolutionary Pedagogy in Post-revolutionary Times: Rethinking the Political Economy of Critical Education." *Educational Theory*, 48(4): 431–462.

——— (2000) *Che Guevara, Paulo Freire, and the Pedagogy of Revolution*. Boulder, CO: Rowman and Littlefield.

——— (2005). *Red Seminars: Radical Excursions into Educational Theory, Cultural Politics, and Pedagogy*. Hampton Press.

——— (2016). *Pedagogy of Insurrection: From Resurrection to Revolution*. New York: Peter Lang.

McLaren, Peter and Petar Jandric (2020). *Postdigital Dialogues on Critical Pedagogy, Liberation Theology and Information Technology*. London: Bloomsbury Academic.

McLaren, Peter and Peter Leonard (1993) *Paulo Friere. A Critical Encounter*. London and New York: Routledge.

McLaren, Peter, Rhonda Hammer, Susan Reily, and David Sholle (1995) *Rethinking Media Literacy: A Critical Pedagogy of Representation*. New York: Peter Lang Publishing Inc.

McLellan, David (1973) *Karl Marx. His Life and Thought*. New York: Harper and Row.

Pinar, William F., Williams M. Reynolds, Patrick Slattery, and Peter M. Taubman (1996) *Understanding Curriculum*. New York: Peter Lang.

Rikowski, Glenn (1996) "Left Alone: End Time for Marxist Educational Theory?" *British Journal of Sociology of Education* 17(4): 415–437.

——— (1997) "Scorched Earth: Prelude to Rebuilding Marxist Educational Theory," *British Journal of Sociology of Education* 18(4): 551–574.

Steinberg, Shirley R. (2001) *Multi/Intercultural Conversations*. New York: Peter Lang.

——— (2018) *Christotainment: Selling Jesus through Popular Culture*. New York and London: Routledge

Steinberg, Shirley R. and Joe L. Kincheloe (editors) (1997) *Kinderculture: The Corporate Construction of Childhood, 1ˢᵗ Edition*. Boulder, CO: Westview Press.

Thompson, E.P. (1963) *The Making of the Working Class*. New York: Pantheon.

Wheen, Francis (2000) *Karl Marx. A Life*. New York: Norton.

Wiggershaus, Rolf (1994) *The Frankfurt School*. Cambridge, UK: Polity Press.

Williams, Raymond (1961) *The Long Revolution*. London: Chatto and Windus.

——— (1962) *Communications*. London: Penquin.

Willis, Paul (1981) *Learning to Labor*. New York: Columbia University Press.

CHAPTER THREE

Exploring the Roots of Digital and Media Literacy through Personal Narrative

My own approach to media and critical media literacy was mediated through in-teraction with Multiple Grand and (God)Fathers, including critical theorists like Herbert Marcuse and Jurgen Habermas, proponents of a political economy ap-proach to media like Noam Chomsky and Herbert Schiller, and a cultural ecology approach inspired by Marshall McLuhan and developed by George Gerbner. I have always maintained that an important part of critical media literacy is more broadly understanding media and their significant economic, political, cultural, and social effects. Understanding media and promoting critical media literacy in its contemporary moment thus led me to engage a variety of media, cultural, and social theorists, which led me to develop a multi-perspectival approach to media with focus on political economy, media texts, audiences, and analyses of the mul-tiple roles and impact of media in contemporary society that made cultivating crit-ical media literacy such an important part of becoming a citizen in today's world (Kellner, 1995 [2020]).

In this chapter, I provide a personal narrative of my encounter with dif-ferent contemporary media theorists and theories, and how I came to synthe-size their work into my own approach to media, focusing on Herbert Marcuse and the Frankfurt School, British Cultural Studies, and critical communications theorists. This multiperspectivist approach involves crossing the divide between political economy and cultural studies, combining humanities and social science approaches to the media, and developing a concept of critical media and digital literacies as a key component of education for today's world. I will provide an autobiographical narrative of how I came to focus upon media and critical media literacy, and of meeting figures who deeply influenced me like Herbert Marcuse, Jurgen Habermas, Noam Chomsky, Herbert Schiller, George Gerbner, and Jean Baudrillard. I will also discuss media theorists who influenced my approach to media and media literacy, those I met through their texts, such as Marshall McLuhan, T.W. Adorno, and Guy Debord. I want to begin, however, with some memories of my own grandfather who taught me to read the daily newspaper, and then having morning paper routes in Falls Church, Virginia and Valley Stream, New York where my first jobs were delivering *The Washington Post* and *The New York Times* and other New York papers on Long Island.

Grandfathers, Paper Routes, and (Theoretical) Godfathers

I was born in the Chelsea Massachusetts Medical Hospital on May 31, 1943. My parents had been married for about three years and had been working for the U.S. government in Washington. My father then joined the Navy, took some courses in economics and business administration at Harvard, and prepared to go to war. My mother gave birth to a child who turned out to be a writer and philosopher, and then she organized a trek across the United States with a six-week-old baby. In a well-documented train ride, my mother and two of her sisters took me from Harvard to Berkeley and then to Carpentaria, California, south of Santa Barbara where the familial unit lived in a paradise overlooking the Pacific Ocean, if one can trust the documentary evidence of home movies of scenes in a small house on a hillside.

The family idyll was short-lived as my father was sent to Hawaii where he served as paymaster in the Navy, roamed the beach with my Uncle Carl, and seemingly avoided trauma or injury in World War II. With the defeat of German and Japanese fascism, my father returned home from war, and got a job with Addressograph-Multigraph business machines as a salesman. My parents rented an apartment in the modest building where my grandparents lived in downtown Los Angeles on South Hope Street.

My young and impressionable body was transported from an ecological paradise in Carpentaria to urban Los Angeles. For the next few years, we lived in downtown LA, and family stories and photographs have my grandfather walking me every day through Bunker Hill, later bull-dozed to build the Bonaventure, the Music Center, and high-rise corporate buildings. According to family legend, my Bunker Hall regime included a daily walk through the neighborhood to the Biltmore Hotel lobby where my grandfather would buy a cigar and a newspaper, and then read to me the current events of the world, surrounded by the swells in the Biltmore lobby. In retrospect, I evidently received an early positive exposure to newspapers that have been a constant feature of my life from childhood on to the present where I begin the day reading a newspaper, before going online and checking other media sources.

My brother John was born in 1947 and the nucleus of the typical American middle-class family was emerging, although we were outgrowing the small LA apartment. My urban flaneur existence came to an end around 1949 when my parents bought a house in Temple City in a new housing development for about $4000. My artistic proclivities at that time were crushed when I decorated the freshly painted downtown LA apartment by drawing pretty pictures on the white walls with crayon. My parents and grandparents were horrified with my aesthetic creations, and for the first-time I can remember I was physically disciplined with my grandfather taking out his belt, putting me across his knees, and spanking out any artistic aptitude I may have had.

It was off to Temple City, a small town east of LA, where Alfred Hitchcock's *Shadow of a Doubt* was set the year of my birth, and which was quickly becoming suburbanized. At that time, the suburbs where relatively new, and so I was among the rising number of suburbanites who would mushroom in the 1950s and become a distinctive form and way of life in American society. Our house on 9828 East Broadway was newly built and new houses were popping up throughout my neighborhood, although there were many homes that had been there for some years so the 'hood was not one of the ticky-tacky little boxes all the same that continue to be satirized to this day (see the opening credit sequence of the TV-series *Weeds*).

I clearly remember walking down East Broadway to start kindergarten, but I do not remember much of what happened in the classrooms or playgrounds, but it was apparently quite benign, as I recall no school traumas. I do remember clearly the first time I watched television, as a neighbor down the street bought the first TV set in the neighborhood and I remember showing up at 5:30 p.m. every weekday afternoon, taking off my shoes and washing my feet, and going in and watching in rapt attention with other neighborhood kids *The Howdy Doody Show*, and, if pressed, could still sing the opening song, "It's Howdy Doody Time!"

Apparently, I started going to church and Sunday school at an early age, and my most traumatic memory of the period is coming home from Sunday school, finding my house full of neighbors, and my grandmother crying, with the terrible news conveyed that my grandfather had a heart attack and died while cutting grass on our front yard with a lawn mower. Tragically, the next day he was scheduled to begin building his own house for my grandmother and himself (he had been a carpenter and built many of the houses in Scribner, Nebraska, where my father and my grandparents grew up).[1]

This was my first memorable encounter with death and family tragedy, I remember my grandmother immediately going into great depression and dying not so long afterwards. Otherwise, suburban living was placid, and I recall no crime, violence, or disruptions in the neighborhood, although I do remember an earthquake with my mother and I standing in the living room feeling the ground shake and some plates and glasses crashing onto the floor.

In the following years I would successively live in Falls Church, Virginia, Valley Stream, New York, Glen Ellyn, Illinois, and Larchmont, New York. After selling business machines for several years in California with Addressograph-Multigraph, my father returned to work for the U.S. government in Washington (1952–1956), and then went back to work for Addressograph-Multigraph again on Long Island (1956–1958). He switched to Arbitron in New York City, a firm that did TV and radio-ratings around 1958 and was transferred to their Chicago office (1961), and then returned to New York, where my parents bought an up-scale house in Larchmont in 1965. Some years later, in the late 1960s, my father was fired in a merger acquisition, and my family learned of the challenges of corporate downsizing. I remember the day he was downsized well as I received a phone call from my father late afternoon from a bar in midtown New York and he told me to meet him there, an event that had never previously occurred. I saw that he had had a couple of drinks and was in a philosophical and reflective mode, telling me that he'd just been fired and decided he would follow my path, choosing an academic career.

Hence, renouncing the corporate rat-race, my father decided to become a professor, finishing his Ph.D. in communications and teaching at Marshall University in West Virginia, where, coincidentally, my brother had settled after some years in hippie communes, supporting himself and his family by renovating homes, businesses, and public buildings, skills he had learned in country-side hippie communes in Iowa and West Virginia, the only one of our family to live a non-urban existence (he is still living in the mountains of Appalachia). My mother had been a high school Latin and English teacher and there were always books around the house. I was a systematic and scholarly reader, starting with all the *Little Golden Books*, and moving up to *Classics Illustrated Comic Books*, of which I had an entire collection. I discovered the library in Temple City and read all the *Winnie the Pooh* books and *Doctor Doolittle* series; I also remember reading and owning a full series of *The Hardy Boys* mystery books. Later summers, while in high school and then college, I would systematically read Poe, Hemingway, Fitzgerald, Steinbeck, dos Passos, Dreiser, and whoever else caught my literary fancy.

My California adventure came to an end as we moved to Falls Church, Virginia, and I learned about race, the South and work. Many of our neighbors were Southerners who were horrified that my brother and I did not hunt nor fish and tried to properly socialize us into approved masculinity. I enjoyed fishing, but abhorred hunting and cannot to this day understand why grown men would want to shoot animals (much less other human beings as is happening in the mass shootings that are intensifying as Congress, so far, has failed to address an out-of-control gun culture). I could also not understand the prejudices of some of my neighbors from the South against Blacks and people of color. I was a rock and roll fan and sports fanatic and many of my favorite singers and athletics were African American and I thought they were *way cool*. I was in awe of Black entertainers and athletes as a teenager and continue to be a fan of multicultural entertainment to this day.

At this time, around nine or ten years of age, my literary career began when my parents bought me a hectograph for Christmas and I started printing out a literary journal, *Ye Olde Courthouse Digest*, an amalgam of my serialized adventure stories, school gossip, and (or so I would like to think), social and political commentary. I was active in the community, making Eagle Boy Scout as our local military folks trained us in survivalism and counterinsurgency through camping trips, and hikes through the Appalachian Mountains. I also played Little League baseball, Church basketball, and was an ace in ping pong, badminton, miniature golf, and other sports. I went to Bible Studies in the summer, was head of the Methodist Young Fellowship, and went to church three times a day on Sunday.

I also became a young capitalist, waking up every morning to deliver *The Washington Post*, invested my earnings in the stock market, and eventually saved enough to later finance a year in Paris. It was at this time, I would begin reading through the newspaper every day, starting, at this time, with sports and then moving to comic strips, followed by early attempts to make sense of the world through newspaper stories, and hence had a close relation with newspapers my entire life, as paper delivery was my introduction to the working day and paid labor.

Once again suburban bliss was disrupted when I was around 12 and approaching my teen years, as my parents moved to Valley Stream, New York. Here, I was quickly initiated into multiculturalism and racism when I discovered that the Jews, Italians, Swedes, Irish, and other ethnicities around me often hated each other, using a variety of nasty names to call one another (ones I'd never heard of). I was interested in cultural difference and cultivated friends from all these groups. I was, however, a bit of a freak with a southern accent, which I quickly lost and assimilated myself by joining the football and track teams (which saved me from having to get into fights every day after school in rough and tumble Elmont High School, where I was regularly teased about my accent, having lived in the South, until I joined the football team which discouraged bullies from messing with jocks).

I discovered New York City at this time and regularly took the bus and subway to Times Square for movies, to the Village to walk around and take in the scene, and to Chinatown to buy firecrackers (I later bought my first ounce of grass in Little Italy when I was in Graduate School at Columbia). In high school, I read existentialism, liked Kerouac and the Beats, and was trying to be cool. I don't remember any teachers or classes that influenced me in high school, except the typing class in the ninth grade, the only boy in the class, I learned speed-typing, clearly my most valuable high school asset. I also remember when I was one of ten to win a New York State Regents Scholarship, my friends howled with glee and the smart kids were surprised, since I was associated with athletics more than academics.

In Valley Stream, I continued early morning labor as a paperboy, waking up before 5:00 a.m. every morning and picked up a bundle of newspapers, including *The New York Times, The New York Daily News, The Herald Tribune,* and the local Long Island newspaper. At my request, the man who delivered my bundle of newspapers every morning put in an extra copy of *The New York Times,* and so as a teenager I began reading daily *The New York Times* and stopped going to church and Sunday school every week, in part to spend the day immersed in reading the quite formidable Sunday *Times.*

My parents moved to Chicago during my senior year in high school and I stayed with family friends to finish up and graduate. In the confusion, all my college acceptance letters got in too late, I was facing my senior year in high school without a college to attend. My parents had gone to Doane College in Crete, Nebraska, my father was on the Board of Regents there, and I got a full athletic and scholastic scholarship, beginning an academic career that was fully subsidized (although my father made me work in Chicago factories during the summers where I discovered the dubious joys of proletarian existence).

I had a philosophy teacher at Doane, Robert Browne, who included Erich Fromm and Martin Buber in his curricula, and the beginnings of a philosophical orientation marked by existentialism and critical social theory that would make the Frankfurt School project sympathetic to me were evolving. I consequently read Marx, Nietzsche, Freud and the like in college, and began to self-consciously study philosophy and imagine myself becoming a philosophy professor.

One of the most eventful college experiences was pulling my ankle tendon in a track meet and ending my athletic career. My Elmont High team came in third in a mile relay in a New York area track meet at Madison Square, and we were jokingly referred to as the "fastest white guys in New York." I had also set a course record in a cross country meet my senior year in high school, after coaches pulled me from the football team and put me into cross country, as they correctly discerned that I could get a track scholarship to college (and had no future as a football player as I was too small). I ran on track and cross-country teams in college, and ending my sports career was a radical change as I had been working out running for hours a day for years on end. I had a big challenge concerning how I was going to spend my life and focus my life-energies.

The existential void was overwhelming and could only be filled with heavy doses of Kierkegaard, Nietzsche, Sartre, Camus, and existential philosophy. A Junior Year Abroad in Copenhagen in 1963–64 aided my Kierkegaard studies and I also discovered socialism at the foreign student club where my attempts to defend U.S. capitalism and democracy were soundly thrashed. A bad flu and free medicine taught me the rationality of socialized medicine and I came to the conclusion that free education was also cool, as was free love, and I have been a partisan of socialism and liberationism since then.

After a junior year abroad in Copenhagen during the summer of 1964 I made a conscious choice to become a philosophy professor. Living with my family in Glen Ellen, Illinois, during the summer, my Uncle Bob got me a job at Cinch Manufacturing with one of his corporate law clients. I thus had my first 9–5 job in which every day I went to work in a factory on the Southside of Chicago and toiled in the mailing room, sorting out and labeling packages. This experience made it clear that I did not want a 9–5 job, but gave me a sense of working-class life, as I spent many evenings and some weekends with my fellow workers. This same summer, Uncle Bob told me that he could get me into Michigan law school, would support my law studies, and would then give me a position in his corporate law firm. I politely declined, however, knowing that I wanted to go into a graduate philosophy program and teach philosophy. The same summer, my next door neighbor gave me a stack of rightwing books to read and invited me to join AT&T's Junior Executive Program after I graduated from college, and he was astounded when I said that I want go to graduate school to study philosophy (this was the Goldwater era, but I was raised in an FDR liberal family, and I did not tell him what I thought of the rightwing books he had given me).

During my senior year in college, I was nominated for a Woodrow Wilson Fellowship and went to the interview in Kansas City, obviously charming the interviewers with my tales of studying Kierkegaard in Denmark and interest in Heidegger and existential philosophy. I was awarded the Woodrow Wilson Fellowship which meant that I could receive a full scholarship to any graduate program that accepted me. At this time, I was focused on living in New York City and made an appointment with James Walsh, the Chairman of the Columbia philosophy department who informed me that with the Woodrow Wilson Fellowship, Columbia would happily accept me, and so I decided there and then to go to Columbia University to study philosophy.

In the meantime, my parents returned to New York, and in summer of 1965 I took courses at the New School, reading Sartre's *Being and Nothingness*, as well as a seminar on Freud and Jung, and I was now well on my way to becoming a philosopher, before even starting my graduate studies in philosophy at Columbia. New York was increasingly capturing my imagination as the place in which I wanted most to live with its museums, films, theatre, and bohemian subculture. I entered Columbia in Fall 1965 and moved to the upper West Side, learning as much philosophy in various parts of New York City as I did from my readings and seminars.

For the next several years, I experienced the joys of New York life in the 1960s. I hung out at the West End bar on Broadway where previous generations of Columbia students had convened, including Ginsberg, Kerouac, and their Beat friends. I went to movies at the Thalia Theater and New Yorker, seeing classical films of global cinema and the new imports from Europe. I went to the Village and saw off-Broadway plays, hung out in coffee shops, and heard music, becoming a great Bob Dylan fan, who I sometimes saw with Joan Baez and others hanging out in the Village.

In the New York of the 1960s there were frequent talks of how we were becoming a media society, the ideas of Marshall McLuhan were en vogue. I devoured *Understanding Media* which gave me a broad overview of the many media of communication that were proliferating during the era and continued reading McLuhan's book which were highly popular at the time. When I began teaching at the University of Texas, Austin, in the 1970s, I devised a course on Philosophy of Communication. I always began with McLuhan and continue to read him and included his work in my Cultural Studies seminars at UCLA where I went to teach in the mid-1990s, as the rightwing took over Texas.

At Columbia in 1969, I heard Herbert Marcuse lecture one evening, and the next day during a reception in the Philosophy Department where none of the philosophy professors showed up, Marcuse asked me and other graduate students to escort him to the West End Bar where earlier Ginsberg and the Beats hung out, where, at the time my fellow graduate students also frequented the bar, for eating, drinking and philosophizing into the wee hours of the night. From Marcuse's writings and lectures, I got the sense that the media were a powerful instrument of the dominant ideology and a great force of reproducing consumer capitalism, a model of the media that Adorno and Horkheimer had earlier developed in their famous analysis of the culture industry in *Dialectic of Enlightenment*.

The Frankfurt School, the Culture Industry, and Media Critique

I began at that time, a sustained study of Marcuse's work that led to publication of my book *Herbert Marcuse and the Crisis of Marxism* (1984). A philosopher, social theorist, and political activist, Marcuse gained world renown during the 1960s as "father of the New Left." Author of many books and articles, and University professor, Marcuse gained notoriety when he was perceived as both an influence on and defender of the "New Left" in the United States and Europe and advocate of revolutionary socialism. His theory of "one-dimensional" society provided critical perspectives on contemporary capitalist and state communist societies and his notion of "the great refusal" won him renown as a theorist of revolutionary change and "liberation from the affluent society" (see Kellner, 1984). Consequently, Marcuse became one of the most influential intellectuals in the United States during the 1960s and into the 1970s.

In 1933, Marcuse joined the *Institut fur Sozialforschung* (Institute for Social Research) in Frankfurt and soon became deeply involved in their interdisciplinary projects which included working out a model for radical social theory, developing a theory of the new stage of state and monopoly capitalism, providing a systematic analysis and critique of German fascism, and developing a theory of the new roles of mass culture and communication in modern societies. Marcuse deeply identified with the "Critical Theory" of the Institute and throughout his life was close to Max Horkheimer, T.W. Adorno, and others in the Institute's inner circle.

The analyses by members of the Institute of the functions of culture, ideology, and the mass media in contemporary societies constitute one of its most valuable legacies. The critical theorists excelled as critics of both so-called "high culture" and "mass culture" while producing many important texts in these areas. Their work is distinguished by the close connection between social theory and cultural critique, and by their ability to contextualize culture within social environments and struggles. Their theory of culture was bound up with analysis of the dialectic of enlightenment (Horkheimer and Adorno, 1972). Culture—once a refuge of beauty and truth—was falling prey, they believed, to tendencies toward rationalization,

standardization, commodification, and conformity which they saw as a conse-
quence of triumph from the instrumental rationality that was coming to pervade
and structure ever more aspects of life in contemporary capitalist societies. Thus,
while culture once cultivated individuality, it was now promoting conformity, and
was a crucial part of "the totally administered society" that was producing "the end
of the individual" (Horkheimer and Adorno, 1972, pp. 17–38).

The critical theorists came to see what they called the "culture industry" as a
central part of a new configuration of capitalist modernity which used culture, advertising, mass communications, and new forms of social control to induce consent
to and reproduce the new forms of capitalist society. The production and transmission of media spectacles which transmit ideology and consumerism through the
means of allegedly "popular entertainment" and information were, they believed,
a central mechanism through which contemporary society came to dominate the
individual.

Adorno and Horkheimer adopted the term "culture industry," as opposed to
concepts like "popular culture" or "mass culture," because they wanted to resist
notions that products of the culture industry emanated from the masses (that is,
from the people). They saw the culture industry as being an administered culture,
imposed from above, as instruments of indoctrination and social control. The term
culture industry thus contains a dialectical irony typical of the style of Frankfurt
School critical theory: culture, as traditionally valorized, is supposed to be opposed
to industry and expressive of individual creativity while providing a repository of
humanizing values. In the culture industry, however, culture has come to function
as a mode of ideological domination and social control rather than of humanization or emancipation.

The culture industry was perceived as the culmination of a historical process
in which technology and scientific organization and administration came to dominate thought and experience. Although Horkheimer and Adorno (1972) carry
out a radical questioning of Marxism and the development of an alternative philosophy of history and theory of society in *Dialectic of Enlightenment*, their theory
of the culture industry provides a neo-Marxian account of mass media and culture
which helps explain both the ways in which the culture industry reproduced capitalist societies and why socialist revolutions failed to take place in these societies.
In this sense, the Institute theory of "culture industry as mass deception" provides
a rebuttal both to Georg Lukács' theory of revolution and "class consciousness,"
and to Bertolt Brecht's and Walter Benjamin's belief that the new forces of mass
communications—especially radio and film—could serve as instruments of technological progress and social enlightenment which could be turned against the

capitalist relations of production and could be used as instruments of political mobilization and struggle (Kellner, 1989).

For Adorno and Horkheimer, by contrast, these new technologies were used as instruments of ideological mystification and class domination. Against Georg Lukács (1972) and others who argued that capitalist society necessarily radicalized the working class and produced class consciousness, Adorno and Horkheimer could argue that the culture industry inhibits the development of class consciousness by providing the ruling political and economic forces with a powerful instrument of social control. The conception of the culture industry therefore provides a model of a technically advanced capitalist society which mobilizes support for its institutions, practices, and values *from below* making class-consciousness more difficult to attain than before. Using Gramsci's terminology (1971), the culture industry reproduces capitalist hegemony over the working class by engineering *consent* to the existing society, and thus establishing a socio-psychological basis for social integration. Whereas fascism destroyed civil society (or the "public sphere") through politicizing mediated institutions, or utilizing force to suppress all dissent, the culture industry coaxes individuals into the privacy of their own home, or movie theater, producing consumers-spectators of media events and escapist entertainment who are being subtly indoctrinated into dominant ideologies.

For the Frankfurt School, mass culture and communications therefore stand in the center of leisure activity, are important agents of socialization and mediators of political reality and should be seen as major institutions of contemporary societies with a variety of economic, political, cultural, and social effects. The critical theorists investigated the cultural industry politically as a form of integration of the working class into capitalist societies. The Frankfurt School theorists were among the first neo-Marxian groups to examine the effects of mass culture and the rise of the consumer society on the working classes, the class that were to be the instrument of revolution in the classical Marxian scenario. They also analyzed the ways that the culture industry and consumer society were stabilizing contemporary capitalism and accordingly sought new strategies for political change, agencies of political transformation, and models for political emancipation that could serve as norms of social critique and goals for political struggle.

The analysis of the culture industry stands, therefore, in a quite ambivalent relationship to classical Marxism. On one hand, the theory is part of the foundation for the critical theory of society, replacing the critique of political economy which had been the foundation for social theories previously in the Marxian tradition. And it served as an important part of the explanation of why the Institute critical theorists no longer placed faith in the revolutionary vocation of the proletariat. Yet in other ways, the analysis of the culture industry employs Marxian arguments through stressing capitalist control of culture, the commodification and reification of culture, its ideological functions, and the ways that it integrates individuals into capitalist society.

For example, Adorno and Horkheimer utilize a model that pits the individual against its "adversary—the absolute power of capitalism" (1972, p. 120), and describe the tendencies toward conformity, standardization, and deception in the culture industry by means of its control by monopoly corporations which themselves are central to the capitalist system (1972, p. 120 ff.). The very processes of production in the culture industry are modeled on factory production where everything is standardized, streamlined, coordinated, and planned down to the last detail. Indeed, Adorno and Horkheimer use their analysis of the culture industry to call attention to what they perceive as the fundamental traits of the administered society, and to carry out a radical critique of capitalism. They suggest that reflection on the culture industries illuminates the processes toward standardization, homogenization, and conformity that characterize social life under what they call "totalitarian capitalism."

The tendencies toward manipulation and domination in the culture industry illuminate similar trends throughout capitalist society in the Frankfurt School analysis. We find similarity to the mass deception present in the culture industries and the deception, false promises, and manipulation in the capitalist economic, political, and social spheres. In this conception, one of the main trends of contemporary capitalist societies is the synthesis of advertising, consumer culture, information, politics, and manipulation that characterizes the culture industries. This dialectical focus on the relationships between the culture industry, capitalism, politics, and social life points to a basic methodological position within the Institute critical theory of society that in turn marks its affinity to Marxian dialectics.

For critical theory, every social phenomenon must be interpreted in terms of a theory of society which itself is part of a stage of capitalism. The theory of the relationships between society and the economy illuminate phenomena like the culture industry, and its analysis in turn sheds light on the economy, politics, culture, and society under capitalism. Consequently, critical theory operates with a dialectic between its topics of analysis (the culture industry, anti-Semitism, or other themes) and its theory of society. In this dialectic, the critical theory of society illuminates the topic under investigation which in turn illuminates the fundamental social trends (i.e., commodification, reification, the culture industry, the authoritarian personality, etc.) described in the social theory (see Kellner, 1989).

In the Dialectic of Enlightenment, Horkheimer and Adorno describe the style of culture industry products and the formulas, conventions, and stereotypes that constitute it, as well as several of the strategies used to indoctrinate its consumers into acceptance of the existing society. "Entertainment," they claim, accustoms the audiences to accept existing society as natural by endlessly repeating and reproducing similar views of the world which present the existing way of life as the way of the world. The eternal recurrence of the same in the culture industry changes, they suggest, the very nature of ideology:

> Accordingly, ideology has been made vague and noncommittal, and thus neither clearer nor weaker. Its very vagueness, its almost scientific aversion from committing itself to anything which cannot be verified, acts as an instrument of domination. It becomes a vigorous and prearranged promulgation of the status quo. The culture industry tends to make itself the embodiment of authoritative pronouncements, and thus the irrefutable prophet of the prevailing order. It skillfully steers a winding course between the cliffs of demonstrable misinformation and manifest truth, faithfully reproducing the phenomenon whose opaqueness blocks any insight and installs the ubiquitous and intact phenomenon as ideal. Ideology is split into the photograph of stubborn life and the naked lie about its meaning -- which is not expressed but suggested and yet drummed in. To demonstrate its divine nature, reality is always repeated in a purely cynical way. Such a photological proof is of course not stringent, but it is overpowering .... The new ideology has as its objects the world as such. It makes use of the worship of facts by no more than elevating a disagreeable existence into the world of facts in representing it meticulously (1972, pp. 147–148).

The culture industry thus tries to induce the individual to identify with society's typical figures and models: "Pseudo-individuality is rife: from the standardized jazz improvisation to the exceptional film star whose hair curls over her eye to demonstrate her originality. What is individual is no more than the generality's power to stamp the accidental detail so firmly that it is accepted as such. The defiant reserve or elegant appearance of the individual on show is mass-produced like Yale locks, whose only difference can be measured in fractions of millimeters" (1972, p. 154). The culture industry thus serves as a powerful instrument of social control that induces individuals to accept their fate and conform to existing society. Advertising progressively fuses in style and technique with the entertainment of the culture industry (1972, pp. 156–167) which in turn can be read as advertisements for the existing society and established way of life.

Herbert Marcuse's Media Critique

In 1955 the Institute critique of the culture industries plays a central role in both Fromm's book *The Sane Society* (1955) and Marcuse's *Eros and Civilization* (1955). Using Freudian and Marxian categories, Marcuse described the process through which sexual and aggressive instincts are tamed and channeled into socially necessary, but unpleasant, labor. Following the Institute analysis of changes in the nature of socialization, Marcuse notes the decline of the family as the dominant agent of socialization and the rise of the mass media: "The repressive organization of the instincts seems to be collective, and the ego seems to be prematurely socialized by a whole system of extra-familial agents and agencies. As early as the pre-school level, gangs, radio, and television set the pattern for conformity and rebellion; deviations from the pattern are punished not so much in the family as outside and against the family. The experts of the mass media transmit the required values; they offer the perfect training in efficiency, toughness, personality, dream, and romance. With this education, the family can no longer compete" (Marcuse, 1955, p. 97).

In Marcuse's view, the mass media were becoming dominant agents of socialization which were displacing the primacy of the family—its role in both Freudian and many U.S. social science theories. The result is the decline of individual autonomy and manipulation of mind and instincts by mass communications: "With the decline in consciousness, with the control of information, with the absorption of individuals into mass communication, knowledge is administered and confined. The individual does not really know what is going on; the overpowering machine of education and entertainment unites him with all the others in a state of anesthesia from which all detrimental ideas tend to be excluded" (p. 104).

Marcuse continued to stress the manipulative effects of the culture industries in his major works and contributed to the wide-spread adoption of the so-called "manipulation theory" of the media by the New Left and others in the 1960s. In *One-Dimensional Man* (1964, p. 25), Marcuse claims that the inanities of commercial radio and television confirm his analyzes of the decline of the individual and the demise of authentic culture and oppositional thought in "advanced industrial society." Throughout the book, he assigns an important role to the media as "new forms of social control" which engender "false needs" and "one-dimensional" thought and behavior necessary for the smooth reproduction of advanced capitalism.

Marcuse's *One-Dimensional Man* (1964) contains a wide-ranging critique of both advanced capitalist and communist societies which theorized the decline of revolutionary potential in capitalist societies and the development of new forms of social control. Marcuse argued that "advanced industrial society" created false needs which integrated individuals into the existing system of production and consumption. Mass media and culture, advertising, industrial management, and contemporary modes of thought all reproduced the existing system and attempt to eliminate negativity, critique, and opposition. The result was a "one-dimensional" universe of thought and behavior in which the very aptitude and ability for critical thinking and oppositional behavior was withering away.

Not only had capitalism integrated the working class, the source of potential revolutionary opposition, but they had developed new techniques of stabilization through state policies and the development of new forms of social control. Thus, Marcuse questioned two of the fundamental postulates of orthodox Marxism: the revolutionary proletariat and inevitability of capitalist crisis. In contrast with the more extravagant demands of orthodox Marxism, Marcuse championed non-integrated forces of minorities, outsiders, and radical intelligentsia and attempted to nourish oppositional thought and behavior through promoting radical thinking and opposition.

One-Dimensional Man was severely criticized by orthodox Marxists and theorists of various political and theoretical commitments. Despite its pessimism, it influenced many in the New Left as it articulated their growing dissatisfaction with both capitalist societies and Soviet communist societies. Moreover, Marcuse himself continued to defend demands for revolutionary change and defended the new, emerging forces of radical opposition, thus winning him the hatred of establishment forces and the respect of the new radicals.

One-Dimensional Man was followed by a series of books and articles which articulated New Left politics and critiques of capitalist societies in "Repressive Tolerance" (1965), *An Essay on Liberation* (1969), and *Counterrevolution and Revolt* (1972). "Repressive Tolerance" (1975) attacked liberalism and those who refused to take a stand during the controversies of the 1960s. It won Marcuse the reputation of being an intransigent radical and ideologue for the Left. *An Essay on Liberation* celebrated all of the existing liberation movements from the Viet Cong to the hippies and exhilarated many radicals while further alienating establishment academics and those who opposed the movements of the 1960s. *Counterrevolution and Revolt*, by contrast, articulates the new realism that was setting in during the early 1960s when it was becoming clear that the most extravagant hopes of the 1960s were being dashed by a turn to the right and "counterrevolution" against the 1960s.

In 1965, Brandeis University refused to renew his teaching contract and Marcuse soon after received a position at the University of California at La Jolla where he remained until his retirement in the 1970s. During this period—of his greatest influence—Marcuse also published many articles and gave lectures and advice to student radicals all over the world. He traveled widely and his work was often discussed in the mass media, becoming one of the few American intellectuals to gain such attention. Never surrendering his revolutionary vision and commitments, Marcuse continued to his death to defend the Marxian theory and libertarian socialism. A charismatic teacher, Marcuse's students began to gain influential academic positions and to promote his ideas, making him a major force in U.S. intellectual life.

Marcuse also dedicated much of his work to aesthetics and his final book, *The Aesthetic Dimension* (1979), briefly summarizes his defense of the emancipatory potential of aesthetic form in so called "high culture." Marcuse thought that the best of the bourgeois tradition of art contained powerful indictments of bourgeois society and emancipatory visions of a better society, and that art had emancipatory pedagogical effects by projecting images of liberation and creating an aesthetic sensibility that rebelled against conformity and oppression. Thus, he attempted to defend the importance of great art for the project of emancipation and argued that cultural revolution was an indispensable part of revolutionary politics, and that revolutionary pedagogy was an important part of revolutionary change (see Kellner, Lewis, and Pierce [2008] and Kellner, Cho, Lewis and Pierce [2009]).

Marcuse's work in philosophy and social theory generated fierce controversy and polemics, and most studies of his work are highly tendentious and frequently sectarian. Although much of the controversy involved his critiques of contemporary capitalist societies and defense of radical social change, in retrospect, Marcuse left behind a complex and many-sided body of work comparable to the legacies of Ernst Bloch, Georg Lukács, T.W. Adorno, and Walter Benjamin.

In retrospect, Marcuse's vision of liberation—of the full development of the individual in a non-repressive society—distinguished his work, along with sharp critique of existing forms of domination and oppression. Primarily, a philosopher, Marcuse's work lacked the sustained empirical analysis in some versions of Marxist theory and the detailed conceptual analysis found in many versions of political theory. Yet he constantly showed how science, technology, and theory itself had a political dimension and produced a solid body of ideological and political analysis of many of the dominant forms of society, culture, and thought during the turbulent era in which he lived, and he constantly struggled for a better world.

In an important essay "On Affirmative Culture," published in *Negations* (1968) Herbert Marcuse provides a dialectical analysis of bourgeois high culture and the ways in which it is both a vehicle of emancipation and of mystification of existing social reality. On his view, culture provides a higher compensatory realm for escape and diversion from the cares of everyday life, as well as a refuge which preserves higher ideals and claims to freedom, happiness, and a better life denied in the existing organization of society. Hence, bourgeois culture is "affirmative" of higher cultural ideals which provide both ideological and potentially critical and emancipatory functions.

Many later analyses of "high culture" within Critical Theory preserve this tension, seeing both regressive and progressive elements within the aesthetic dimension. Yet the Institute tended to ascribe the higher, more progressive functions of culture to "art" (i.e., "high culture") and its more debased ideological functions to mass culture.

The Frankfurt School and Critical Theory

"Critical theory" stood as a code for the quasi-Marxist theory of society of a group of interdisciplinary social theorists collectively known as the Frankfurt School. The term, Frankfurt School, refers to the work of members of the *Institut für Sozialforschung* (Institute for Social Research) that was established in Frankfurt, Germany, in 1923 as the first Marxist-oriented research center affiliated with a major German university. Max Horkheimer became director of the institute in 1930, and gathered around him many talented theorists, including Erich Fromm, Franz Neumann, Herbert Marcuse and Theodor W. Adorno. Under Horkheimer, the Institute sought to develop an interdisciplinary social theory that could serve as an instrument of social transformation. The work of this era was a synthesis of philosophy and social theory, combining sociology, psychology, cultural studies, and political economy, among other disciplines.

In a series of studies carried out in the 1930s, the Institute for Social Research developed theories of monopoly capitalism, the new industrial state, the role of technology and giant corporations in monopoly capitalism, the key roles of mass culture and communication in reproducing contemporary societies, and critiques of mass culture, conformist pedagogy, the authoritarian personality, and the decline of democracy and of the individual. Critical theory drew alike on Hegelian dialectics, Marxian theory, Nietzsche, Freud, Max Weber, and other trends of contemporary thought. It articulated theories that were to occupy the center of social theory for the next several decades. Rarely, if ever, has such a talented group of interdisciplinary intellectuals come together under the auspices of one institute. They managed to keep alive radical social theory during a difficult historical era and provided aspects of a neo-Marxian theory of the changed social reality and new historical situation in the transition from competitive capitalism to monopoly capitalism.

During the Second World War, the Institute split up due to pressures of the war. Adorno and Horkheimer moved to California, while Lowenthal, Marcuse, Neumann and others worked for the US government as their contribution in the fight against fascism. Adorno and Horkheimer worked on their collective book

Dialectic of Enlightenment (1947 [trans. 1972]), which discussed how reason and enlightenment in the contemporary era turned into their opposites, transforming what promised to be instruments of truth and liberation into tools of domination. In their scenario, science and technology had created horrific tools of destruction and death, culture was commodified into products of a mass-produced culture industry and conformist schooling, and democracy terminated into fascism, in which masses chose despotic and demagogic rulers. Moreover, in their extremely pessimistic vision, individuals were oppressing their own bodies and renouncing their own desires as they assimilated and made their own repressive beliefs and allowed themselves to be instruments of labor, authoritarian institutions and government, and war and militarism.

After the Second World War, Adorno, Horkheimer and Pollock returned to Frankfurt to re-establish the institute in Germany, while Lowenthal, Marcuse and others remained in the USA. In Germany, Adorno, Horkheimer and their associates published a series of books and became a dominant intellectual current. At this time, the term, "Frankfurt School" became widespread as a characterization of their version of interdisciplinary social research and of the particular critical theory developed by Adorno, Horkheimer, and their associates. They engaged in frequent methodological and substantive debates with other social theories, most notably "the positivism dispute," where they criticized more empirical and quantitative approaches to theory and defended their own more speculative and critical brand of theory.

The Frankfurt School eventually became best-known for their critical theories of "the totally administered society," or "one-dimensional society" (Marcuse 1964). which analyzed the increasing power of capitalism over all aspects of social life and the development of new forms of social control. During the 1950s, however, there were divergences between the work of the Institute relocated in Frankfurt and the developing theories of Fromm, Lowenthal, Marcuse and others who did not return to Germany, which were often at odds with both the current and earlier work of Adorno and Horkheimer. It is misleading to consider the work of various critical theorists during the post-war period as members of a monolithic Frankfurt School. Whereas there were both a shared sense of purpose and collective work on interdisciplinary critical theory from 1930 to the early 1940s, thereafter critical theorists frequently diverge, and during the 1950s and 1960s the term the "Frankfurt School" can really be applied only to the work of the institute in Germany under Horkheimer and Adorno.

I began reading the Frankfurt School, especially Herbert Marcuse at Columbia University in the mid-1960s. At this time, while I was taking seminars in German philosophy and U.S. pragmatism, I obtained John Dewey's desk. One day in the Columbia Philosophy Department, one of the secretaries was dismayed that Dewey's desk was being thrown away. I told her that I would love to have it and rounded up several graduate students, we lugged the desk down Broadway for twenty blocks and over to 105th St. and West End where we carried it up five floors of stairs. Placing it next to my window overlooking Riverside Park. I now had the desk of the figure who overlooked us in our Philosophy Seminar Room and whose books we needed to read for our comprehensive exam so through the desk I appropriated the spirit of Dewey whose view that communication was at the center of life deeply impressed me. Perhaps the spirit of Dewey, however, was mediated by Jack Kerouac's semi-autobiographical novel *Vanity of Duluoz*, I deduced that I was living in the same apartment as he described the fifth walkup pad at the end of 105th overlooking Riverside Park and a Buddhist temple that gonged out the prayer hour every morning, hence I absorbed the texts and ideas of Herbert Marcuse and the Frankfurt School, John Dewy and American pragmatism, and the philosophy of Hegel in my philosophy studies, mediated by my intense immersion in Jack Kerouac and the Beats and the emerging U.S. counter-culture and anti-war movement as the Vietnam war heated up and we faced the dangers of being drafted in that unpopular war.

My first course as a teacher at Columbia in 1967 resulted from an extremely fortunate invitation, an award, to teach in their famous Great Books program. A few graduate students were allowed to teach in Columbia's Humanities Great Books program along with major professors like Lionel Trilling, Robert Belknap (a major Dostoyevsky scholar), Howard Porter (a renowned Homer scholar) and other specialists. We were privileged to have lunch once a week with the Columbia Great Men of Literary Studies, each of whom gave us a seminar on the various Great Books of the week, starting with the Bible, Homer, Plato, Greek tragedy, Dante, Boccaccio, and others. Hence, since the beginning of my teaching at Columbia, I adopted a Great Books approach, a pedagogy I continued as Assistant Professor of Philosophy at University of Texas-Austin where I was later hired to teach Marxism and Continental philosophy.

My first day as an instructor in Humanities at Columbia in 1968, I entered the classroom modestly with long hair and blue jeans, sitting in front of a class of undergraduates, many from prep schools who had read the classics I was supposed to teach, perhaps in their original languages. I confessed to the students that I hadn't previously read many of the books but had read Homer and Plato and the Greek dramatists and was looking forward to working with the class to read these books together. I sat on top of the desk, provided introductory remarks, attempted to engage, sometimes successfully, the students in conversation. Later, when I read Paulo Freire's *Pedagogy of the Oppressed*, I learned that I was practicing spontaneously a proper dialogical teaching method, learning from the students as I taught, and I have followed this pedagogy ever since.

In 1968, I was studying for my philosophy comprehensive exams at Columbia and teaching my first course when a student uprising erupted, with SDS radicals occupying the President's Office. Other student groups took over other campus buildings at Columbia University in one of the first and most dramatic student strikes of the era. The Grateful Dead came on campus to give us a free concert, and one day Stokley Carmichael, R. Rap Brown, Eldridge Cleaver, and other Black radical leaders came on to campus us to tell us we needed to get serious and join with them to carry out a real revolution, and not just a campus shutdown. Not much came out of this, but we had the feeling that we were at the heart of revolutionary upheavals in the U.S. and globally when a representative from France came and told us of the French student and worker uprising that was shutting down the whole of Paris and briefly was erupting throughout France.

My philosophical allegiances at the time were primarily to phenomenology and Existentialism, and while I was unprepared for the explosiveness and impact of the student rebellion, I became active in New Left politics, participating in major anti-war demonstrations. Indeed, students all over the United States and Europe were demonstrating against the Vietnam War, taking over University buildings and even campuses, and in Paris in May '68, it appeared that a new French revolution was in the making. To help understand these events, I went back and read the works of Herbert Marcuse, and by the time of the publication of *An Essay on Liberation* (1969), I both better understood Marcuse's writings and the philosophical underpinnings of the student movement to which I was increasingly attracted and involved.

During this time, the Vietnam war was raging and many of my generation were being sent over as cannon fodder for a cause that we did not understand. One day around 1968 I went over to Barnard College and heard a packed lecture by Noam Chomsky. At the time, Chomsky was a Professor of Philosophy at MIT, known to philosophy students for his controversial philosophy of mind, but proved himself a brilliant public lecturer, providing an entire history of post-World War II Vietnam, the National Liberation Movement that drove out the French, their Civil War, and how the US intervened against the Communist North, providing a sharp critique of U.S. interventionism and imperialism. I walked away with a much deeper understanding of the dynamics of Vietnam and great respect for Noam Chomsky who I would later meet and whose writings had an impact on my view of media and politics, creating the desire to be, like Chomsky, a public intellectual who applied their academic training and knowledge to analyze contemporary events.

In 1969, I left Columbia to write my dissertation on "Heidegger's Concept of Authenticity" with the support of a German government fellowship (DAAD). I chose to pursue this project at the University of Tubingen, in the small southwestern German town where Hegel, Hölderlin, Schelling, and other luminaries had studied, and which had a reputation as an excellent place to study a broad range of German philosophical traditions. Tubingen was permeated with the spirit of '60s radicalism and I bought pirate editions (*Raubdruck*) at the University Mensa of Karl Korsch's writings on Marxism, Georg Lukács' *History and Class Consciousness*, Max Horkheimer and T.W. Adorno's *Dialectic of Enlightenment*, and other texts of the Frankfurt School. I also became involved in a Critical Theory study group, and sat in on Ernst Bloch's seminars, which alternated between seminars on the great philosophers and ones on topics such as imperialism, fascism, and other political topics. From Bloch, among other things, I learned that philosophy was political, that politics required philosophical analysis and critique.

I was rapidly moving toward the Critical Theory of the Frankfurt School, a move intensified by a year in Paris. After two years in Germany, I had almost completed my dissertation on Heidegger and received a good grounding in German philosophy. I was eager to improve my knowledge of French, and to immerse myself in French philosophy and culture. During a thirteen-month sojourn in Paris during 1971–1972 while subsidized by my paper route savings, I devoted myself to French language and philosophy, and drafted the first version of a book on Herbert Marcuse whose work continued to interest me.

While in Paris, I meant an Algerian philosophy student, and he took me to hear the lectures of Levi-Strauss, Foucault, Deleuze, and Lyotard, inspiring me to read their recent works, as well as the texts of Baudrillard, Derrida, and other French thinkers currently in vogue. Listening to Foucault's lectures was like being in Church, as he intently read from lecture notes in a hushed darkened auditorium. Levi-Strauss was more lively and was very friendly when another friend took me to his office to meet him; Levi Strauss had lived in the U.S. and spoke charming English and was happy to discuss his work with a young American philosopher who was moving more toward poststructuralism as many of the new French theorists were moving away from the structuralism of Levi-Strauss, Althusser, and others in favor of more complex theories of language, meaning, social institutions, and power – a move I later took at the University of Texas where I met Gayatry Spivak and Jacques Derrida.[2]

Upon returning to the States in 1972, I went to visit my parents now living in Huntington, West Virginia, where my father was a Professor of Communications at Marshall University. Earlier, one day in 1969, before leaving for Germany, I received a call from my father to meet him downtown in a bar, an event that had never previously happened. At the time he was one of the top Vice Presidents at Arbitron, which did television ratings, and, as I learned when I saw him drinking alone in a downtown bar, he had just been fired, as the company had just hired a new President who immediately fired my father and others at the top positions to get his own flunkeys into position (previously my father had risen the corporate ladder as there were frequent corporate buyouts of the company, leading to the top echelon being fired when new management came in). Having experienced years of corporate viciousness, my father explained that he was giving up "the corporate rat race" and had decided "to take your route and become a professor." My father already had an M.A. in business and friends at the University of Ohio communications department accepted him for its Ph.D. program and in two years he received a Ph.D. in communications with a dissertation on how the television ratings system worked in the U.S. and got a job teaching at Marshall University.

In December 1972, I offered myself for sale for a position in continental philosophy at the American Philosophical Society (APA) job market, selling myself to the University of Texas at Austin, where I labored in continental philosophy for some twenty-plus years. I remember traveling to Boston with a group of other philosophy graduate students and sleeping on the floor in a room where someone could afford to foot the bill for the philosophy convention where we were seeking jobs. I had only a couple of prearranged interviews so had to hustle to try to organize a job interview. At a "smoker" (i.e., a mass gathering of philosophy professors and graduate students), I saw a name tag on a flamboyant looking man with the name tag "Douglas Browning, University of Texas-Austin." I knew that Texas had a job in continental philosophy so I cornered Browning, told him of my Ph.D. dissertation on Heidegger, that I had studied at Columbia and then Tubingen and Paris and knew a broad range of continental philosophies and would like a job in Texas. He sized me up and put me on the schedule for a 9:00 a.m. interview the next day. I could see that the group of interviewers was just waking up and drinking cups of black coffee so I joined in and bantered about Boston Celtics basketball, UT football, and other trivialities until the interview begin. I noticed one prominent figure as Ed Allaire, a maven of analytic philosophy, extremely hostile to the continentals, who had taught at the University of Iowa where my brother had studied for a couple of years and noted to Ed that my brother had enjoyed his philosophy lectures. When I presented my dissertation, I did so in the language of analytic philosophy, it sounded like I was a down-to-earth continental theorist.

Curiously, UT's position was specifically for someone to teach Marxist philosophy (some "know your enemy" conservative had managed to get the philosophy department to offer one of the few courses on Marxist philosophy in the country). The previous holders of this position had been fired after several years and it was clear that the Department was not seeking a red-flag waver so when asked whether I would be willing to teach a course on Marxism, I replied in the affirmative, saying that although most of my work had been in existentialism, phenomenology, Hegel, and contemporary German and French philosophy, I was interested in Marx and would be pleased to teach the course, and shortly thereafter I was offered a position as Assistant Professor of philosophy at the University of Texas at Austin, starting in Fall 1973 for a salary of $12,000.

My study in Europe had indeed provided a good grounding in the Marxian tradition and made the Texas offer attractive, and although I received a couple of other offers, I decided to go to Texas. This choice was fortunate, as Texas had a strong tradition in continental philosophy and a pluralistic department that allowed a broad range of different types of philosophical inquiry (although an anti-continental philosophy police squad would emerge and become hegemonic in the mid-1990s, ending this phase of my philosophical adventures).

Media Culture, the Public Sphere, and U.S. Politics

In the mid-1970s I was involved in Marxist studies groups at the University of Texas at Austin. After going through key Marxian texts, including the *Grundrisse* and *Capital*, we decided to study American political economy and in particular television. We saw corporate control of television, a la the Frankfurt School, as a major source of corporate hegemony, but we were also impressed with the Trilateral Commission report that the media, universities, and other institutions were promoting too much democracy and threatening corporate hegemony, and we wondered what we could do to contribute to this crisis for capital.

Our study group became with sustained study and discussion of Horkheimer and Adorno's model of the culture industry in *Dialectic of Enlightenment* and Herbert Marcuse's critique of the media within one-dimensional society. The group also became involved in alternative media and were given a chance to do a weekly public access TV show, *Alternative Views*. Accordingly, from 1978 to the mid-1990s, Frank Morrow, myself and others taped hour-long interviews combined with documentary programs producing a show a week for years on end, that were eventually syndicated around the United States, and briefly made me a celebrity in New York City, where the program was shown several times per week on the NY CUNY (City University of New York) access channel. This project helped me to become a Deweyean/Chomskyean public intellectual, and to apply philosophical notions and abilities to issues of public concern in a public forum.

At the time, I also become involved in study of the media and ideology and published in the 1970s in *Socialist Review,* one article on the concept of ideology and another on television ideology and emancipatory popular culture. Hence, at that time I was aggressively using the concept of ideology and doing ideology critique. Later, I read Foucault and others' critique of the concept of ideology, as too reductive or totalizing, and briefly questioned the salience of the concept of ideology for cultural critique. Yet later, I encountered Stuart Hall and British cultural studies, which expanded the concept of ideology to include dominant ideas of gender, race, sexuality, religion, and other major ideologies, as well as ideologies of class and capitalism. I thus took up their expanded concept of ideology, also informed by the Italian Marxist Antonio Gramsci (1971) that there are dominant ideologies in many dominant of social life that are all the time in contestation, such as racism vs anti-racism, or religious ideologies versus secular ones. For Gramsci, there are always struggles between different ideologies in society at any given time, but there can be dominant ideologies, like state capitalism and then neoliberalism, in certain historical moments. In other conjunctures, fascism became a dominant ideology, and Marxism-Leninism became a dominant ideology in the Soviet bloc all over the world during the Cold War.

The term "ideology" has descriptive and critical uses, and after writing those early articles on ideology and popular culture, I studied British cultural studies and agreed with Stuart Hall on the need to expand the concept of ideology and ideology critique to encompass gender, race, class, sexuality, and other domains. There are, for instance, dominant gender ideologies and there are contestations of them, which is in part what feminism does. There are dominant homophobic, heteronormativist ideologies, there are racist ideologies, religious ideologies, and so on.

In researching a project of investigating the genealogy of critical communications research in the U.S. and the impact of the Frankfurt School, I went to the Annenberg School of journalism at the University of Penn where George Gerbner held sway and edited the *Journal of Communication* to hear lectures and discuss communications with Gerbner. He was very cordial and recalled how as a refugee from Nazi Germany he was an assistant of Adorno working on his study of television and himself took on study of television and violence as a major research project, influenced by Adorno and the Frankfurt School but developing his own cultural ecology approach, seeing the media, in McLuhanist terms, as a cultural environment which in Gerbner's most famous study involved study of television and the indicators that demonstrated growing violence on TV and the media (see, for example, Gerbner and Signorielli 1988).

I also interviewed Herb Schiller when we were on a panel in New York in a conference on television held in the late 1970s. After my presentation of television as a contested terrain and providing a multiperspectivist analysis of television as a story-teller, business, and screen where the battles over race, class, gender, sexuality, and politics are fought, Herb countered with the declaration that compared to the previous speaker (me) his talk would be reductive, economistic, simplistic, and—true! As he would often do, Herb picked up the day's *New York Times* and analyzing its front page would deconstruct its view of the world and then present his own political economy approach. Later in life, I would become increasingly friendly with Herb and had a nice visit presenting to Herb's department in San Diego, a few years before his death, and learned that Herbert Schiller would drive Herbert Marcuse, who himself did not have a driving license, to work at the University of California, La Jolla in the 1970s.

I became as well involved in cultural studies in the 1970s and have remained active in this field through the present. Around 1976, I wrote Stuart Hall who was head of the then little-known Centre for Contemporary Cultural Studies in Birmingham England, asking about his work and his program. Stuart sent a three-page, single-spaced typed letter and a stack of his Centre's fabled stenciled papers and my media study group devoured them. The combination of philosophy, social theory, and cultural studies that I was engaged in eventually produced a series of works, including this book. Later, I was present at Urbana, Illinois, for a conference organized by the Institute for the Marxist Interpretation of Culture, in the summer of 1983 and met Stuart Hall whom I found to be extremely engaging, generous, and impressive as a pedagogue. I attended lectures that Hall, Perry Anderson, and Fredric Jameson gave in the pre-conference summer school lecture course, and found the summer school and conference extremely stimulating, shaping my work for the next decades with its discussions of Marxism, postmodernism, and cultural studies, literarily introducing the latter two themes to the U.S. academic world, which would be concerned with postmodernism and cultural studies to this day.

Although I was associated with Herbert Marcuse's wing of Frankfurt School critical theory after publishing my book *Herbert Marcuse and the Crisis of Marxism* (Berkeley and London: University of California Press and Macmillan Press, 1984), I liked Habermas' work on communicative action, theory and practice, and other works and did not see this either/or choice, introduced by Habermas's student Albrecht Wellmer who came to New York to lecture on Habermas and presented Habermas's work as far superior to Marcuse and Horkheimer and Adorno, in a proselytizing mode. This was the beginning of the development a Habermasian camp, that would be a global intellectual subculture which continues to this day.

Habermas himself was very friendly to me, inviting me to conferences in Germany and eventually writing a letter for tenure for me in the philosophy department (as did Marcuse, Gouldner, and George Gerbner who also published work of mine on media in his *Journal of Communication*). Around this time, I invited Habermas to the University of Texas, he agreed to come, give a University Lecture, a talk with my critical theory seminar, and participate in a conference on Brecht, organized by Betty Weber, a close friend in the German Department. I remember going to pick Habermas up at the Austin airport and when he arrived with his wife and young girls, I was pushed aside by Siegfried Unseld, Habermas's German publisher and head of Suhrkamp, who was teaching in the German Department at UT. Habermas saw me, introduced me to Unseld who I had already met, and informed Herr Unseld that Herr Kellner was his host in Austin, so of course Unseld would invite Herr Kellner to the dinner that Unseld was planning for Habermas that night, and Herr Unseld graciously responded, "Sicher ist Herr Kellner zu Abendessen mit uns eingeladen."

In the following days, Habermas lectured on Hannah Arendt and communicative action, and in my seminar filled the blackboard with diagrams outlining the distinctions in *Knowledge and Human Interests* and his developing theory of communicative action. At the Brecht conference, Habermas was excited to meet the German playwright Heiner Muller who would soon have a year's guest professorship at Austin. Learning that I was teaching Marxism, Muller came over one night with a bottle of scotch, and we spent the night discussing Marxism. But he was ultimately excited that I had a collection of the Westerns of people like Sam Peckinpah, Robert Aldrich and others and eagerly consumed this cultural fare on my Betamax and TV set.

Later in the 1980s, I was visiting Habermas in his office in Frankfurt, and we were discussing the ongoing battles between French postmodern versus German critical theory, a theme central to Habermas' *The Philosophical Discourse of Modernity*, which drew a sharp distinction between German critical rationalist traditions and what he saw as irrational French traditions and fiercely attacked these postmodern theorists. Habermas complained that he worried what he saw as irrationalist tendencies in French (and some German) thought could lead to fascism, as happened in Germany in the 1930s. While he was arguing, I noted that my plane back to the U.S. was leaving in less than an hour and Habermas leaped into action, assembling his driver and putting me and my suitcases in the car. He accompanied us to the airport, and when it was clear that I was not going to make the plane, Habermas called Lufthansa, the German national airline, announced himself, said that a colleague was close to the airport and to hold his flight. As we sped up to the departure area there was a phalanx of Lufthansa employees handing me my boarding pass, rushing me through customs to the waiting plane, demonstrating that a philosopher in Germany could have serious clout.

In the 1980s, I had a *Big Idea* that was to shape my work for the next decades: that was that our culture was a media culture, that it was media which were shaping the patterns of Everyday Life, of our economy (through advertising and promotion); of our politics, increasingly mediated; and of our culture was which becoming a media culture in which all cultural forms were directly constructed or mediated through the media (i.e., we knew which artists or music was hot or cool through the media).(Ronald Reagan was president so it was clear that part of politics was acting, image construction and spectacle).

This concept comes part from Marshall McLuhan who in *Understanding Media* (1964) argued that with new forms of media we have new forms of culture, consciousness, and Everyday Life, and partly from the Frankfurt School's culture industry thesis that that capital and technology were creating new syntheses that were coming to dominate culture, the economy, politics, and all forms of Everyday Life. As noted, I also agreed with Gramsci and British Cultural Studies that culture is a contested terrain rather than an instrument of domination and manipulation which was view of Frankfurt School, but also Althusser and structuralists, and other Marxist theories of media at the time.

I set out to develop a critical theory of media and technology that would articulate both the ways that media could be used as instruments of power, domination, and social control, and how the media could be used as forms of resistance to hegemonic power and could be used for alternative forms of pedagogy, politics, and communication. I also recognized that media were so powerful, so proliferating and omnipresent, that it was impossible to really grasp their complex, singular, and often weird effects (as noted, I also was open to poststructuralist theories of the media).

I have long tried to synthesize German and French traditions, rather than to oppose them, and this project animated a book co-authored with Michael Ryan, *Camera Politica: The Politics and Ideology of Contemporary Hollywood Film* (1988). The idea was to combine critical theory and post-structuralist methods to interrogate the politics and ideology of Hollywood film. Ryan and I saw film as emerging as an especially powerful form of culture at a time when video cassettes and video rental stores made it possible to see a many of the world's films at one's home and to make personal copies of films and build-up a film library –as I did and continue to do. I literally bought the first Betamax video recorder in Austin after reading about it previously; I knew it was what I needed to do cinema and media studies. At this time cable and satellite television was also proliferating and I remember being one of the first to hook up to cable TV in Austin and recall that

Taxi Driver was the first film I saw on HBO and one of the first that I recorded and could carefully study (as well as to take tapes into class and play and discuss scenes with students, making video recorders a transformative teaching tool as well as instrument of research and pleasure). Of course, my Betamax was soon obsolete and replaced by VCRs (and later DVDs, Blu-ray, and digital), but I followed this trajectory with resignation, changing video recorders yearly just as one would do during the first years of personal computers when every year improvements were qualitative.

Working on *Camera Politica*, Ryan and I saw film as a contested terrain in which political battles over gender, class, race, sexuality and more broadly politics and ideology were transcoded, hence the name of our book *Camera Politica*. We saw that dominant film genres, auteurs, and specific films transcoded the social and political struggles and passions of the day in ways that their decoding and interpretation could provide insights into the social and political struggles and passions of the day, as well as dominant fantasies, fears, hopes, and dreams.

My two books on television during the Reagan/Bush era also drew on both German and French traditions, attempting to rethink the problematics of the Frankfurt School critique of the culture industries through a concrete study of American television. This project informed my *Television and the Crisis of Democracy* (1990) and *The Persian Gulf TV War* (1992). *Television and the Crisis of Democracy* (1990) argued that in the Reagan era television was used as a powerful instrument of governing and power, and that capital and the construction of images and spectacle were coming to play ever increasingly powerful roles in society and politics, creating a crisis of democracy. I employed a structuralist model of economy, state, and the media in writing this book and argued that corporations were coming to control the state and media. Liberal theories of a democratic society had postulated separation and division of power between the executive, legislative and judiciary, with the media serving as a "fourth estate," to provide part of a system of checks and balances that could criticize misuses of power and corruption and provide voices and venues of participation. Of course, by the 1980s in U.S. society giant corporations controlled the media, especially television, and used media to promote their own corporate interests (through advertising and glamorizing the consumer society in entertainment), as well as to support whatever political party or candidate best served their corporate interests. In the 1980s it was of course Reagan and Bush Daddy (i.e. George Herbert Walker Bush also known as "Poppie") who provided tax breaks for the rich, deregulation, and whatever policies their corporate overloads and bagmen would demand. To be sure, there might be conflicts between various economic interests, but the Reagan and Bush regimes relentlessly promoted corporate interests overlooking the interests and needs of ordinary people, workers, and the middle class.

In *The Persian Gulf TV War* (1992), I argued that Bush Daddy's Gulf War directed against Iraq and Saddam Hussein when he invaded Kuwait in 1990s was orchestrated as a TV war to promote U.S. power and hegemony in the Middle East, to demonstrate that the U.S. military was a superior global force, and to help Bush Daddy with his re-election. Although Bush had a 90 % approval rating after the Gulf War and appeared a shoo-in for re-election, a young upstart from Arkansas, Bill Clinton, the Man from Hope, ended up beating Bush Daddy in the 1992 election, making the whole sordid affair of the Gulf War for naught (and a few billion dollars to the military-industrial complex). The media had played a role of cheerleader throughout the war, had transmitted whatever lies and propaganda the Bush administration and Pentagon utilized, and whipped up a patriotic fervor in support of the war, as if it were a sports event and the media were cheerleaders for the home team. It demonstrated to me the intensifying crisis of democracy, the corruption of the mainstream media, and the frightening ability of the media to promote whatever agenda is pushed by the dominant political and corporate elite.

I had one of my great academic moments serving on a panel with two of my Godfathers, Noam Chomsky and George Gerbner at the Association of Journalism and Mass Communication meetings in Boston, August 1991. Still the time of the Gulf War, I had the book out (noted above), and presented a paper, "The Media Propaganda War." Following Gerbner's spirited denunciation of the media and the Gulf War and Chomsky's dissection of U.S. foreign policy and how the mainstream media advances US imperialist interventions, I took a Chomskyean position that indeed during the Gulf War the corporate media were mainly promoting the interests of the U.S. military and military-industrial complex and providing propaganda for an imperialist U.S. foreign policy.

That day, Chomsky was honored with a life-time achievement award and presented an interesting talk on his early politics and how he got into activism, telling how he was influenced by Jewish anarchist and socialist groups and always took a critical position toward the state and its policies, especially military interventions. Spending the day with Chomsky was a real treat and I continue to read his books and follow the documentary films he participates in like *Manufacturing Consent: Noam Chomsky and the Media* (1992) and, most recently, *Is the Man Who is Tall Happy?* (2013).

In all my own writings on media and politics, I use philosophy and critical social theory as providing weapons of critique and tools of analysis that can be applied to concrete issues and problems. I thus do not use philosophy as abstract dogmas to be religiously worshipped, but as a body of living thought to apply to contemporary problems and issues. The best of continental philosophy is critical and dialogical (i.e., Hegel, Marx, Kierkegaard, Nietzsche, Sartre, et al.), and its major thinkers have often drawn on the most productive elements of their predecessors, while overcoming those aspects that are no longer useful or relevant. I thus see philosophy as dialectical, assimilating new theories and ideas into its arsenal of theory and critique, making connections between different spheres of social existence, culture, and ideas, laying out dominant conflicts in the worlds of society and ideas, negating certain ideas and critiquing what are discerned to be oppressive social, political, and cultural reality, and providing new syntheses of theory and politics, just like Hegel, Marx, Dewey, Gramsci, and the Frankfurt School in earlier eras. With poststructuralism, I would also say that philosophy can articulate differences, ambiguities, and complexities of the present moment and would resist any notion of completeness, certitude, or closure to a specific analysis and interpretation, as history is always open, always subject to new interpretations and events, and the times, indeed, are always changing, just as Bob Dylan clearly saw.

I have continued to apply the insights and methods of philosophy to a vast array of cultural phenomena and my book *Media Culture: Cultural Studies, Identity, and Politics, Between the Modern and the Postmodern* (1995) attempted to reconceptualize the project of cultural studies by using the tools of philosophy and critical social theory. Within cultural studies, I have argued for a multiperspectival model that combines political economy, textual analysis, and study of audience reception and media effects. The various philosophical positions I have studied—ranging from Marxism to feminism to poststructuralism—can be applied to the interpretation and critique of cultural and political phenomena and contribute to developing a critical, multicultural, and political cultural studies.

Becoming My Own(Theoretical)God-Father

During my twenty-five years+ of service at UCLA as George F. Kneller Chair in the Philosophy of Education, I focused on researching the relevance of new digital technologies for education, politics, and everyday life, as well as continuing work in philosophy, social theory, and cultural studies. In education from the mid-1990s to the present, I have been especially concerned to expand the notion of literacy to include critical media literacy and critical media and digital literacies. By the mid-1990s, it was clear to me that our culture was a media culture, and that the media were becoming increasingly powerful instruments of socialization, political indoctrination, and sources of meanings and identities as cable and satellite television mushroomed, talk radio and channels of broadcasting expanded as the

Internet absorbed video, audio, and the culture of image and spectacle, and as new technologies and social media continued to proliferate.

I had long been an advocate of media literacy, once receiving a grant during the Carter presidencies in the 1970s to teach media literacy to teachers in lower income high schools in the Mississippi Delta area. For months, I taught workshops in helping teachers provide curricula that would educate their students to critically read and decode media messages, including representations of gender, class, sexuality, and race to help students and educators discern racist, sexist, homophobic, classist, and other negative representations in the media, while also looking for positive images, meanings, role models, and programming. At Texas, I devised a course on philosophy of Culture and Communication which introduced theories of media, cultural studies, and taught critical media literacy which aimed at promoting knowledge of media ownership and programming, taught textual analysis, and developed theories of media power and alternative progressive uses of media for politics, pedagogy, and social transformation. At UCLA, I transformed this course into an Introduction to Cultural Studies seminar that uses my book *Media Culture* and a Blackwell reader *Media and Cultural Studies: KeyWorks*, co-edited with Gigi Durham (2001; second edition 2012), which brings together key texts in contemporary approaches to media culture and communication ranging from Roland Barthes and Guy Debord to studies of YouTube, Facebook, Twitter, and social media.

While at UCLA in the 1990s, it became clear to me that the Internet and new digital technologies were dramatically transforming culture, consciousness, and Everyday Life, and I organized a seminar at UCLA to explore technology and new media. During this period, I published articles on new technologies and new literacies in *Educational Theory* and related articles in various books and journals, including a series of studies of the Internet and politics, and studies of new digital media and social networking, some of which I draw upon and expand and update in this book. I argue that new technologies require new literacies, and that being technoliterate does not just involve knowing how to use computers and new technologies, as in some academic forms of technoliteracy, but also involves understanding the multiple functions of new technologies and new media in Everyday Life, understanding how they are transforming communication, social interaction, scholarly research, politics, culture, and economics.

In exploring how digital technologies and social media could be used for education, I worked with my students to produce web sites for courses in technology and society, cultural studies, and philosophy of education, as well as helping to develop websites on postmodern theory and critical theory, all on my webpage (which unfortunately disappeared when a server at UCLA burned Up—before the cloud – although I have been able to retrieve some of this material through Internet sites that had preserved some of the material). I was thus one of the first academics to develop a website that made available my articles, papers, and even books as they went out of print. I am now working on a series of projects to bring together my essays on new technologies, literacies, education, cultural studies, social theory, and democracy, that would follow the Deweyean project of democratizing education as an instrument of progressive social transformation and of which the essays in this book are a part.

Whereas much of the dominant literature on the new digital technologies and social media from the beginning to the present tends to be either celebratory or derogatory, I provide what I intend to be a balanced appraisal of the costs and benefits of deploying digital technologies and social media. In debates concerning whether books or computer data bases and on-line resources provide the basis for contemporary education, I mediate between these extremes, arguing that education today should be based on a balance between book material and digital and multimedia-based material. Likewise, I argue that traditional literacy in print culture and traditional skills of reading and writing are more important than ever today, but that we need to teach new literacies to supplement the skills of the past.

In the 2000s, I began a collaboration with Jeff Share which produced several articles and a book *The Critical Media Literacy Guide: Engaging Media and Transforming Education* (2019). We conceived this book as a handbook that teachers could use to teach the methods and concepts involved in learning critical media and digital literacies. Yet we also conceived the book as one that students and citizens could use on their own to become insightful and critical readers, interpreters, and analysts of media culture in their own society and lives.

My views on media and media literacy have evolved over a long period of different historical and cultural experiences and under the influence of different Grandfathers and Godfathers who influenced and promoted my work in various ways. As my generation moves on in its senior years and positions, it is our obligation to similarly find younger colleagues to mentor and help evolve, as the previous generation helped myself and my generation, which also involves dialogue in which we can learn from the younger generation!

Notes

1   Later, however, I learned from my father's sister Aunt Helen that at one time my grandfather was a successful carpenter/builder and that their family was one of the more affluent families in Scribner, Nebraska. Then, as we consumed a bottle of bourdon in her trailer in a camp outside of Kansas City, Kansas, she told me how twice during the depression the family moved, because

there were no more construction jobs, eventually moving to the other side of the tracks before my grandparents retired and moved to Los Angeles where my parents joined him and my grandmother in a modest apartment during the outbreak of World War II and Helen and her sister, my Aunt Shirley, married..

2   See Spivak's translation of Derrida, *Of Grammatology* (2016), Fortieth Anniversary Edition.

References

Derrida, J. (2016) *Of Grammatology.* Fortieth Anniversary edition, Baltimore: Johns Hopkins University Press.

Durham, M. G., and D. Kellner. (2001). *Media and Cultural Studies: KeyWorks.* Malden, MA: Blackwell; second edition 2012.

Gerbner , G. and .N Signorielli (1988) *Violence and Terror in the Mass Media: An Annotated Bibliography.* Greenwood Press. Westport, Conn.

Gramsci, A. (1971). *Prison Notebooks.* New York: International Publishers.

Horkheimer, M., and T. W. Adorno. (1972). *Dialectic of Enlightenment.* New York: Herder and Herder.

Kellner, D. (1984). *Herbert Marcuse and the Crisis of Marxism.* Berkeley and London: University of California Press and Macmillan Press.

———. (1989). *Critical Theory, Marxism, and Modernity.* Cambridge, UK and Baltimore, MD: Polity Press and John Hopkins University Press.

———. (1990). *Television and the Crisis of Democracy.* Boulder, CO: Westview.

———. (1992). *The Persian Gulf TV War.* Boulder, CO: Westview.

———. (1995). *Media Culture: Cultural Studies, Identity, and Politics Between the Modern and the Postmodern.* London and New York: Routledge; second revised edition 2020.

———, and J. Share. (2019). *The Critical Media Literacy Guide: Engaging Media and Transforming Education.* Rotterdam, The Netherlands: Brill-Sense Publishers.

Lukács, G. (1972). *History and Class Consciousness: Studies in Marxist Dialectics.* Translated by Rodney Livingstone. Cambridge, MA: MIT Press.

Marcuse, H. (1955). *Eros and Civilization.* Boston: Beacon Press.

———. (1964). *One-Dimensional Man.* Boston: Beacon Press; second edition, Beacon and Routledge Press, 1999.

———. (1965). "Repressive Tolerance," in *A Critique of Pure Tolerance*, edited by Robert Paul Wolff, Barrington Moore, Jr., and Herbert Marcuse (pp. 95–137). Boston: Beacon Press.

———. (1969). *An Essay on Liberation.* Boston: Beacon Press.

———. (1972). *Counterrevolution and Revolt.* Boston: Beacon Press.

———. (1979). *The Aesthetic Dimension.* Boston: Beacon Press.

McLuhan, M. (1964). *Understanding Media: The Extensions of Man.* New York: McGraw-Hill.

Ryan, M., and D. Kellner. (1998). *Camera Politica: The Politics and Ideology of Contemporary Hollywood Film.* Bloomington: Indiana University Press.

CHAPTER FOUR

Critical Pedagogy, Cultural Studies, and Radical Democracy: Reflections on the Work of Henry Giroux

After publishing a series of books that many recognize as major works on contemporary education and critical pedagogy, Henry Giroux turned to cultural studies in the late 1980s to enrich education with expanded conceptions of pedagogy and literacy.[1] This cultural turn is animated by the hope to reconstruct schooling with critical perspectives that can help us to better understand and transform contemporary culture and society in the contemporary era. Giroux provides cultural studies with a critical pedagogy missing in many versions and a sustained attempt to link critical pedagogy and cultural studies with developing a more democratic culture and citizenry. The result is an intersection of critical pedagogy and cultural studies that enhances both enterprises, providing a much-needed cultural and transformative political dimension to critical pedagogy and a pedagogical dimension to cultural studies.

Crucially, Giroux has linked his attempts to transform pedagogy and education with the project of promoting radical democracy. Giroux's earlier work during the 1970s and 1980s focused on educational reform, pedagogy, and the transformation of education to promote radical democracy. In *Border Crossings* (1992), Giroux notes "a shift in both my politics and my theoretical work" (1). The shift included incorporation of new theoretical discourses of poststructuralism and postmodernism, cultural studies, and the politics of identity and difference embodied in the evolving discourses of class, gender, race, and sexuality that proliferated in the post-1960s epoch. Giroux criticized those who ignore "the sea changes in social theory" within the field of education and called for a transformation of education and pedagogy in the light of the new paradigms, discourses, and practices that were circulating by the 1990s.

One of the key new discourses and practices that Giroux was henceforth to take up and develop involved the burgeoning discipline of cultural studies. In his initial appropriations of cultural studies, he presented his shift as a "border crossing" that involved transformative transdisciplinary perspectives which overcame the disciplinary abstractions and separations of fields like education, social theory, and literary studies. In metatheoretical discussions, Giroux presented reasons for the importance of cultural studies in reconstructing contemporary education, the need for new understandings of culture, cultural politics, and pedagogy that went beyond the orthodoxy of both Left and Right, focusing on how the transformation of education and pedagogy could contribute to the project of radical democracy. Giroux thus uses cultural studies to transform and enrich critical pedagogy and to provide new intellectual tools and practices to transform education. In turn, Giroux argues that cultural studies should see the importance of pedagogy and to continue its commitment to radical democratic social transformation, rather than to merely indulge in textualist readings or audience studies of how people use and enjoy popular culture, as in some versions of cultural studies that have emerged in the past decade.

In the past decades, Giroux has accordingly focused on developing the relationship between critical pedagogy, cultural studies, and radical democracy in a series of books, including *Border Crossings* (1992), *Living Dangerously: Multiculturalism and the Politics of Culture* (1993), *Disturbing Pleasures: Learning Popular Culture* (1994), *Fugitive Cultures* (1996), *Channel Surfing: Racism, the Media, and the Destruction of Today's Youth* (1997), *The Mouse that Roared: What Disney Teaches* (1999), *Stealing Innocence* (2000), and *Impure Acts. The Practical Politics of Cultural Studies* (2000).[2] This rich and productive corpus crisscrosses the borderlines of educational theory and pedagogy, cultural studies, social theory, and radical democratic politics, promoting a genuinely transdisciplinary and transformative reconstruction of education, theory, society, and politics. In the 2000s, Giroux has also produced a series of works on public pedagogy, engaging the intersection between politics, education, culture, and society in the 2000s.

My study will accordingly engage Giroux's writing in these arenas over the past decades, highlighting what I see as the most significant contributions to transforming education and society, as well as some limitations of his work. At stake is developing a critical pedagogy and cultural studies that will help empower the next generation and enliven democracy as we enter a situation perilous to democracy and the individual in the new millennium.

Giroux's Big Themes: Youth as Hope and Scapegoat

Giroux's work is important because it takes on many of the big issues of the contemporary era. Several of his major books have focused on the social construction and media representations of youth, in explorations of how youth have been both scapegoated for social problems and commodified and exploited by the advertising, consumer, and media industries (Giroux, 2001, 2009). Giroux always situates his cultural analyses within a political and historical context so that, for instance, the war against youth is seen as part of an attack on the welfare state, public schooling, and democratic culture during the Reagan-Bush-Clinton years.[3] Giroux also takes care to contextualize his writings within his own working class background, his history as a critical educator, and emergence as a radical critic of existing culture, society, politics, and the educational establishment. Giroux combines the personal and the political, the theoretical and the practical, in taking on the key issues of the day.

In the light of the ongoing attack on youth and youth culture over the past decades, it is interesting to read in Giroux's 1996 *Fugitive Cultures* analyses of how media were then scapegoating youth, especially youth of color, as the source of social problems and the escalation of violence in society. Giroux cites the disturbing statistic that "close to 12 U.S. children aged 19 and under die from gun fire each day. According to the National Center for Health Statistics, 'Firearm homicide is the leading cause of death of African-American teenage boys and the second-leading cause of death of high school age children in the United States'" (cited in Giroux, 1996: 28).

Giroux correctly notes that the proliferating media stories about youth and violence at the time generally avoid critical commentary on racism and on the connections between the escalation of violence in society and the role of poverty and social conditions in promoting violence: a blind spot that continues into the present. In addition, he astutely notes that the media scapegoating of youth also neglects dissection of the roles of white men in generating violence and destruction, such as "the gruesome toll of the drunk driver who is typically white" (1996: 37).[4]

At the same time, working class youth and youth of color have been represented in the media and conservative discourses for decades as predators, as threats to existing law, order, and morality. Most disturbingly, at the very time that poverty and division between the haves and the have nots are growing, a conservative-dominated neo-liberal polity has been cutting back the very programs—public education, job training and programs, food stamps, health and welfare support—that provide the sustenance to create opportunities and hope for youth at risk.[5] Giroux correctly rejects the family values and moralistic critique of media culture of such conservatives who lead the assault on the state and welfare programs while supporting prisons, harsher punishment, and a "zero tolerance" for youthful transgressions (Giroux, 2001).

Instead, Giroux targets the corporations who circulate problematic images of youth and the rightwing social forces that scapegoat youth for social programs at the same time they attack programs and institutions that actually could help youth. Giroux is clearly aware of the importance of media culture as pedagogy and calls upon cultural critics to see the pedagogical and political functions of such cultural forms that position youth as objects of fear or desire. In a series of studies, Giroux notes how corporations exploit the bodies of youth to sell products, manufacturing desires for certain products, and constructing youth as consumers.

In a brilliant critique of a series of Benetton fashion ads, Giroux argues that the 1985 United Colors of Benetton campaign used images of racial harmony to sell both its clothing line and a banal view of cultural unity that erased class, racial, gender, and sexual difference, inequalities, oppression, and suffering (1994: 3 ff.). In his sharp critique of the 1991 Benetton campaign which included compelling images of a person with AIDS, poverty, war, and environmental destruction, Giroux argues that the purported social realism of these ads was used to aestheticize suffering and to sell an image of the Benetton corporation as a vehicle of social responsibility. Giroux deconstructs the campaign by disclosing the corporations' commitment to neo-liberal anti-government positions, hostility to unions, and its attempt to position its fashion-line within a global clothing market. Carrying out a detailed analysis of the production and reception of the Benetton campaign, Giroux dissects how a major global corporation uses images as vehicles of ideology and promotion of its wares. His studies demonstrate the need for a visual pedagogy which engages the production and reception of corporate images, as well as providing a hermeneutical reading of the specific images and texts.

Giroux continued his pedagogy of the corporate image and advertising in a critique of 1995 Calvin Klein ads. This advertising campaign deployed photos of youthful bodies by Perry Meisel, posed in provocative sexual displays bordering on the pornographic, to sell high-end clothing (1997, Chapter One). The ironic use of underclass youth to sell expensive clothes underlines what Giroux sees as the dual process of scapegoating youth while objectifying and commodifying them to sell products. Young bodies are positioned in such images not as sources of agency or resistance, but as a "site of spectacle and objectification, where youthful allure and sexual titillation are marketed and consumed by teens and adults who want to indulge a stylized narcissism and coddle a self that is all surface" (1997: 21).

Giroux also critically interrogates a Calvin Klein "heroin chic" campaign that portrayed emaciated bodies and covertly romanticized drug use and youth decadence (1999: Chapter Two), advertising images that fall in line with conservative attacks on youth as decadent and immoral. His intention, however, is not to engage in a moralistic critique of such ads. Rather, Giroux undertakes to show how they merge fashion and art to shape images of the youthful body in the interests of commodification that serve corporate profits while providing highly problematic role models and forms of identity for youth. Giroux is concerned that youth are being increasingly driven from the public sphere, active democratic citizenship, and empowering creativity into privatized spaces where they are positioned as consumers and provided with identities that replicate commodified models and ideals.

Channel Surfing (1997) and *Stealing Innocence* (2000) provide examples of critical pedagogy that demonstrate that "childhood" and "youth" are social constructions and sites of struggle between opposing political ideologies and forces. "Children" and "youth" in Giroux's view are a complex site of hope and possibility, as well as domination and exploitation. Giroux critically engages the pedagogies in locales ranging from schooling to media culture and everyday life that shape youth. In particular, he provides sustained critique of representations that scapegoat youth for public problems while the political and media establishment carry out attacks on public schools and programs and policies which provide opportunities and hope for youth. Giroux criticizes in these texts representations of youth such as are found in Calvin Klein ads, depictions of irresponsible sex and drug use in films like Larry Clark's *Kids* (1996), and a variety of urban films that especially vilify youth of color and help foster public images of youth as decadent, corrupt, and in need of discipline and control.

Against the scapegoating and commercialization of youth, and the promotion of attitudes of despair and hopelessness, Giroux wants to foster an ethic of hope and possibility, conceptualizing youth as a contested terrain, as an arena both of oppression and struggle. Giroux argues that by criticizing misrepresentations of youth in media culture and the scapegoating of youth through negative media images and discourses, we are combatting an attack on youth used to justify cutbacks in education, harsher criminal penalties and other punitive measures that are arguably part of the problem rather than the solution.

Giroux sees culture and the media as forms of pedagogy, every bit as important—and in some cases more so—than schooling. He calls for a cultural studies that provides a counterpedagogy to the teaching that is provided by mainstream schooling and corporate and media culture, noting: "For years, I believed that pedagogy was a discipline developed around the narrow imperatives of public schooling" (1994: x). And yet, he notes that his own identity was largely fashioned on the terrain of popular culture and everyday life that shaped him more significantly than public education. Accordingly, he argues that pedagogy needs to be theorized in terms of a variety of public sites that shape, mold, socialize, and educate individuals. Indeed, Giroux convincingly demonstrates in book after book that it is precisely corporate media culture that is shaping our culture and everyday life, as well as institutions such as schooling and cultural sites like museums, theme parks, shopping centers, advertising, and the like.

For Giroux, "the politics of culture provide the conceptual space in which childhood is constructed, experienced, and struggled over" (2000a: 4). Culture is both the sphere in which adults exercise control over children and a site where children and youth can resist the adult world and create their own cultures and identities. It is thus important to critically question "the specific cultural formations and contexts in which childhood is organized, learned, and lived" (1994: x).

In a study of child beauty pageants (2000a, Chapter 1), Giroux shows how this competitive sphere imposes adult models on children, promotes restricted and problematic gender roles, and displays provocative sexual displays in young girls. Giroux does not, a la Neil Postman, lament the "adultifying" of the child and disappearance of childhood (pp. 12 ff. and 40), but focuses on the exploitation of children in these "nymphet fantasies" in which adults project their desires and impose their models upon girls.[6] Giroux's concern is with how children and youth are exploited and socialized by commercial consumer culture and the lack of public spaces and sites for the young to develop agency and learn democratic and cooperative social relations and values in an increasingly commodified and privatized culture and society.

Giroux's analysis of the genealogy of child beauty pageants calls attention to often neglected source of childhood construction that need to be engaged by a critical cultural pedagogy. As an example of corporate pedagogy, Giroux devotes sustained study of the multiple roles in childhood socialization, ideological indoctrination, and commercialization of the Walt Disney corporation, resulting in a book on Disney and its pedagogies (1999). Giroux's 1999 study of "the Wonderful World of Disney" cultural production, a slogan that he suggests itself stands as a metonym for the United States, analyzes certain Disney Touchstone films, targeted mainly at teenagers and adults.

Hollywood Pedagogy

Giroux notes how the terrain of Hollywood film provides an important ground of pedagogy and takes on the politics of representation in two Disney Touchstone films of the era, *Good Morning, Vietnam* (1987) and *Pretty Woman* (1990). Giroux presents Barry Levinson's take on Vietnam as an attempt to recuperate the sense of U.S. loss over the Vietnam war, to establish an ethos of innocence for American memory, and to erase from history the turbulence and violence of the Vietnam era. The suffering and tragedy of Vietnam is displaced by Robin Williams' "comic, manic improvisation" (1994: 35). Williams plays a DJ for an Army radio station in Saigon circa 1965. Conflict in the film focuses on what sort of music the DJ could play, and Giroux suggests that cultural struggle over music replaces the dynamic of contestation over the war itself, while the U.S. intervention is clothed in innocence, presenting U.S. soldiers as tourists to an exotic locale.

Giroux also criticizes the racism and sexism in the film, as in the representations of the Black sidekick to the DJ, played by Forest Whitaker, who is presented as "a shuffling, clumsy grunt," and is positioned as the obedient servant to the colonial master. Not surprisingly, the representations of the Vietnamese are racist, with women displayed as sexual commodities for U.S. servicemen, while in general the Vietnamese are present as exotic Others who are purveyors of criminality and lawlessness.

Pretty Woman, in Giroux's reading, also presents ideological representations of recent U.S. history, this time in the Cinderella story of a working-class prostitute, played by Julia Roberts, who is groomed and redeemed by a corporate raider (Richard Gere). Assimilating appropriate fashion and style imagery, in the Disney redoing of the Pygmalion myth, the prostitute reconstitutes herself as a suitable corporate trophy wife, and patriarchal relations and family values thus triumph over sordid and inappropriate sex and style. The predatory business practices of the corporate raider are erased in the chivalrous behavior of the businessman, whose questionable business practices are justified when he takes over his father's corporation, who had mistreated him and his mother.

The Disney world of innocence and family values is thus able to triumph and redeem even disturbing and base historical and social conditions. Giroux's second sustained critique of Disney ideology involved critical scrutiny of Disney animation cartoons aimed at children (1996: Chapter 3 and its continuation in Giroux 1999). He notes that while cultural studies traditionally focused on youth culture, it has largely ignored children's culture, such as animated films (1996: 89–90). Giroux scrutinizes the narrow gender roles in these films and finds that although some of the young women portrayed, such as the woman-mermaid Ariel in *The Little Mermaid* (1989) or the young woman in *Beauty and the Beast* (1991), are initially depicted as feisty and active, they are positioned to find true love and happiness in submission to male-dominated romance. Other Disney films like *Aladdin* (1992) simply portray women as handmaidens to male pleasure, or like *The Lion King* (1994) are strictly patriarchal, depicting women in subordinate roles.

Giroux dissects the stereotyping and covert racism in Disney animation films. Arabs are depicted in vile racist representations and many of the villains in Disney animation "speak through racially coded language and accents" (106). The heroes and heroines in these films, however, speak standardized American and are portrayed in images modeled after idealized American youth. A Disney cultural worker, for instance, admitted that the figure of *Aladdin* was modeled after Tom Cruise (106), and, as Giroux suggests, heroines such as the little Mermaid or Pocahontas are modeled after Southern California nubile teen models. Such representations normalize whiteness and American fashion and style as the ideal for youth, fostering insecurities and feelings of inferiority in youth of color or other nationalities.

In addition, and notoriously, Disney films erase the scars and ugliness of colonial history, as in *Pocahontas* (1995) which shows no trace of the displacement, suffering, and death inflicted indigenous peoples by the European colonists. Moreover, Disney films like *The Lion King* display "deeply antidemocratic social relations" (107), naturalizing authority, hierarchy, structural inequality, and royalty as part of a natural order. Class, gender, and racial inequalities are presented as benign and justified in this world, displaying Disney nostalgia for a simpler and more harmonious world that erases from cultural memory the turbulence and pain of history and the continuation of social inequalities, injustice, and suffering in the present.

Giroux thus critically dissects the sorts of pedagogy involved in the Disney world.[7] He analyzes "what Disney teaches" and the implications of a big corporate conglomerate playing such a major role in pedagogy and socialization, as well as the ways that this influences education, politics, and our cultural and public life, here in the U.S. and globally. Giroux's book on Disney includes dissection of the structure and power of Disney Corporation, and raises questions about the effects of the possession of so much cultural power. Demonstrating the immense range of cultural sites occupied by the Disney corporation, Giroux discloses the diversity of its products in critical analyses of Disney's films, its forays into education and community building, and its extensive marketing operations of toys, merchandise, and theme parks spun-off from its films. Critically engaging such a cultural empire requires combining historical, social, and political analysis, textual readings, and studies of cultural effects of a wide range of artifacts. Giroux thus produces a cultural studies which deploys transdisciplinary perspectives, including analysis of political economy and production, cultural artifacts and sites, and their reception and effects.

Hence, Giroux offers a wide-ranging model of cultural studies and greatly expands the domain of pedagogy, demonstrating the importance of critically engaging the pedagogy of a broad spectrum of cultural artifacts, often ignored by educators. Since youth today are the subjects of education, critical teachers must understand youth and their problems and prospects, hopes and fears, competencies and limitations. Understanding and productively engaging youth in the context of their everyday lives is clearly one of the big issues for educators, parents, citizens, and those of us concerned about the future. For youth are the future, and the quality of life and the polity of the new millennium depend on educating youth and helping produce generations who can themselves create a better, freer, happier, and more just society.

Giroux constantly argues that educators, parents, and citizens should be deeply concerned with youth. This involves attempting to understand its culture and problems, combating the ways that youth are being misrepresented in the media and miseducated in the schools, and developing pedagogical strategies and cultural politics that will reform and democratically transform media, education, and society. Cultural studies is useful because it provides access to youth culture, to the actual culture that socializes and educates youth—or in some cases miseducates it—, and thus potentially increases our understanding of the youth we are teaching and working with. Clearly, Giroux demonstrates the importance of media education for a reconstruction of schooling and the importance of cultural studies for a transformative critical pedagogy. He also consistently argues that key social phenomena such as the situation of youth can only be grasped through their race, gender, and class configurations, that youth are articulated by these concrete social determinants which must be addressed in any adequate analysis.

The Intersection of Class, Race, and Gender

For Giroux, culture matters precisely because such constituents of everyday experience as youth, gender, race, class, sexuality, and so on are constructed in and through cultural representations. Often, these representations are invisible, and their effects are unperceived. Hence, a critical cultural studies must make visible how representations construct a culture's normative views of such things as class, race, ethnicity, gender, sexuality, place, occupation, and the like, and how these representations are appropriated to produce subjectivities, identities, and practices.

Some of Giroux's first concrete cultural studies of the 1990s involve analysis and critique of how Hollywood celluloid culture constructs a pedagogy of class, race, and gender. He indicates the need for critical media pedagogy to disclose how these texts are constructed and to help enable students to critically dissect and interpret media representations, narratives, and their effects. In a reading of *Dead Poets Society* (1993: 40 ff.), Giroux tells how his students initially identified with the rebellious teacher Mr. Keating, played by Robin Williams. Keating set out to reinvigorate education at a conservative boys' boarding school, Welton Academy, which functioned to prepare elite males for Ivy League colleges and ruling class life. At first, Giroux notes, students saw the Williams' figure as an ideal of transformative education, passionately committed to teaching, and helping to change his students' lives in an emancipatory fashion.

Yet a closer reading of the film, Giroux remarks, discloses a "politics and aesthetics of nostalgia" which looks back to past cultural forms (e.g., romantic poetry) as privileged cultural texts, thus in effect affirming a conservative canon as the heart and soul of pedagogy. Hence, while the film does provide a critique of authoritarian and disciplinary education, it does not go beyond conservative individualism and aestheticism and fails to engage the problems, conflicts, and struggles of the present, to see the past as a contested terrain, or to engage those voices and texts that more radically contest the inequities and injustices of Western civilization. Moreover, when Keating himself is challenged by the authorities for his unorthodox teaching practices and unjustly dismissed over the suicide of a student, he politely and respectfully submits to his fate, rather than exhibiting any critique, resistance, or struggle against the repressive and authoritarian power structure that rules the institution.

Furthermore, Giroux criticizes the representations of women in the film "that are misogynist and demeaning" (1993: 47). Women are positioned primarily to support and provide pleasure to men, they are relegated "to either trophies or appendages of male power" (48). Women are not presented in the film as active subjects with their own dreams and agency, but as "reified object[s] of [male] desire and pleasure" (48).

Not surprisingly, race is invisible in *Dead Poets Society* which "privileges whiteness, patriarchy, and heterosexuality as the universalizing norms of identity" (42). The film takes for granted the equation of whiteness with class privilege and does not trouble its nostalgic narrative with the disruptive dynamics of race and sexuality. Likewise, in another probing cultural study of the period, Giroux shows how the contemporary conflicts over gender, race, and class are ideologically smoothed and absorbed in the narrative machine of *Grand Canyon* (1993: 104 ff.). In this film, the white yuppie family of the story come to recognize racial and cultural difference in the present, but in a manner that reassures them that they do not have to surrender power and privilege and that difference can be harmoniously absorbed into the existing order.

Indeed, Giroux has intensely engaged over the past decades the problematics and dynamics of race—clearly one of the major issues of our time—as well as the intersections of race, class, gender, multiculturalism, and the crisis of democracy and public schooling in the U.S. (see especially Giroux, 1993, 1996, and 1997 and many of his works of the 2000s). He enriches these topics with his combination of critical pedagogy, cultural studies, and a sustained political situating of representations and struggles over race within the context of burning issues and conflicts of the day.

In discussing issues of violence in the media and the effects of media violence on youth and society, Giroux argues that discussions of violence and media must include race, gender, and class (1997, Preface and passim). In a series of texts, he has carried out sustained critiques of media stigmatizing of youth as the source of social ills through analysis of depictions of violent youth in the media and journalism, cinematic representations of youth in Hollywood film, and political discourses that call for "zero tolerance" of youth indiscretions and crimes (2001).

Giroux shows how media representations of Black people stigmatize Black youth and, more broadly, Youth of Color. In *Fugitive Cultures* (1996), Giroux documents the role of media presentations of Black people which have helped promote what he calls "a white moral panic" (1996: 97). During the era of the O.J. Simpson trials in the mid-1990s, major magazines featured threatening Black males on their covers with stories like "A Predator's Struggle to Tame Himself" and "The Black Man Is in Terrible Trouble. Whose Problem is That?" (ibid). Giroux points out that the endless repetition of these images "reproduce racist stereotypes about Black people by portraying them as criminals and welfare cheats;" it also "remove whites from any responsibility or complicity for the violence and poverty that has become so endemic to American life" (1996: 66).

Racial coding of violence and the association of crime with youth of color was evident in the attacks on rap music and hip-hop culture that circulated throughout the 1990s.[4] As an example, Giroux cites the hypocrisy of Bob Dole's attack on rap and Hollywood films' depiction of violence, drugs, and urban terror in communities of color. For Dole refused to criticize violence in the films of the Hollywood right, such as those of Republicans Bruce Willis and Arnold Schwarzenegger. Moreover, he was a fervent supporter of the NRA and critic of stricter gun laws and failed to address the ways that poverty and worsening social conditions generated violence (produced in part by Republican policies that Dole spearheaded). Moreover,

Dole had often not even seen the films nor heard the music that he attacked (1996: 67 ff.).

Always clearly pointing to the political consequences of such cultural and political discourses and representations, Giroux notes that "such racist stereotyping produce more than prejudice and fear in the white collective sensibility. Racist representations of violence also feed the increasing public outcry for tougher crime bills designed to build more prisons and legislate get-tough policies with minorities of color and class" (1996: 67). Hence, racist and brutal depictions of people of color in media culture contribute to intensification of the culture of violence, and fuel campaigns by rightwing organizations that stigmatize racial groups. Such representations also promote social and political conditions that aggravate rather than ameliorate problems of crime, urban decay, and violence.

Indeed, throughout the 1990s and continuing into the new millennium there have been copious media spectacles featuring dangerous Black youth, including sustained attacks on rap music and hip- hop culture,[8] Black gangs and crime, and urban violence in communities of color. Latinos are also stigmatized with political (mis)measures such as Proposition 187 "which assigns increasing crime, welfare abuse, moral decay, and social disorder to the flood of Mexican immigrants streaming across the borders of the United States" (Giroux, 1996: 66). Social scientists contribute to the stigmatization in books like *The Bell Curve* which assert Black inferiority and provide "a respectable intellectual position" for racist discourse in the national debate on race (1996: 67).

Hollywood films and entertainment media contribute as well to negative national depictions of people of color. In his discussion of Hollywood cinematic portrayals of inner city youth, Giroux analyzes how communities of color are shown as disruptive forces in public schools, contributing to white moral panic that youth of color are predatory, violent, and are destroying the moral and social fabric of the country. *Boyz N the Hood* (1991), *Juice* (1992), *Menace II Society* (1993), and *Clockers* (1995) are films which present negative representations of Black youth which Giroux argues feed into rightwing moral panics and help mobilize support for harsher policing and incarceration of ghetto youth. Against these prejudicial and sensationalistic fictional representations, Giroux valorizes Jonathan Stack's documentary *Harlem Diary* (1996) in which urban youth are themselves provided with cameras and cinematic education to explore their situations and to give voice to their own fears and aspirations (1997: 62).

In addressing the culture of violence in *Fugitive Cultures* (1996), Giroux engages what he calls "hyper-real" violence in the films of Quentin Tarantino's *Reservoir Dogs* (1992) and *Pulp Fiction* (1994). Giroux argues that Tarantino's use of excessive and exaggerated violence in these films aestheticizes the brutality of violence, contributing to a cynical and nihilistic cinema. *Reservoir Dogs* uses a gritty realism and stylized violence to represent extremely ruthless crime in ways that "revels in stylistic excess in order to push the aesthetic of violence to its visual and emotional limits" (1996: 71).

Pulp Fiction, in Giroux's reading, promotes the same cynical ethos of Tarantino's earlier films, but in the register of a more hip, cool, and stylized postmodern idiom. A pastiche of the crime genre of "pulp fiction," Tarantino fragments his narrative structure, deploys a sadistic irony and ultra-hip talk and music, and puts on display a misanthropic amorality to promote what Ruth Conniff has called "a culture of cruelty" (1996: 76). Tarantino, in Giroux's reading, deploys violence for shock and schlock effects, playing with cinematic conventions, without critically analyzing, contextualizing, or contesting the patterns of violence in his films. Violence in Tarantino's films is gratuitous, contingent, and ubiquitous, rather than emerging from specific contexts and social conditions. It can erupt anywhere, anytime, to anyone, rather than being generated by specific social causes and conditions. It is aestheticized and used for shock effects rather than to probe into what causes violence and its horrific effects on human beings and communities. Such films thus contribute to promoting a culture of brutality by naturalizing and romanticizing major forces of human suffering and tragedy.

Giroux critiques the racism and sexism in Tarantino's film, noting the racist language and obsessive use of the "N-word," as well as the highly problematic representations of women and homophobia. Indeed, Giroux suggests that the rape of a Black man by two white thugs in *Pulp Fiction* combines homophobia with racism (82), presenting at once highly derogatory images of gay sex and positioning the Black man as a deserving target of white male rage (he is about to kill the Bruce Willis character for honorably refusing to throw a fight, as the Black thug ordered). Giroux also points out how the sociopath Jules (played by Samuel Jackson) misuses the African American tradition of prophetic language in his pretentious use of religious discourse in the context of committing heinous crimes (82).

Giroux insists that such cinematic transgression and irony is not innocent or merely playful but has harmful political and cultural effects. Yet Giroux does not himself stigmatize Hollywood films or the media alone for the alarming escalation of violence in the U.S., calling attention instead to conditions of poverty, social injustice, and urban decline that contribute to the larger problems of the contemporary era. Attacking Bob Dole's and other hypocritical assaults on Hollywood and the media, Giroux argues that it is precisely conservative policies which cut back public institutions that would provide adequate education, welfare, employment, public spaces, and life opportunities for youth that helped generate the alienation, violence, and nihilism that is all too evident in contemporary American life—and not only in communities of color, as we are aware in the era of Black Lives Matter, in which a powerful movement has arisen to protest the epidemic of police brutality and murder of Blacks and people of color.

Hence, a critical cultural studies and pedagogy should at once carry out critical discussion of the politics of representation in media culture, focusing on the images and discourses of race, gender, class, and sexuality, but at the same time contextualize the critique within broader social conditions, discourses, and struggles. While ethical and ideological critique of specific forms and texts of media culture are certainly appropriate, the critical pedagogue avoids moralizing assaults on media culture per se. The focus is instead on how racism, sexism, poverty, political discourses and policies, and the social context as a whole produce phenomena like violence and suffering. Although media culture can be contributory, it is not the origin of human suffering, and thus censoring media images alone is not the solution to problems like societal violence and injustice. Rather there are a complex nexus of conditions that cause violence and youth nihilism, and while media culture can be criticized for its representations it should not be scapegoated.

The political contextualization, critique, and focus of Giroux's work, however, sometimes lead his exercises in cultural studies and critical pedagogy to what might be called a political and ideological overdetermination of his readings of specific cultural texts. While Giroux increasingly focuses on the importance of cultivating the ethical dimensions of education and critical pedagogy, his readings of specific cultural texts usually privilege political critique over valorization of positive ethical, aesthetic, and philosophical dimensions to the text (a critique sometimes made of my work to which I plead guilty). There is in Giroux a perhaps too quick collapse of the aesthetic and textual into the political in some of his readings, as I also have done, mea culpa. This procedure is arguably justified in discussions of films like the works of Tarantino or *Fight Club* (Giroux 2001), which aestheticize violence and indeed themselves collapse aesthetics into politics. This is also the case with ad campaigns that Giroux criticizes for their aestheticizing and commodification of youthful bodies, promoting "heroin chic" and other dubious ideals for youth. And Benetton ads or other images that aestheticize urban deprivation and suffering in glossy images also merit sharp critique.

Yet certain cultural texts have an aesthetic excess, a polysemic overdetermination of meaning, contradictory moments and aspects that can be read against the ideological grain even of conservative texts and those that aestheticize violence. For instance, although I agree with Giroux that Larry Clark's *Kids* is highly problematic and can be read as part of a set of representations and discourses which demonize youth as nihilistic, decadent, and immoral (1997: 45), the film also provides a cautionary morality tale warning of the consequences of causal drug use and unsafe sex. While visiting at Wake Forest University, I attended a showing of the film in which afterwards a visibly shaken audience seriously discussed the danger of AIDS and unsafe sex. There was also a heated discussion of race and representation provoked by the film. While *Kids* does depict urban youth as "decadent and predatory," as Giroux argues, it also allows for a diagnostic critique of children going astray without responsible parenting, or adequate mentoring. The film shows adults as almost completely absent from children's life and society at large as negligent and failing to provide adequate parenting, supervision, education, and spaces to provide youth the opportunity to develop agency, moral responsibility, and healthy communities.

In addition to political and ideological critique, films and other media texts can be read diagnostically to provide critical insight into contemporary society (see Kellner, 1995). Consequently, on one hand, one can agree with Giroux that in films such as *Boyz n the Hood* (1991), *Menace II Society* (1993), and *Clockers* (1995), Black male youth are framed through narrow representations that fail to challenge and in effect reiterate the dominant neoconservative image of "Blackness as menace and 'other'" (1997: 45). Yet a diagnostic critique can also discern how these films provide insights into the constraints that Black youth face and the need to fight the injustice of racial oppression and inequality.[9] Hence, in addition to enacting ideological and political critique, a critical cultural studies can read texts to gain critical knowledge of their conjuncture and can valorize oppositional or utopian moments that can work against the grain of their otherwise conservative or hegemonic problematics.

Nonetheless, Giroux is right to call for political critique of cultural texts, to take culture seriously as a site of pedagogy and the construction of our sense of gender, race, class, sexuality, and other potent markers of contemporary experience and practice. His politicizing of cultural studies provides a salutary alternative to depoliticizing or aestheticizing cultural studies that either focus on banal consumer use of media artifacts, that refuse ideological or hermeneutical critique, or that flatten cultural texts into one-dimensional non-signifying surfaces as in some "postmodern" versions of cultural studies. By contrast, Giroux's political readings and critique of cultural texts, his contextualizing of media artifacts in the social and political struggles in which they emerge, and his insistent focus on the politics of representation encompassing the full dimensions of class, race, ethnicity, gender, and sexuality provide productive models for cultural studies and critical pedagogy. This work demonstrates the need for their articulation to provide more responsible and responsive theoretical and political models and practice.

Critical Pedagogy, Radical Democracy, and Social Justice

Throughout his work within cultural studies, Giroux sees "culture as the site where identities are constructed, desires mobilized, and moral values shaped" (2000b: 132). Importantly, culture "is the ground of both contestation and accommodation" and "the site where young people and others imagine their relationship to the world; it produces the narratives, metaphors, and images for constructing and exercising a powerful pedagogical force over how people think of themselves and their relationship to others" (2000b: 133). Hence, culture is intrinsically pedagogical and political, it forms, shapes, and cultivates individuals and groups and is thus in important site for radical democratic politics.

While culture can be conservative and shape individuals into conforming to dominant modes of thought and behavior, it also presents a site of resistance and struggle. A critical pedagogy and cultural studies thus attempt to give voice to students to articulate their criticisms of the dominant culture and to form their own subcultures, discourses, styles, and cultural forms. Navigating the tricky and treacherous shoals between those who would claim that culture has nothing to do with politics and would engage in elitist or textualist pedagogy abstracted from concrete political and historical conditions and struggles, contrasted to those, mostly on the Left, who deny that culture is crucial for politics, Giroux wants to insist that both culture and politics have an important pedagogical dimension. In *Impure Acts. The Practical Politics of Cultural Studies* (2000b), Giroux notes the irony that in a time of technological and cultural revolution marked by new media, technology, and forms of culture, there is crisis of democratic culture. This era is marked, Giroux argues, by rampant consumerism, the suppression of dissent, corporate conglomerate control of major culture sites, and reduction of schooling to prepare students to get better test scores and fit into the new global economy. In this context, he calls upon teachers, theorists, and cultural activists to perceive that "struggles over culture are not a weak substitute for a 'real' politics but are central to any struggle willing to forge relations among discursive and material relations of power, theory and practice, as well as pedagogy and social change" (2000b: 7).

In the contemporary conjuncture, Giroux stresses the importance for teachers and other cultural workers to reinvigorate democratic culture and to intervene in the new cultural spaces to revitalize democracy. For Giroux, cultural studies deals with media culture contextually and politically, seeing the ways that media texts either reproduce existing relationships of domination and subordination in relation to gender, class, race, and other hierarchies, or resist modes of inequality, injustice and domination. Culture can promote democracy by projecting images of a more egalitarian and just social order, or providing more empowering images of youth, women, people of color, and other oppressed groups. Further, media culture can provide useful moral education, critical knowledge of contemporary conditions, and empowering representations which can help generate more informed, educated, and active subjectivities.

By combining cultural studies and critical pedagogy, Giroux took a postmodern turn that saw the potentiality for a reconstructive project democratically transforming education, pedagogy, culture, and society. For Giroux, the new "post" theories provided the resources for new discourses, pedagogy, practices, and politics. They supplied the material and tools for reinventing education and radical democratic politics. Giroux's main focus was the reconstruction of education and pedagogy in the service of radical democracy. This involved a heightened focus on culture in which cultural studies not only engaged contemporary cultural texts but helped to cultivate the ability to retrieve histories and imagine new futures. Giroux's critical pedagogy sought not only new media literacies and ways of reading culture, but also ways of reinventing education in the service of a transformative democratic politics.

Toward a Public Pedagogy

While some versions of the postmodern turn took their avatars into the realms of increasingly abstract and pretentious discourse, Giroux sought a new language for critical pedagogy and radical democracy and new theoretical perspectives to help critique the current system of education, culture, and society, and to create democratic alternatives.[10] Whereas some champions of the postmodern turn (especially followers of Baudrillard, Virilio, and some of the more exotic brands of French postmodern theory) fell into a hopeless nihilism and pessimism, perceiving the collapse of Western civilization and modernity in the implosive postmodern realms of new media, technology, and social conditions, Giroux called for a reconstruction of Enlightenment narratives of democracy, emancipation, and social justice and transformation. He sought new subjects for a transformative practice that would help realize the progressive promises of the Enlightenment rather than promoting anti-Enlightenment and anti-rational thought and practice (which themselves, as Habermas constantly reminds us, can be enemies of democracy and social justice).

Avoiding extreme and problematic versions of the postmodern turn, Giroux was able to develop radical critiques of modern theory, pedagogy, and politics, while providing reconstructive alternatives that draw on both modern and postmodern traditions. His reconstructive and radical democratic politics are evident in his deployment of the categories of identity and difference. Whereas modern theory tends to erase or cover over difference with its emphasis on unified subjects, common culture, universal reason, truth, and values, Giroux defends an affirmation of difference that also articulates shared experiences, goals, and democratic values. Thus, while an extreme postmodern valorization of difference would erase all universals, commonalties, and shared identities, Giroux deploys a dialectic of identity and difference which sees the complexity, multiplicity of social identities and the possibility for producing more democratic and just subjectivities, discourses, and practices.

Likewise, where an extreme postmodern identity politics would verge toward separatism, or reduce politics to construction of highly specific racial, gender, sexual or other identities that often fetishize difference, Giroux calls for a "border politics" where individuals cross over and struggle together for democracy and social justice—a notion illuminating by the concept of intersectionality and a politics of alliance and solidarity (Kellner, 2020). Giroux has developed a pedagogy of representation, place, performance, and transformation. His pedagogy of representation and place involve grasping the larger historical contexts that produce various oppressions, resistance and struggle, identity, and differences. His pedagogy of representation involves perceiving how media, education, political discourses and practices, and other institutional forces generate cultural images and discourses that produce and reproduce forms of oppression and domination, but also generate transformative struggles for a freer and more just society.

Yet his pedagogy of representation also involves the construction of subjectivities and practices that would be able to give voice and expression to their own histories, oppressions, and aspiration, to fight against domination and for transformative democracy and social justice. Here Giroux's pedagogy of place cultivates the ability to retrieve hidden or submerged life histories and those of one's groups, to situate these histories in the political context of the present, and to activate them within the political struggles for the future (see, for instance, Giroux, 1993, Chapters 2 and 4).

Giroux has promoted a pedagogy that cultivates both a retrospective grasp of one's historical past, a perception of the dominant forces of oppression and resistance in the present, and an anticipation of a better future rooted in historical struggle and vision. The pedagogy of place and representation in Giroux's work involves also cultivating a pedagogy of the popular. For it is the popular forms of media culture that often shape an individual's sense of history, the present, and the future, as well as one's understanding of the dynamics of race, gender, class, sexuality, and so on. Here, a critical cultural studies provides the critical tools to provide competencies that enable teachers, students, and citizens to develop the ability to analyze and criticize cultural representations that promote domination and oppression. It also, as Giroux argues, can help foster resistance and the construction of transformative concepts of history, possibility, and a more democratic and egalitarian configuration of class, gender, racial, and other identities.

Yet in linking cultural studies with critical pedagogy, Giroux also wants to animate capacities to produce alternative subjectivities and practices in the struggle for radical democracy and social justice. This involves seeing teachers as cultural workers and intellectual who provide the theory, language, and skills to both dissect the dominant culture and construct a new more democratic culture and more empowered and ethical identities. In this vision, intellectuals and teachers are cultural workers engaged in a struggle to represent the present, past, and future. Giroux has a democratic faith in the potential of teachers, students, and citizens to educate themselves and to struggle together for a better world.

Indeed, in the 2000s, Giroux has stressed the central importance of development a public pedagogy in which teachers and students become public intellectuals and activists, fighting against injustices and for radical democracy.[11] Giroux has focused on major issues of the 2000s ranging from the 9/11 terrorist attacks, to the Iraq war and the assaults on democracy by the Bush-Cheney administration, and most recently on Trump's multiple assaults on democracy and escalating gun violence. Throughout, he insists that teachers, students, and citizens should be actively engaged in the public sphere and fight for democracy, equality, and social justice. He ascribes education and educators a key role in the struggle for democracy as schooling can either produce active citizens, passive consumers, or alienated individuals who sit on the sidelines. Yet education itself for Giroux needs to be connected with activist cultural politics as I note in the conclusion.

Conclusion

Giroux sees cultural politics as encompassing education, artistic work, the pedagogy of social movements, and a public pedagogy aligned with the struggle for radical democracy. His performative pedagogy (see the Introduction to Giroux and Shannon, 1997; Giroux, 2000b, Chapter 6) attempts to demonstrate how cultural texts enact broader societal and political issues in a pedagogy that makes visible relations of power, domination, and resistance in media culture and the public sphere. For Giroux, educators and radical intellectuals are cultural workers who should struggle to nurture and keep alive democratic culture, educating individuals for democracy and promoting citizenship and moral education. Giroux has always been steadfastly on the Left but has long opposed a form of Marxist orthodoxy which privileges the working class as the primary agent of social change and that valorizes economic issues over all other cultural, social, or political issues and struggles. In *Living Dangerously* (1993), Giroux wrote: "Contrary to the conventional left thinking, ... the greatest challenge to the right and its power may be lodged not in the mobilization of universal agents such as the working class or some other oppressed group, but in a cultural struggle in which almost every facet of daily life takes on a degree of undecidability and thus becomes unsettled and open to broader collective dialogue and multiple struggles" (36).

Giroux has stressed how education, youth, race, gender, and culture in general have been contested terrains. Schooling, in his view, is a site of struggle between conservative, neo-liberal and more democratic forces—and continues to be as we move through a new millennium. Likewise, youth is a site of contestation with corporate and conservative forces attempting to colonize, commodify, and control youth, while more democratic and emancipatory forces attempt to educate and empower young people, stressing hope, possibility, and the possibility of collectively creating a better world – and young people themselves have been passionate participants in contemporary social movements from Occupy to Black Lives Matter, MeToo, the Dreams, environmental struggles, and struggles for rational gun safety measures. The intense struggles over race and gender during the past decades bring cultural representations and a wealth of political, cultural, and social issues to the fore which require that critical pedagogy, cultural studies, and a radical democratic politics work to struggle for social justice and equality in an environment often hostile to such ideals.

As we proceed further into this millennium, the turbulence of the technological revolution, global restructuring of capitalism, and the expansion of rightwing authoritarian populist movements creates a volatile situation where established orthodoxies and authorities are becoming questioned, new digital technologies and devices, proliferating social media, and new oppositional practices and social movements are emerging, in response to the continued repression of people of color, women, youth, and poor and the ravages of neo-liberalism and the authoritarian presidency of Donald Trump and threats to democracy from rightwing politicians and activists who on January 6, 2021 tried to overturn the democratic election of Joe Biden and who continue to threaten voting rights, fair elections, and other constituents of democracy.

In the highly divided, contested, and over-heated context of the 2020s, the entire social field is one of contestation between authoritarian, corporate, conservative, neoliberal, and democratizing forces. Giroux's contribution over the past decades has been to always side with radical democratizing forces on the issues of the restructuring of education, political transformation, and a democratization of all forms of social, political, and cultural life. Giroux thus advances forms of radical democratization and social justice which balance support for the rights of children and youth, civil rights, women's rights, an egalitarian democratic culture, and a revitalized public sphere with respect for difference. This project provides marginal and excluded voices a chance to participate and creates the democratic institutions: schooling, media, cultural forms, and public spaces which make possible a genuine participatory democracy. It directs critical pedagogy and cultural studies to struggle for democratization and against injustice and not just to provide more sophisticated methods of reading or teaching cultural texts. In these ways, Giroux encourages those of us involved in the project of critical pedagogy, cultural studies, and the theory wars to not forget democratic politics and social struggle as we attend to our pedagogical and public performances.

Notes

1   For his first sustained presentation of the importance of cultural studies for critical pedagogy and the reconstruction of education, see Giroux (1992: 161 ff.); on the need for a richer understanding of culture, cultural politics, and pedagogy than in conventional orthodoxies, see Giroux (1992; 180 ff.); some of the positions in his cultural turn were anticipated in Giroux and Simon (1989). For my own takes on media culture and cultural studies, see Kellner (1995 [second revised edition, 2020]).

2   Giroux also co-edited a series of books on critical pedagogy and cultural studies, signaling the collaborative nature of the enterprise; see Giroux and Simon (1989), Giroux and McLaren (1989, 1994), Giroux, McLaren, Lankshear, and Cole (1994), and Giroux and Shannon (1997). One might also cite Giroux's collaborations with Stanley Aronowitz who also worked to combine cultural studies, critical pedagogy, and radical democratic politics (1991, 1994).

3   For an excellent studies of the ongoing and escalating war against youth, see Giroux (2001, 2009).

4   On Rap and Hip Hop, see Kellner (1995).

5   It is important for critical educators, students, and activists to put pressure on the Biden-Harris administration to reverse these policies. See the Brooking Institution analysis of the challenges of "The Biden Presidency and a New Direction in Education Policy," December 17, 2020 at https://www.brookings.edu/blog/brown-center-chalkboard/2020/12/17/the-biden-presidency-and-a-new-direction-in-education-policy/ (accessed in April 5, 2021).

6   The Dark Side of the sexualizing of youth has emerged at the end of the Trump presidency with Jeffrey Epstein and other members of the corporate and political elite getting caught up in child prostitution scandals, while Republican Congressman and hardcore Trump supporter Congressman Matt Gaetz is also caught up in involving paying for sex with teenage girls. See Justin Vallejo, "Matt Gaetz campaign hires Jeffrey Epstein lawyer in connection to Justice Department investigation, report claims The probe has reportedly expanded from sexual

misconduct to include campaign finance issues.," *The Independent*, Sep 27, 2021 at https://www.independent.co.uk/news/world/americas/us-politics/gaetz-campaign-hires-epstein-lawyer-in-connection-into-doj-investigation-report-claims-b1927922.html (accessed June 4, 2022).

7   Curiously, as I revise this essay for the collection of my essays on education which the reader has in hand, the rightwing has been attacking Disney for Disney opposition to the "don't say gay" bill, sponsored by Gov. Ron DeSantis (R) and the Florida state legislature. See Michael Feola "Why Republicans are attacking Disney for 'grooming' on LGBTQ rights. The 'new right' believes that to win in politics, it first has to break what it sees as the left's stranglehold on the culture." *The Washington Post*, May 5, 2022 at https://www.washingtonpost.com/politics/2022/05/05/dont-say-gay-disney-desantis-gay-trans/ (accessed June 4, 2022).

8   For my own analysis of the political attack on rap in the early 1990s, see Kellner (1995, Chapter Four).

9   Giroux's reading of *Juice* is more nuanced and provides a better context for productive engagement with contemporary films dealing with Black urban youth (1996: 39 ff.). While Giroux is rightfully concerned that the film could help promote "white panic" and negative images of Black youth, he notes the critique of violence in the film. While I would agree with Giroux (1996: 44) that one needs to go beyond mainstream Hollywood films to texts like Julie Dash's *Daughters of the Dust*, or Leslie Harris's *Just Another Girl on the IRT*, to find more progressive and complex representations of African-Americans, I would argue that even films which have negative representations can be engaged by a critical cultural studies to produce productive discussions and insights into contemporary social conditions and the dynamics of race, gender, sexuality, class, and other sites of representation and contestation.

10 For Giroux's defense of theoretical language, see 1993, Chapter 6 and 1994, Chapter 6. In retrospect, I would agree with Giroux on the usefulness of theory and need for new theoretical languages to describe emergent social, cultural, and political conditions and to develop more complex discourses to capture the turbulence, intense changes, and novelties of the present. But in the present conjuncture, I would want to mediate between those who call for clarity and accessibility in discourse and writing contrasted to those who defend high theory and complexity. Hence, while I believe it was salutary to appropriate and deploy the new theoretical discourses of the past decades, and have done so myself, I think in the present conjuncture, it is important to try to become as clear and accessible as possible. Moreover, I would argue that a virtue of Giroux's work is that it is indeed always lucid and accessible to a broader public, even while he was, like were many of us, learning new languages and developing new theories and pedagogies. Finally, I would suggest that engaging the always-proliferating cyberculture and transformations of education and everyday life brought on by digital technologies and social media, requires complex theoretical language and analysis, as well as new pedagogies and a democratic restructuring of education, as I am arguing in this book.

11 Giroux continues to be a highly active public intellectual. During the 2020s, he has an email listserve to which I subscribe where he send out texts addressing current social and political issues, interviews he does on pedagogy, and articles or posts on the intersection of education and politics, always championing radical democracy. See, for example, a couple of days ago I got a posting by Giroux reading: "Hi Everyone, thought you might be interested in this video interview I did on what mass shootings tell us about America with the remarkable Sonali Kolhatkar. https://freespeech.org/stories/what-mass-shootings-tell-us-about-america/." Keep on going Henry! Right on!

References

Aronowitz, Stanley and Henry Giroux (1985; second edition 1993) *Education Still Under Siege*. Westport, CT: Bergin and Garvey.

—————— (1991) *Postmodern Education*. Minneapolis: University of Minnesota Press.

Giroux, Henry (1992) *Border Crossings. Cultural Workers and the Politics of Education*. New York: Routledge.

——————(1993) *Living Dangerously: Multiculturalism and the Politics of Culture*. New York: Peter Lang Publishers.

—————— (1994) *Disturbing Pleasures. Learning Popular Culture*. London and New York: Routledge.

—————— (1996) *Fugitive Cultures*. New York: Routledge.

—————— (1997) *Channel Surfing: Racism, the Media, and the Destruction of Today's Youth*. London: Palgrave MacMillan.

—————— (1999) *The Mouse that Roared: What Disney Teaches*. Lanham, MD: Rowman and Littlefield.

—————— (2000a) *Stealing Innocence*. New York: St. Martin's Press.

—————— (2000b) *Impure Acts. The Practical Politics of Cultural Studies*. New York and London: Routledge.

—————— (2001a) *"Zero Tolerance and Mis/education: Youth and the Politics of Domestic Militarization,"* Tikkun, March/April: 29–35.

—————— (2001b) "Private Satisfactions and Public Disorders: "Fight Club", Patriarchy, and the Politics of Masculine Violence," *JAC* 21(1) (Winter 2001): 1–31, on-line at https://www.jstor.org/stable/20866386?seq=1 (accessed April 5, 2021).

—————— (2009) *Youth in a Suspect Society: Democracy or Disposability?*. London: Palgrave Macmillan.

Giroux, Henry and Patrick Shannon (1997) *Cultural Studies and Education: Toward a Performative Practice*. New York and London: Routledge.

Giroux, Henry and Peter McLaren (editors) (1989) *Critical Pedagogy, the State, and the Struggle for Culture*. Albany, NY: SUNY Press.

—————— (1994) *Between Borders: Pedagogy and Politics in Cultural Studies*. New York and London: Routledge.

Giroux, Henry, Peter McLaren, Colin Lankshear, and Mike Cole (1994) *Counternarratives*. New York and London: Routledge.

Giroux, Henry and Roger Simon (1989) *Popular Culture, Schooling & Everyday Life*. Granby, MA: Bergin & Garvey.

Kellner, Douglas (1995; second revised edition 2020) *Media Culture*. London and New York: Routledge.

———— (2001) "New Technologies/New Literacies: Reconstructing Education for the New Millennium." *International Journal of Technology and Design Education* 11: 67–81.

———— (2008) *Guys and Guns Amok: Domestic Terrorism and School Shootings from the Oklahoma City Bombings to the Virginia Tech Massacre.* Boulder, CO: Paradigm Press, 2008.

CHAPTER FIVE

Multimedia Pedagogy and Multicultural Education for the New Millennium

Rhonda Hammer and Douglas Kellner

New technologies provide tools to reconstruct education as we traverse a new millennium. Multimedia technologies produce new resources and material for expanding education. In examining the Shoah Project, which documents the experiences of survivors of the Holocaust, we demonstrate how it provides important tools for historical and religious education, as well as making the reality of the Holocaust vivid and compelling in the contemporary moment. In this context we discuss how multimedia can provide an important supplement to multicultural education, bringing the experiences of marginal and oppressed groups to the mainstream. Yet we also argue that effective multimedia education requires historical contextualization, the skills of critical media literacy, and engaging pedagogical presentation in the classroom to make it effective as a supplement to traditional classroom and print-based education. We show how educational technologies, such as those produced by the Shoah Foundation and the UCLA Film and Television Archives, can help reconstruct education for the 21st Century.

New technologies are dramatically altering every aspect of life from work to education. While television has been regularly denounced by educators for the "dumbing-down" of youth, new multimedia technologies are providing innovative and exciting teaching tools. During the first week of February 1998, we viewed two sets of cutting-edge multimedia production at the Shoah Institute just outside of Hollywood and at the UCLA Film and Television Archives in Los Angeles.

In this essay, we explore the potentials of multimedia technology for developing multicultural education and the ways that digital technologies can enhance the educational process.

Teachers of 20th century history and religious education confront the problem of how to teach the Holocaust. Simply citing statistics and retelling the story of the concentration camps and murder of more than six million Jews and other ethnic nationalities and minorities cannot adequately convey the enormity of this event. To supplement existing accounts of the Holocaust and to dramatize its effects, we believe that multimedia technology can help re-create the experience and provide a better sense of its horror, inhumanity, and magnitude. The multimedia dimension enables students to experience the sounds, sights, and images of history as well as to learn basic facts. Testimonies of ordinary citizens, as well as political leaders, help demonstrate the personal dimension of history and dramatize the effects of historical events on ordinary people. The interactive dimension of multimedia technology potentially can involve students more integrally in historical research and enhance moral understanding, thus providing powerful pedagogical tools to teach tolerance and promote a multicultural and an antiracist curricula. Hence, we see the virtue of multimedia technology in providing new tools for historical documentation and pedagogy that can help reconstruct education for the 21st century.

Teaching the Unthinkable: The Shoah Project

The Shoah Visual History Foundation is tucked within the dream factories in the Hollywood Hills, not far, in fact, from the infamous "Hollywood" sign. The Shoah Foundation utilizes the most advanced multimedia digital technology to document the impact of the Holocaust. Founded by Steven Spielberg, the Shoah Project combines technological inventiveness with audio-video historical documentation to capture the experiences of Holocaust survivors. The result is a highly impressive set of multimedia materials that show how new media can provide significant teaching tools for the information age.

Shoah, the Hebrew word for "destruction" or "annihilation," has become a metaphor for one of the most heinous programs of genocide in 20th century history. Although some films and television productions have attempted to depict some of the stories of more than sixteen million to eighteen million victims and survivors of the Nazi Holocaust, until this project there had been a serious lacuna of audiovisual material that attempted to capture the testimonies of those who had survived. However, rather than simply documenting the stories and memories in stock footage and traditional linear, static, talking-head video or film, this project uses advanced digital technology. The project utilizes top-quality video documentary footage archived and distributed by fiberoptic interactive multimedia, produced by creative collaboration in technology, education, and media production. In taking advantage of computerized multimedia technology, producers used additional material to accompany the testimonies, maps, archival historical footage, related music, and sound effects. These devices provide the capacity to experience multiple dimensions of the historical ordeals being described, as well as to gain better contextual understanding.

The Shoah Project thus combines video documentary footage, historical texts and commentary, and interactive archives to provide educational material concerning the Holocaust. It is in this sense that the educational potential is significant, demonstrating how digital technologies can supplement traditional teaching materials. Video testimony of survivors in conjunction with interactive multimedia material both humanizes the Holocaust and enables in-depth involvement that makes the facts and horrors more striking and real.

It is therefore ironic that this nonprofit and imaginative prototype of a new form of politicized, contextual, humanistic multimedia pedagogy is due, in large part, to the inspiration, commitment, and initial financial support of Steven Spielberg, one of the most successful members of the Hollywood community. Hollywood is frequently demonized for its role in the production of commercial media "junk" often said to underlie many of the problems affecting young people. Yet it was during Spielberg's filming of *Schindler's List* (1993), his movie about the relationships between Holocaust survivors and a Catholic German war profiteer responsible for saving many of his Polish, Jewish employees, that he decided to initiate the Survivors of the Shoah Visual History Foundation. Rather than just depicting representative victims and survivors—through actors—Spielberg was provoked, largely through personal encounters with survivors throughout production of his award-winning film, to apply this new video and multimedia technology to developing new types of educational and historical tools. The result is perhaps the most significant historical archive of an oppressed people ever produced, and a dramatic demonstration of the pedagogical potential of new multimedia technology.

Incorporating the expertise of numerous scholars, historians, and specialists from a variety of fields, the USC Shoah Foundation was initially directed by Michael Berenbaum, a respected Holocaust scholar. Berenbaum was the director of the Research Institute of the United States Holocaust Memorial Museum in Washington, D.C., before he accepted the position of president and CEO of the foundation;[1] he has been succeeded by Douglas Greenberg and Stephen Smith and at this time is seeking a new Director.[2] The project has, since 1994, archived more than 51,000 eyewitness accounts in thirty-two languages from fifty-seven countries. Freelance videographers and interviewers undergo training sessions organized by the foundation and base their interviews primarily on a specially designed questionnaire. Within this context, individuals who experienced life in the camps are asked to address three areas: pre and postwar experiences, as well as the substantive portion involving their firsthand wartime ordeal in concentration camps, and other World War II experiences.

The unedited videotapes are duplicated once they arrive at the Shoah Institute headquarters. Copies are made not only for the participants, but also for storage on both the East and West Coasts of the United States. One copy is housed in California and the other, which will eventually be preserved permanently in Israel, at the Holocaust Museum in Washington, D.C. In addition, a digitalized version exists for interactive computer accessibility, as well as a copy coded for documentation purposes. The taped interviews are also periodically checked for "quality control" at the Institute, and/or provide assistance to individual interviewers. The "cataloging," or "customized cataloging interface," as it is called, is one of the most impressive aspects of the project in both technical and pedagogical terms. Through a complex computer documentation system, comprised of an ever-growing number of key categories or terms, each testimony is analyzed and documented by professionals. This process provides not only a computer record of the participants' words, but the grouping of each testimony into three- to four-minute vignettes. In addition, multiple aspects of the survivors' experiences are indexed under a diversity of topics that can be referenced for future use.

Each interview takes about eight hours to index, using digital technology. The final version of the text includes multimedia and interactive documentary footage, maps, and spoken materials, as well as the option to access associated interviews and places of learning. Eventually the Shoah institutional holdings will link through networks to museums, educational institutions, and nonprofit organizations worldwide. The foundation is also producing documentaries, books, and educational CD-ROMs to further distribute its groundbreaking archival material. Cumulatively, these products provide valuable educational material and documentation of human nobility, spirit, and courage in the face of the Nazi system.

These archives not only chronicle individual experience and perseverance, but also provide an innovative pedagogical approach to understanding, studying, and better contextualizing the horrors of the Holocaust. Materials allow one to contextualize individual instances of oppression against the more general features of German fascism. Moreover, the tapes put in question the pernicious stereotype of Jews as sheep being led to the slaughter, a myth that has been perpetuated for far too long and that has done significant damage and disservice to the Jewish people. Such stereotypes of passivity, by covering over resistance and struggle, also do injustice to many other victims of the abuse and torture that remain prevalent in the contemporary world.

Consequently, one of the most moving portions of each video is a segment at the end that allows the interviewee to introduce their families, to show pictures and news clippings, to read from letters or journals, and to include material he or she feels is relevant. This material is often the most accurate way of commemorating the families, friends, and loved ones of the millions victimized. The project is not confined to video documentation and databases but enables the production of documentary films that incorporate its material and expand on its techniques. The Academy Award-winning documentary, *The Last Days* (1998), for example, effectively incorporated Shoah Foundation material as do a number of other documentaries made from, or utilizing, the footage.

We cannot begin to describe "the undescribable" in the collection of Holocaust testimonies. It would be difficult to recount the experiences captured in these records in a fashion that adequately summons the emotions they evoke, as well as the human frailties, talents, courage, love, altruism, fortitude, and horrors on display. Yet we should stress the documentary value of the archival material and its pedagogical significance, as well as the potential empowerment these testimonies realize in form and content. The project provides strength for those who, until exposure to the graphic ordeals of other survivors' experiences-may have felt alone, isolated, or marginalized by their victimization. It also helps those inspired by their courage to carry on in the face of horrific suffering and evil.

Moreover, the interactive archive's strongest application may reside in its potential to recontextualize contemporary history and the place of the Holocaust, combined with its cultivation of a politics of hope with which individuals and groups can overcome horrible deprivation and oppression. For disenfranchised students who will have access to these documents, the experiences should be instructive, thus transcending the often-abstract modes of teaching which frequently fail to capture the human dimension of history, especially of suffering and struggle. The multimedia presentation of the Holocaust also overcomes the tendency in some circles to divide one subject from another. Such abstracted and decontextualized education often neutralizes associations among disparate areas. By contrast, combining multimedia material provides more than one dimension to events like the Holocaust. The combination of historical documentation and personal testimony enhances the possibility of both historical and moral education.

New Educational Technology: Challenges and Potential

Hence, we believe that a mechanistic and all-too-common reductive abstraction of teaching from human experience and multidisciplinary perspectives can be overcome in part, through the use of digital multimedia as teaching devices. Narrow, print-based pedagogy often reduces the eloquent dialectic of real history to the banal versions that so often masquerade as "the real thing" in many schools and universities. Multimedia education, however, can help access lived experience, as well as dramatize and concretize basic historical facts and knowledge.

Many current criticisms of the role of computer and multimedia technology in schools stem from an inability to grasp the importance of computer and digital literacies and to understand how new technologies can help revitalize education. This failure has been preceded by uneven classroom use of film and television. Such "media" were often used as a supplement, or as an excuse for the teacher to take a break from the arduous activity of interacting creatively with students—and are still used in this way. Yet all-too-infrequently has critical media literacy been taught, or has there been imaginative use of multiple media in the classroom. Within K-12 classrooms and in higher echelons, wherever teachers are taught how to teach, media, computer, and technological literacies are rarely discussed, although this situation may soon change given the computerization of education (see Luke, 1997; Kellner, 1998) and expansion of media literacy education throughout the world (see Kellner and Share 2019).

It appears as if a form of elitist blindness has emanated from leading educational theorists and so-called experts regarding the role of media in the everyday lives of both teacher and student. There is also a pervasive failure to employ these shared materials in a manner that enhances education, such as through teaching about the semiotic codes and ideological frames that structure much of media culture. There is also failure in empowering both teacher and student to analyze and interpret media culture. Media and digital literacies are necessary in the computer era for navigating more complex technological and ideological forms, such as DVDs, the Internet, and social media.[3]

Media and computer literacy will enable students to seek information and knowledge more actively, but also provides the skills to develop their own cultural artifacts within the educational setting and within a wider pedagogical, philosophical, and practical context. It is inspiring to see websites and other artifacts that students have already produced, often collaboratively, with computer and multimedia technologies. In view of the increased role of computers in business, higher education, and everyday life, such skills will be necessary for creative participation in the future.

It is therefore unfortunate that many influential educators and pedagogues have discredited media and computer literacies in favor of outdated arguments which privilege the written word. This may be the bias of the university professor, immersed in the publish-or-perish domain, and it is translated into hostility toward alternative, multimedia pedagogies. The prejudice against new technologies and interactive multimedia may reflect technological incompetence and phobia among teachers who, themselves have not mastered these technologies, while hostility toward teaching critical media and digital literacies may result from conservatism and vested interests, as well as lack of vision.

There are, of course, limitations to the use of media and computer technology in education, and we believe that, in an information society, print literacy and other fundamentals are more necessary than ever. In a world of information overload, it is increasingly important to teach critical reading and analysis, and clear and concise writing. Further, we ourselves continue to be active writers, readers, and lovers of book culture and printed media, perhaps to excess. Moreover, a good classroom teacher can provide context, application of class material to the situation of the students, and a forum for discussion and live interaction that computers cannot. Hence, far from suggesting the obsolescence of the classroom and traditional models of good teaching or of book culture, we argue that sound classroom pedagogy and constructive dialogue are as important as ever. Yet we also believe that it is the responsibility of educators to use the most advanced technologies in addition to teaching the basic skills of reading, writing, and mathematics. Obviously, teaching tools cannot fully replace teachers. We believe that the relationship between print media and multimedia technology, as well as between classroom teaching and computerized teaching tools, is not a choice of either-or, but is one of both-and. In this conception, multimedia is used to supplement print material and digital technologies are deployed to supplement classroom teaching exercises.

We owe it to our students to prepare them for new labor markets, forms of information and entertainment, and a society mediated by ever expanding and developing technology. Yet rather than deploying multimedia technologies, traditional educators persist in blaming media and technology for declining test scores and an alleged dumbing-down of youth, not unlike blaming the victim. These educators often propose or defend problematic tools like "V-chips" in televisions to censor so-called sexually explicit or violent programming-often misidentified or misdefined by the "experts," rather than teaching students to analyze and dissect representations of violence or other objectionable material. Likewise, it is now fashionable to defend programs that will block home or school computers from objectionable content as the solution to allegedly debased use of computer technologies.

It seems more productive, however, to teach students how to access and appreciate worthwhile educational media and cultural material rather than to censor and condemn, although learning skills of critique is an essential part of media pedagogy and education in general. Censoring material often makes it more appealing and seductive, so we recommend critical engagement with media rather than simple prohibition. Moreover, the incorporation of media literacy programs within the public school and university systems hardly requires anything more than a television set, VCR monitor, pretaped programs, and a teacher or professor trained, committed, and knowledgeable in media literacy theory and practices. As Carmen Luke argues :

> TV is today's mass social educator, with powerful influence on social life, people's worldviews, consumer behavior and the shaping of public sentiment. The network of commodity and visual symbolic sign systems within which we live is already so dense and pervasive that we fail to make much note of it. Television takes up more of children's time than any other activity except sleeping and school-aged children watch on average between 18–30 hours a week. By age 18, the average viewer has watched some 14,000 hours of TV, and yet during that same time has spent only 12,000 hours in classrooms in front of teachers and texts. These figures do not include time spent reading comic books and magazines, playing video games, or playing with media spin-off toys. (1996, 1)

Luke goes on to emphasize the everyday situations of the typical student writing: "In my estimation, the everyday televisual and popular cultural texts that students encounter are at least as, if not more significant sources of learning than the print texts educators deem as culturally relevant literacy text (ibid). Her appraisal of contemporary student consciousness regarding the significance of media is a common sense and shared assumption, yet it is at odds with how media and computers are regarded in everyday teaching practice. While Luke focuses on television, it would be appropriate, given the current explosion of such technologies, to also include computer and multimedia culture in discussing media pedagogy, as both Alan and Carmen Luke have long done, along with ourselves.

For example, even with the widespread availability of inexpensive video equipment within schools and universities, teachers rarely teach students how to analyze media or promote critical media literacy, let alone teach students how to use the equipment to produce their own media. Production of alternative or parodic forms of commercial media, for instance, could break barriers and extend the educational process in many exciting pedagogical directions (see Hammer, 1995). Yet this inexpensive and accessible option is rarely employed by university or K-12 classroom teachers. Unfortunately, it seems far more common for teachers to supplement oral and written teachings with a film or video as a far less valued corollary text.

Moreover, if practical applications of media production are taught, they are often addressed with condescension and allocated to a less-socially credible school employee, usually technical support staff. Such staff are often not interested in or qualified to teach the necessary semiotic skills and analytical conceptualizations. Furthermore, the main authority figure, the classroom teacher or professor, often diminishes the importance of this kind of literacy, typically in a subtly dismissive manner, by the very lack of demonstrated skill and/or interest in such work. The teacher thus abdicates to "techies" the pedagogical responsibilities.

Hence arises the illogical but common practice of blaming the victim, or student in this case, and the technology itself in a fashion that obscures its potential pedagogical significance. Media culture, digital technologies, and social media have become a common object of disdain within the educational context. Like TV and Hollywood films that many educators have earlier blamed for students' educational and human failings, digital technologies and social media are also being demonized. Many educators and critics denounce out of hand new digital technologies rather than studying how such tools can enhance education. In a similar vein, criticisms also proliferate concerning student use of the computer and Internet to plagiarize and cheat on term paper assignments, rather than seriously investigating the ways that digital technologies and multimedia could advance research and education. Such criticism also obscures the real epistemological and behavioral shifts that an expanding computer and media culture are producing and the need to develop pedagogies to use these technologies for educational purposes.

The criticisms often call attention to the challenge and ubiquity of the new technologies and dramatize the need for teachers and curriculum developers to become literate in these domains. Such emergent pedagogical forums deserve the respect with which the written, published word is afforded within the academic realm, often, we might add, uncritically. News stories depict youth using computers to access pornography, to cheat, or to play trivial games. It is as if we are being revisited by 1950s' morality. Cruising the Web, as well as other controversial activities like chat rooms or virtual interactive sites, is generally considered corrupting, like early involvement in rock and roll.

Moreover, some educators have adopted a counterproductive attitude toward these new technologies and their incorporation into both the classroom and everyday lives. They hence shirk their responsibilities as practical and critical pedagogues to use the most advanced technologies for educational purposes. Too many educators and critics employ the (admittedly compelling) argument that the new technologies are more accessible to the privileged and therefore reinforce class hierarchies, which will eventually enable children of the predominantly white-middle and upper classes to become more computer literate. Critics often use this argument to imply that computers will generate more rigid class-based divisions in employment and social position, rather than devising strategies to make sure that disadvantaged groups have access to digital technologies and education concerning their use (and misuse!).

Merely dismissing new technologies manifests a refusal to address the need to promote multimedia, computer, and digital literacies among all social groups. In fact, the admittedly growing disparity between the haves and have-nots must become part of an educational epistemology and politics. This cause needs the active participation of educators in political coalitions that seek to make these technologies more accessible to the underprivileged student populations. Such coalitions require teachers and educational professionals who are networked in grassroots organizations, official and unofficial lobbying groups, and research and grant-making organizations, as well as participants in and perhaps subverters of the educational and social systems that benefit ruling groups along the axes of class, gender, and race.

What is needed therefore is an epistemological shift toward deploying multimedia and digital technologies for educational purposes. This turn should aim to empower and enlighten both teachers and students, and to assist them in recognizing the differences among good and bad, mediocre, and beneficial, media and digital culture. Teachers and students should evaluate multimedia with the same seriousness that educators judge print media. This approach, however, necessitates a commitment to teaching media, computer, and multimedia literacies and the active incorporation of the best programs within the pedagogical forum. It is within this context, then, that the Shoah Project could prove an innovative teaching resource. Any liberatory educational form must be pedagogically efficacious in both form and content. Projects like the Survivors of the Shoah Visual History Foundation can provide models of how multimedia material can enhance education, if, of course, the material is used appropriately.

Multimedia technology also has potential for multicultural education. To non-Jews, Jews are an Other; they exist in an area of strangeness, just as Black people are alien to non-Blacks who have not interacted with them. Multimedia technology makes representations of those perceived as Other accessible. These images can personalize individuals; they make it possible to experience the views, practices, and culture of groups outside one's life. Multimedia can dramatize oppression, making intolerance and bigotry vivid, showing the evil effects of racism and prejudice.

Digital multimedia can thus help document racism and teach tolerance by providing vivid examples of prejudicial behavior, racial, and other forms of oppression. Such documentation enables students and citizens to empathize with the victims in situations that are often abstract and objectified. Hence, well-produced multimedia can help teach tolerance and ethical behavior, as well as history, religion, philosophy and any subject.

We are therefore encouraged that the Shoah Foundation will depict many forms of fascist oppression, in addition to the slaughter of millions of Jews in the Holocaust. The next phase of its work involved documentation of other groups and individuals oppressed by German fascism, including many who have sometimes been forgotten in literature and research dedicated to the vitriolic hatred of the Nazis toward the Jewish people. The complexities involved in expanding parameters of the Shoah are powerfully expressed by Bohdan Wytwycky in *The Other Holocaust: Many Circles of Hell* (1982), which provides an excellent supplement to the Shoah material.

To grasp the full range of fascist atrocities, one must understand the Nazi policies that extended beyond Jews and encompassed an additional nine million to ten million who shared the same or similar fates (Wytwycky, 1982, 17). Wytwycky draws on Dante to attempt to clarify the Nazis' genocidal pathology.

> In his classic medieval trilogy, *The Divine Comedy*, Dante managed to portray nine different "circles" of damnation. The Nazi hell, too, consisted of different circles into which victims were consigned and in which they suffered a variety of cruel fates. The Nazi hell differed from Dante's, of course, because its victims were innocents whose only "crime" was to belong to peoples whom Nazis and racism had decreed to be unworthy of sharing in the Thousand Year Reich. (17)

Hence, rather than restricting its archival project to audiovisual documentation of Jews, the Shoah Foundation has been expanding its mandate. It will actively collect the testimonies of other pariahs of the Nazi genocide. These groups include Roma people (previously referred to as *Gypsies*), Slavs, homosexuals, Jehovah's Witnesses, communists, individuals deemed physically or mentally challenged or different, as well as any individual or group who resisted the official doctrines of the so-called Germanic master race. Moreover, the Shoah Institute is also attempting to chronicle those who refused to collaborate, who put their lives on the line by assisting those identified as the enemies of the Third Reich. The power of fascism was due in large part to the legions of collaborators rewarded for cooperation that cost the lives of brothers, sisters, friends, and loved ones. Celebrating the lives and sacrifices of those who resisted fascism is an important lesson for the future and a necessary aspect of understanding the past.

The magnitude of the Shoah Project helps show how new technologies can revitalize education for today's student. Creative use of new technology depends on those who implement it. The technologies' real efficacy is predicated on the convictions and sustainable teaching programs that must accompany these kinds of projects. Such reconstruction requires the commitment and critical intelligence, as well as hard work of teachers, who with the students desperately need these resources to learn about the world, and hence about themselves and their place in it.

Historical Education and Multimedia: UCLA's *Executive Order 9066*

The Shoah Project, to be sure, had tremendous economic resources, but as Steve Ricci, director of the Film and TV Archives at UCLA, and his colleagues have demonstrated, it is not necessary to have more than forty-five million dollars to produce a highly effective, interactive supplement. While the Shoah Foundation has a large budget and multiple funding sources, unlimited use of state-of-the art equipment, and the contributions of at least 240 paid staff members and more than 3,600 volunteers, Ricci and his colleagues have done fine work. With the Japanese American National Museum, Ricci and the UCLA center co-produced a CD-ROM which is highly sophisticated and arresting in both form and content. And like the Shoah Project, *Executive Order 9066: The Incarceration of Japanese Americans during World War II* bursts disciplinary boundaries to depict one of the most blatantly racist programs in U.S. history.[4]

The UCLA-produced CD-ROM documents an often-obscured episode. Emphasizing particularly the situation of Japanese Americans in the United States, this riveting multimedia, interactive project documents, at many levels how 120,000 Japanese Americans were incarcerated by the U.S. government in numerous so-called internment concentration camps primarily in the West, Midwest, and Texas. Allowing users to navigate from photographs, diaries, and home videos of life in the camps to newsreels, essays, and other texts, the CD-ROM provides a context in which to understand the events and humanizes the experience of victims and survivors. It also contains information often omitted from accounts of the war, such as the collusion of thirteen Latin American countries with U.S. agents in the displacement and internment in the United States of more than two thousand people of Japanese ancestry from these countries, on the highly dubious charges that they posed security risks.

Like the Shoah Project, the UCLA CD-ROM stresses the necessity of reexamining legitimized programs of persecution and inhumanity to others. The incarceration of Japanese Americans was rationalized and justified solely on the basis of bigoted myths and practices, and the CD-ROM helps ensure that we do not forget and repeat, falsify, or gloss over these atrocities. One learns, for example, that much of the land or property owned by the Japanese was legally stolen or "repossessed" by U.S. government agencies.[5]

Employing archival and documentary footage, maps, photographs, and oral histories, *Executive Order 9066* interrogates the arrests and incarceration of more than 120,000 Japanese Americans, of whom more than two-thirds were American citizens. Drawing on both UCLA owned material and the resources of the Japanese American National Museum, the project includes artistic blends of computer graphics and stunning virtual reality to make the experience concrete. Moreover, the CD-ROM incorporates Japanese American actors and celebrities as narrators and includes many of their own testimonies. This content further humanizes the shameful episode, as well as demonstrating the courage of those too often portrayed as victims.

The CD-ROM thus clearly demonstrates, in various ways, that propensities toward intolerance and persecution lie within ourselves and within systems of government and lifestyles defined as democratic, liberal, and egalitarian. The production reveals that crimes against humanity are not restricted to peoples and nations commonly identified as evil, totalitarian, fascist, undemocratic, or Other.

Rather than relying on the "bells and whistles" that often typify educational CD-ROMs, or emulating the brain candy of computer games, *Executive Order 9066* permits students to learn at their own speed. It also facilitates individualized and classroom-based multimedia tutorials, studies, and assignments. The CD-ROM thus exemplifies calls for multimedia projects that enhance and transform public pedagogies. Consequently, this is the kind of multimedia project essential for contemporary teaching.

Digital transdisciplinary multimedia projects make it possible to teach not only mathematics, reading, study skills, geography, history, and some science, but also disciplines such as political science, economics, and sociology. They do so without the often tedious and dull subject divisions that generally infect these subjects. Instead of decontextualizing historical events-divorcing them from reality-the multimedia and digital projects we have discussed provide contextualized understanding of political oppression. They also teach tolerance and the importance of resisting racist and oppressive political behavior. By bringing human dimensions of persecution to the fore, multimedia technology can also serve as an instrument of moral and political education.

Notes

1 "Dr. Michael Berenbaum to Join Survivors of the Shoah Visual History Foundation USC Shoah Foundation," November 25, 1996 at https://sfi.usc.edu/news/1996/11/10333-dr-mich ael-berenbaum-join-survivors-shoah-visual-history-foundation (accessed June 4, 2022). The announcement of Berenbaum appointment as also notes: "The Shoah Foundation is a non-profit organization dedicated to videotaping and preserving interviews of Holocaust survivors all over the world. Working with the world's leading Holocaust museums, educators, archivists, documentary filmmakers and with Holocaust survivors, the Foundation is compiling the most comprehensive library of firsthand survivor testimonies ever assembled. The archive will be used as a tool for global education about the Holocaust and to teach racial, ethnic, and cultural tolerance. The initial five Shoah Foundation repositories are Yad Vashem in Jerusalem, the United States Holocaust Memorial Museum in Washington D.C., the Simon Wiesenthal Center in Los Angeles, the Fortunoff Video Archive at Yale University, New Haven, and the Museum of Jewish Heritage in New York City."

2 See Grayson Schmidt, "USC Shoah Foundation approaches 30 years and begins a leadership transition. Executive Director Stephen D. Smith will step down at the end of 2021 but continue to serve the institute as executive director emeritus." October 6, 2021, at https://news.usc.edu/192810/usc-shoah-foundation-stephen-smith-leadership-transition/ (accessed June 4, 2022).

3 For detailed discussion of the evolution of media literacy and the major literature and debates, see Luke (1997), Kellner (1998), and Kellner and Share (2019).

4 Other allied countries colluded with the United States in perpetuating this government-authorized bigotry against Japanese citizens and residents of the United States, Canada, and South America. For information on ordering *Executive Order 9066*, write Film and TV Archives, UCLA, 302 E. Melnitz, Los Angeles, CA 90095, or visit their Web site www.cinema.ucla.edu/publications.html (accessed June 4, 2022).

5 The Civil Liberties Act of 1988 apologized formally and allocated forty million dollars in reparations-half to fund educational programs, and the other half to compensate about 81,000 Japanese Americans directly. The legislation hardly addresses the grievances, suffering, loss, and long-term consequences of this injustice.

References

Hammer, Rhonda (1995) "Strategies for Media Literacy," in *Rethinking Media Literacy: A Critical Pedagogy of Representation*, edited by Peter McLaren et al. (pp. 225–35). New York: Peter Lang.

Kellner, Douglas (1998) "Multiple Literacies and Critical Pedagogy in a Multicultural Society." *Educational Theory* 48 (1): 103–22.

Luke, Carmen (1997) *Technological Literacy.* [Adult Literacy Research Network/The National Language and Literacy Institute of Australia] Melbourne: Language Australia.

Wytwycky, Bohdan (1982) *The other Holocaust: Many Circles of Hell.* Washington, D.C.: Novak Report.

CHAPTER SIX

Reading Images Critically: Toward a Postmodern Pedagogy

Modernity is interpreted as both the best and worst of things. It has been characterized in terms of progressive advances over premodern, or traditional, societies, and as a motor of innovation, creativity, change and progress. Modernity has been identified with individuality, enlightenment, science and technology, the industrial and political revolutions, and thus with democracy and freedom (Berman, 1982; Cahoone, 1988; Habermas, 1987; Kolb, 1986). More negative postmodern critiques, however, associate modernity with repression, homogeneity, and a totalitarian domination which has epistemological, sexual, political, and cultural dimensions. Postmodern theorists, such as Jean Baudrillard, Jean-Francois Lyotard, Arthur Kroker, and David Cook, claim we have left modernity behind for a new postmodern condition or scene. An extreme version of postmodern theory (Baudrillard, Kroker/Cook) claims that postmodernity constitutes a fundamental break or rupture in history which forms an entirely new society, while Lyotard, Michel Foucault and others simply recommend new ways of knowing, doing, and being which *Lyotard characterizes as postmodern knowledge*, or a "postmodern condition."[1] These theorists recommend postmodern positions over modern ones and thus positively valorize the discourse of the postmodern, while it is presented in more negative terms and images in the pessimistic writings of Baudrillard and some of his followers.

Fredric Jameson (1984), by contrast, represents postmodernism as both progressive and regressive, both positive and negative. With this and some other exceptions, most responses to the postmodern debate have been one-sided some enthusiasts jump on the bandwagon to trumpet the latest advances in Theory, Culture, and Society while others aggressively assault the postmodern attacks on the modem (e.g., Habermas, 1987), deny that anything like a postmodern condition even exists (e.g., Britton, 1988), or react with ambivalence and perhaps confusion.

Some of my own studies (Kellner, 1987, 1988, 1989a, 1989b) have taken a primarily critical posture toward what I considered to be the pretensions and inflated bombast of much postmodern theory, while exhibiting, no doubt, some degree of ambivalence (found in the postmodern theory trilogy I co-authored with Steven Best (Best and Kellner, 1991, 1997, and 2001). In this article, however, I will assume a different posture by stressing some of the positive openings in postmodern thought and those postmodern positions that might be productive for critical pedagogy. Yet I will continue to deflate certain pretensions and criticize certain excesses and dubious or reactionary aspects of so-called postmodern thought.

I should stress in advance that I do not believe that any coherent and shared postmodern theory exists, nor that we are in something like a completely new postmodern condition or scene. Rather, we should be aware of the diversity of postmodern theory and positions and read postmodern theory as pointing to new trends and social conditions that require a loosening up and development of our old theories and that might be productive for new theoretical syntheses. The latter will be the aim of this study, which will sketch outlines of a critical pedagogy that makes use of both modern and postmodern theory and positions.

Postmodern Positions: Some Theoretical Advances and Openings

One such postmodern position that I find salient to pedagogical concerns is the breakdown of the boundaries between "high" and "low" culture which Jameson (1983, 1984) and others claim is at the very heart of the postmodern. Jameson argues that one of the defining features of postmodernism

> is the effacement in it of some key boundaries or separations, most notably the erosion of the older distinction between high culture and so-called mass or popular culture. This is perhaps the most distressing development of all from an academic standpoint, which has traditionally had a vested interest in preserving a realm of high or elite

culture against the surrounding environment of philistinism, of schlock and kitsch, of TV series and *Reader's Digest* culture, and in transmitting difficult and complex skills of reading, listening and seeing to its initiates. (Jameson, 1983, p. 112; compare Jameson, 1984, pp. 54*ff.*)

Other postmodern positions (associated with Jacques Derrida, Michel Foucault, Gilles Deleuze, and Felix Guattari, among others) extend notions of reading, writing, and textuality to a variety of cultural texts, ranging from philosophical treatises to Harlequin novels and films. Through critiques of the boundaries between high and low culture and the emphasis on extension of such notions as textuality and writing, G.L. Ulmer (1985) and others have developed a postmodern populism. They attack the elitism inscribed in the conservative model of education which canonizes great books, complex literary skills, and the artifacts of high culture. Although traditional high culture provides unique pleasures and enticements, its enshrinement and canonization also serve as an instrument of exclusion, marginalization, and domination by oppressive sex, race, and class forces. Furthermore, it operates with a highly limited concept of culture and excludes from the domain of serious cultural artifacts precisely those phenomena which most immediately engage most individuals in our society. Consequently, one of the merits of certain postmodern positions is that they expand the concept of culture while breaking down barriers between "high" and "low" culture, thus opening a vast terrain of cultural artifacts to scrutiny and critical discussion.

These positions are important, I believe, in developing a new critical pedagogy which attempts to expand literacy. Modem pedagogy is organized around books and gaining literacy in reading and writing, centering its notion of education and literacy on the acquisition of skills that are especially applicable to print culture. Conservative educators bewail decline in this sort of print literacy and prescribe traditional educational curricula and methods as the solution, calling for a return to the great books, the established canons, and traditional methods for teaching literacy (see the discussion in Aronowitz and Giroux, 1985 and in Giroux, 1988). Other, more liberal, commentators (Hirsch, 1987) prescribe a broader notion of cultural literacy; they urge teaching a wide spectrum of cultural knowledge and skills, applied to texts ranging from the great books to classified ads to make its recipient a more adequate learner and doer in the contemporary society. Although this liberal program has its merits in contrast to the conservative model, it also has its limitations. Giroux (1988), by contrast, argues for a notion of critical literacy connected to a discourse of emancipation, possibility, hope, and struggle.

Building on this program, I will make some proposals concerning developing *critical media literacy* and the development of competencies in reading images critically, concentrating on some examples from print advertisements. These examples pose in a provocative way the need to expand literacy and cognitive competencies in order to survive the onslaught of media images, messages, and spectacles which are inundating our culture. The goal will be to teach a critical media literacy which will empower individuals to become more autonomous agents, able to emancipate themselves from contemporary forms of domination and able to become more active citizens, eager and competent to engage in processes of social transformation.

Reading Images Critically

One insight central to postmodern theory is the emphasis on the increasingly central role of image in contemporary society. Baudrillard (1981, pp. 185) describes the transition from a metallurgic society, defined as a society of production, to a semiurgic order characterized by the proliferation of signs, simulacra, and images. For Baudrillard, postmodern society is one defined by radical semiurgy, by the proliferation and dissemination of images and the entry into a new culture saturated with images. Indeed, from the moment we wake up to clock radios and/or tum on the television for the morning news, or check our email or cell phone for messages, to our last moments of consciousness at night with Steven Colbert and the Late Show, Bruce Springsteen or Bob Dylan music , or films by Spike Lee or Ava DuVernay we find ourselves immersed in an ocean of images, in a culture saturated with a flora and fauna of diverse species of images and spectacle which contemporary cultural theory has only begun to sort out.

Building on this postmodern position without presenting it as such, Neil Postman (1985) argues that around the tum of the 20th century, Western society left print-typographical-culture behind and entered a new "Age of Entertainment" centered on a culture of the image. Accompanying the new image culture, Postman argues, is a dramatic decline in literacy, a loss of the skills associated with rational argumentation, linear and analytical thought, and critical and public discourse. In particular this sea change in literacy and consciousness has led to a degeneration of public discourse and a loss of rationality in public life.[2] Postman attributes this "great transformation" primarily to television, which indeed can be interpreted as the most prolific image machine in history; it generates between fifteen and thirty images per minute and thus millions, or even billions of images per day with the expansion of cable TV.

Other image machines generate a panoply of print, sound, environmental, and diverse aesthetic artifacts within which we wander, trying to make our way through this forest of symbols. We need to begin learning how to read these images, these fascinating and seductive cultural forms whose massive impact on our lives we have only begun to understand. Surely, education should attend to the new image culture and should teach a critical pedagogy of reading images as part of critical media literacy. Such an effort would be part of a new radical pedagogy that attempts to get at the roots of our experience, knowledge, and behavior and that aims at liberation from domination and the creation of new, plural, enhanced, and more potent selves, ideals characteristic of both modem and some postmodern theory.

Reading images critically involves learning how to appreciate, decode, and interpret images, concerning both *how* they are constructed and operate in our lives and *what* they communicate in concrete situations. Certain postmodern theory (e.g., Foucault, Derrida, Deleuze/Guattari, and Lyotard) helps make us aware of how our experience and selves are socially constructed, how they are overdetermined by a diverse range of images, discourses, codes, and the like. This strand of postmodern theory excels in deconstructing the obvious, taking the familiar and making it strange and unfamiliar, and thus in making us attend to how our language, experience, and behavior are socially constructed and are thus constrained, overdetermined, and conventional, subject to change and transformation. Following an anti-hermeneutical thrust of structuralism, however, one strand of postmodern thought (Deleuze/Guattari) is overly restrictive concerning what it wants critical theory to do. This approach limits theoretically correct inquiry to either descriptive analysis of how phenomena work, or formal analysis of how signification and representation function, eschewing hermeneutical interpretation of ideological content for a more formal and structuralist type of analysis (although they also have poststructural/postmodern proclivities (see Best and Kellner 1991).

Some postmodern theory, indeed, claims that in the contemporary society of simulacra, images are by nature flat, one-dimensional, and glitzy, referring only to themselves or to other images (a strong version of this thesis is found in Baudrillard (1983a) while a weaker version is found in some of the essays in Gitlin (1987); see the critique in Best and Kellner, 1987).[3] Such a formal postmodern image critique, then, would content itself with describing these images, much as Susan Sontag (1969) urged in her strictures "against interpretation." Sontag's work anticipated postmodern positions and the postmodern sensibility which is ironic, erotic, and playful. Such a formal and anti-hermeneutical temptation will be resisted here. It may make our critical activity easier and cleaner, while yielding new insights and ways of seeing, yet it is too restrictive and one-sided for certain pedagogical tasks, such as the one which I undertake here.

Indeed, I find Derrida's method of deconstruction (1976) more suggestive for the process of reading images critically. Just as Derrida finds texts to be saturated with metaphysical oppositions and positions, so too are the images and scenes of mass-mediated culture. In the following reading of some familiar advertisements, I will show that their images contain precisely the sort of metaphysical oppositions that Derrida finds in texts and that the images serve to cover over or occlude the metaphysical oppositions which often turn out to be social contradictions. Advertising metaphysics are linked, as I will try to demonstrate, to dominant ideologies; thus, deconstructive critique of advertising and other artifacts of mass-mediated culture is also a critique of ideology.[4]

As a test case for a critical pedagogy of images, I will take advertising, a prolific and potent source of cultural imagery. Elsewhere I develop a general theory of advertising and fashion and review new critical perspectives on advertising (Harms and Kellner, 1989; Kellner and Harms, 1991). Here I will focus on developing tools to decipher, interpret, and criticize those ubiquitous advertising images that saturate our culture. The phenomenon of advertising (and hence the importance of learning to read advertisements critically) is far from trivial, as U.S. society invests over $102 billion a year in advertising, fully 2 % of our gross national product, far more money than in education (Association of National Advertisers, 1988, p. 4). This is a crime and a national scandal which alone should concern educators.

Postman argues that before the 20th century advertising tended to be generally informative, or at least used the media of print, rational argumentation, and verbal, rhetorical persuasion to induce consumers to buy the products offered (1985, pp. 60). By the 1890s, however, advertisements began to make increased use of photographs and illustrations and their text degenerated into slogans, jingles, and simple rhymes, with image replacing discursive rationality. In a sense, advertising became a dominant public discourse of the 20th century with its portrayals of commodities, consumption, lifestyles, values, and gender roles displacing other forms of public discourse. In this way, imagistic discourses of the private life, of commodity gratification, eroded more discursive political discourses and constituted a radical displacement of the public sphere, which postmodern theorists claim has been destroyed in the contemporary consumer and media society (compare Habermas, 1989 with Baudrillard, 1983b).

The significance of advertising for education is many-sided. Advertising constitutes one of the most advanced spheres of image production, with more money, talent, and energy invested in this form of culture than practically any other in our hyper-capitalist society. Advertising itself is a pedagogy which teaches individuals what they need and what they should desire, think, and do to be happy, successful, and genuinely American. Advertising teaches a worldview, values and socially acceptable and unacceptable behavior. Advertising, as Jules Henry (1963) argued, contains a morality and a view of truth which stresses self-indulgence, instant gratification, hedonism, and relativism. Henry argued that advertising constitutes an entire philosophical system which incorporates the values of our most powerful social force (corporate capitalism) and which itself is a major pillar of consumer capitalism.

Moreover, advertising is an important social text and social indicator which provides a repository of information concerning social trends, current fashions, contemporary values, and what really concerns the denizens of consumer capitalism. Much can therefore be learned from studying advertising. It may also be a major force in shaping thought and behavior. I will bracket, however, the debate concerning whether advertising is or is not a powerfully efficacious force in directly shaping consumer behavior and simply assume that advertising exists as a major sector of the cultural industry whose products a critical pedagogy should engage. Far from being merely flat, one-dimensional exemplars of a postmodern image culture, I will argue that advertisements are multidimensional cultural texts with a wealth of meaning which require sophisticated decoding and interpretation. As an exercise in this direction, let us take up the task of learning to read and criticize some familiar cigarette ads and to discern what this critical process tells us about ourselves and our society.

Symbolic Images in Virginia Slims and Marlboro Ads

In order to provide an introduction to reading the symbolic images of ads critically, I shall examine some print ads which are readily available for scrutiny and which lend themselves to critical analysis. Print ads are an important section of the advertising world, with about 50 % of advertising revenues going to various print media while 22 % goes to television (Association of National Advertisers, 1988, p. 4). Although apologists for the advertising industry claim that advertising is predominantly informative, careful scrutiny of magazine, television, and other imagistic ads indicates that it is overwhelmingly persuasive and symbolic and that its images not only attempt to sell the product by associating it with certain socially desirable qualities, but they sell a worldview, a life-style, and a value system congruent with the imperatives of consumer capitalism.

To illustrate this point, let us look first at two cigarette ads: a 1981 Marlboro ad aimed primarily at male smokers and a 1983 Virginia Slims ad which tries to convince women that it is cool to smoke and that the product being advertised is perfect for the "modern" woman (see Figures 1 and 2).[5] Corporations like those in

Figure 1.

the tobacco industry undertake campaigns to associate their product with positive and desirable images and gender models. Thus, in the 1950s, Marlboro undertook a campaign to associate its cigarette with masculinity, associating smoking its product with being a "real man:" Marlboro had been previously packaged as a milder women's cigarette, and the "Marlboro man" campaign was an attempt to capture the male cigarette market with images of archetypically masculine characters. Since the Western cowboy image provided a familiar icon of masculinity, independence, and ruggedness, it was the preferred symbol for the campaign. Subsequently, the "Marlboro man" became a part of American folklore and a readily identifiable cultural symbol.

Such symbolic images in advertising attempt to create an association between the products offered and socially desirable and meaningful traits in order to produce the impression that if one wants to be a certain type of person, for instance, to be a "real man," then one should buy the sponsor's product. Consequently, for decades, Marlboro used the cowboy figure as the symbol of masculinity and the center of their ads. In a postmodern image culture, individuals get their very

Figure 2.

identity from these figures; advertising thus becomes an important and overlooked mechanism of socialization, as well as a manager of consumer demand.

Ads form textual systems with basic components which are interrelated in ways that positively position the product. The main component of the classical Marlboro ad is its conjunction of nature, the cowboy, horses, and the cigarette. This system associates the Marlboro cigarette with masculinity, power, and nature. Note, however, in Figure 1 how the cowboy is a relatively small figure, dwarfed by the images of snow, trees, and sky. Whereas in earlier Marlboro ads, the Marlboro man loomed large in the center of the frame, now images of nature are highlighted. Why this shift?

All ads are social texts which respond to key developments during the period in which they appear. During the 1980s, media reports concerning the health hazard of cigarettes became widespread, a message highlighted in the mandatory box at the bottom of the ad warns that "The Surgeon General Has Determined

That Cigarette Smoking is Dangerous to Your Health!" As a response to this attack, the Marlboro ads now feature images of clean, pure, wholesome nature, as if it were "natural" to smoke cigarettes, as if cigarettes were a healthy "natural" product, an emanation of benign and healthy nature. The ad, in fact, hawks Marlboro Lights, one of the captions describes it as a "low tar cigarette." The imagery is itself "light," white, green, snowy and airy. Through the process of metonomy, or contiguous association, the ad tries to associate the cigarettes with "light;" "natural;" healthy snow, horses, the cowboy, trees, and sky, as if they were all related "natural" artifacts, sharing the traits of "nature." The ad thus covers over the fact that cigarettes are an artificial, synthetic product, full of dangerous pesticides, preservatives, and other chemicals.[6]

Thus, the images of healthy nature are a Barthesian mythology (Barthes, 1972). They attempt to cover over the image of the dangers to health from cigarette smoking and to "naturalize" cigarettes and smoking. The Marlboro ad also draws on images of tradition (the cowboy), hard work (note how deeply in the snow the horse is immersed; this cowboy is doing some serious working!), caring for animals, and other desirable traits, as if smoking were a noble activity, metonomically equivalent to these other positive social activities. The images, texts, and product shown in the ad thus provide a symbolic construct which tries to cover over and camouflage contradictions: between the "heavy" work and the "light" cigarette, between the "natural" scene and the "artificial" product, between the cool and healthy outdoors scene and the hot and unhealthy activity of smoking, and between the rugged masculinity of the Marlboro man and the Light cigarette, originally targeted at women. In fact, this last contradiction can be explained by the marketing ploy of suggesting to men that they can both be highly masculine, like the Marlboro man, and smoke a (supposedly) "healthier" cigarette, while also appealing to macho women who might enjoy smoking a "man's" cigarette which is also "lighter" and "healthier," as women's cigarettes are supposed to be.

The 1983 Virginia Slims ad (Figure 2) also attempts to associate its product with socially desired traits and offers subject positions with which women can identify. The Virginia Slims textual system classically includes a vignette at the top of the ad with a picture underneath of the Virginia Slims woman next to the prominently displayed package of cigarettes. In the example pictured, the top of the ad features a framed box that contains the narrative images and the message, which is linked to the changes in the situation of women portrayed through a contrast with the "modern" woman below. The caption under the boxed image of segregated male and female exercise classes in 1903 contains the familiar Virginia Slims slogan "You've come a long way, baby." The caption, linked to the Virginia Slims woman, next to the package of cigarettes, connotes a message of progress, metonomically linking Virginia Slims to the "progressive woman" and "modern" living. In this ad, it is the linkages and connections between the parts that establish the message which associates Virginia Slims with progress. The ad tells women that it is progressive and socially acceptable to smoke, and it associates Virginia Slims with modernity, social progress, and the desired social trait of slimness.

In fact, Lucky Strike carried out a successful advertising campaign in the 1930s which associated smoking with weight reduction ("Reach for a Lucky instead of a sweet!"), and Virginia Slims plays on this tradition, encapsulated in the very brand name of the product. Note too that the cigarette is a "Lights" variety and that this ad, like the one for Marlboro, tries to associate its product with health and well-being. The pronounced smile on the woman's face also tries to associate the product with happiness and self-contentment, struggling against the association of smoking with guilt and dangers to one's health. The image of the slender woman, in turn, associated with slimness and lightness, not only associates the product with socially desirable traits, promotes the ideal of slimness as the ideal type of femininity.

Later ads for Capri cigarettes advertise the product as "the slimmest slim!," building on the continued and intensified association of slimness with femininity. A 1988 Capri ad pictures its happily smoking woman as more stylishly and modly attired than the more conventional and conservatively dressed 1983 Virginia Slims woman, replicating the increased emphasis on expensive clothes and high fashion in the "Yuppie" era where high consumption as a way of life has become a much-advertised goal. A 1988 Virginia Slims ad (Figure 3), in fact, reveals a considerable transformation in its image of women during the 1980s and a new strategy to persuade women that it is all right and even "progressive" and ultramodern to smoke. This move points to shifts in the relative power between men and women and discloses new subject positions for women validated by the culture industries.

Once again, the sepia-colored framed box at the top of the ad contains an image of a woman serving her man in 1902; the comic pose and irritated look of the woman suggests that such servitude is highly undesirable. Its contrast with the Virginia Slims woman (who herself now wears the leather boots and leather gloves and jacket as well) suggests that women have come a long way, while the ever-present cigarette associates a woman's right to smoke in public with social progress. This time the familiar "You've come a long way, baby" is absent, perhaps because the woman pictured would hardly tolerate being described as "baby" and because indeed women's groups had been protesting the sexist and demeaning label in the slogan. Note, too, the transformation of the image of the woman in the Virginia Slims ad. No longer the smiling, cute, and wholesome potential wife of the earlier ad, she is now more threatening, more sexual, less wifely, and more masculine. The

Figure 3.

sunglasses connote the distance from the male gaze which she wants to preserve and the leather jacket with the military insignia connotes that she is equal to men, able to carry on a masculine role is stronger and more autonomous than women of the past.

The 1988 ad is anti-patriarchal and expresses hostility toward men: the over-weight man with glasses and handlebar mustache looks slightly ridiculous and it's clear that the woman is being held back by ridiculous fashion and intolerable social roles. The "new" Virginia Slims woman, who completely dominates the scene, is the epitome of style and power. This strong woman can easily take in hand and enjoy the phallus (i.e., the cigarette as the sign of male power accompanied by the male dress and military insignia) and serve as an icon of female glamor as well. This ad links power, glamor and sexuality and offers a model of female power that is associated the cigarette and smoking. Ads work in part by generating dissatisfaction and by offering images of transformation, of a "new you!" This particular ad promotes dissatisfaction with traditional images and presents a new image of a more powerful woman, a new lifestyle and identity for the Virginia Slims smoker.

Although "Lights" and "Ultra Lights" continue to be the dominant Virginia Slims types, the phrase does not appear as a highlighted caption noted before and the package is not shown either. No doubt this "heavy" woman contradicts the "light" image and the ad seems to want to connote power and (a dubious) progress for women rather than slimness or lightness. Yet the woman's teased and flowing blonde hair, her perfect teeth which form an obliging smile, and especially her crotch (positioned in the ad in a highly suggestive and inviting fashion) code her as a symbol of beauty and sexuality, albeit more autonomous and powerful. In these ways, the images associate the advertised products with certain socially desirable traits and convey messages concerning the symbolic benefits that will accrue to those who consume the product.

The point I am trying to make is that it is precisely the images that are the vehicles of the symbolic meanings and messages. Therefore, critical literacy in a postmodern image culture requires learning how to read images critically and how to unpack the relations between images, texts, social trends, and products in commercial culture. My reading of these ads suggests that advertising is as concerned with selling lifestyles and selling socially desirable subject positions, which are associated with their products, as with selling the products themselves. Putting it another way, advertisers use symbolic constructs, with which the consumer is invited to identify, to induce her to use their product. Thus, the Marlboro man (i.e., the consumer who smokes the cigarette) is smoking masculinity or natural vigor as much as a cigarette, while the Virginia Slims woman is exhibiting modernity, thinness, or female power when she lights up her slim.

Making these connections enables individuals to discern the hidden compulsions and enticements behind certain forms of consumer behavior. Enabling individuals to gain critical literacy in regard to advertising and other forms of popular culture provides emancipatory competencies which enable individuals to resist manipulation by consumer capitalism. Beyond that, it provides us with skills which enable us to read current trends in society and to note significant changes. For example, the two Virginia Slims ads suggest that at least a certain class of women (white, upper-middle and upper-class) were gaining more power in society and that women were being attracted by stronger, more autonomous and more masculine images.

A comparison of a 1988 Marlboro ad (Figure 4) with the company's earlier ads also yields some interesting results. The ads once centered on the Marlboro man, and in the early 1980s continue to feature this figure; curiously, by the late 1980s, human beings disappeared altogether from some Marlboro ads, which projected pure images of wholesome nature associated with the product. The caption "Made especially for menthol smokers," green menthol insignia on the cigarette package and the blue and green backdrops of the trees, grass, and water all attempt to incorporate icons of health and nature into the ads, as if these menthol "Lights" would protect the buyer from cigarette health hazards. In particular, the prominent use of water provides a purifying and refreshing paleosymbolic aura to the totality of the scene, attempting to wash away fears that smoking might indeed damage one's health.

Undoubtedly, this transformation in the Marlboro ads was a response to the growing concern about the health hazards of cigarettes, which required even purer emphasis on nature. Indeed, the mandatory warnings on the ads are becoming larger and even more threatening with the Marlboro ad telling the customer that

Figure 4.

"Cigarette Smoke Contains Carbon Monoxide" and recent captions on woman's cigarette ads warning that "Smoking Causes Lung Cancer, Heart Disease, Emphysema, that it "May Complicate Pregnancy," and "Smoking by Pregnant Women May Result in Fetal Injury, Premature Birth, And Low Birth Weight." Against these dire warnings, recent Marlboro ads have therefore abandoned the human figure, the familiar Marlboro man, featuring instead ad images of pure nature. The romantic use of nature in these ads codes nature as a site of innocence and tries to appropriate such images for the hardly innocent cigarette. This nostalgia for innocence is arguably a feature of a fallen postmodern culture and shows the magical ways that advertising attempts to produce another world, a transformed utopia. Such advertising seeks to blot out the dystopia of modern technological society with its dangerous products, health hazards and its spoil-sport government regulatory apparatus which forces advertisers to warn consumers that their products may well kill them.

Yet the absence of the Marlboro cowboy might also point to the obsolescence of the manual worker in a new postmodern information and service society where significant sectors of the so-called "new middle class" work in the industries of symbol and image production and manipulation. The prominent images of the strong and energetic horses, however, point to a continued desire for power, for identification with figures of power. The actual powerlessness of workers in contemporary capitalist society makes it in turn difficult to present concrete contemporary images of male power that would appeal to a variety of male (and female) smokers. Eliminating the male figure also allows appeal over a wider range of social classes and occupational types, including both men and women who could perhaps respond more positively to images of nature and power than to the rather obsolete cowboy figure. Further, and these images are clearly polysemic, subject to multiple readings, the new emphasis on "Great refreshment in the Flip Top box" not only harmonizes with the "refreshing" images of green and nature, but points to the new hedonist, leisure culture in postmodern society with its emphasis on the pleasures of consumption, spectacle, and refreshment. The refreshment tag also provides a new legitimation for cigarette smoking as a refreshing activity (building on the famous Coca Cola "pause that refreshes"?) which codes an obviously dangerous activity as "refreshing" and thus as health-promoting.

Other readings are, of course, possible. The absence of human figures in the recent Marlboro ads could be read as signs of the erasure of the human in postmodern society, giving credence to Foucault's claim that in a new episteme the human itself could be washed away like a face drawn on sand. Or, more mundanely, the absence of the Marlboro man might be an effect of the death by cancer of one of the men who posed for the ad-who, in fact, appeared before his death in videotapes warning against the dangers of the product that he had once represented. Thus, these ads are multidimensional, polysemic, and open to a variety of readings. A Freudian reading of Figures 1–3 might focus on the phallic images of the cigarette, with the white, phallus figure standing up firm and erect in Figure 1, while in Figure 2 the Virginia Slims woman firmly yet daintily holds the icon of phallic power. Note by contrast that in Figure 3 she holds it more casually and ambiguously, glove on hand and dark sunglasses over her eyes, raising the question: what *will* these women do with the phallus!? A Freudian reading might note that although the phallic cigarette protrudes more hesitantly from the Marlboro package in Figure 4, the horses can also be read as strong images of virility and phallic power. Yet the cigarette image can also be read in the ads as an example of humans dominating and controlling nature, or as an example of how humans can use a synthesis of nature and culture for their own pleasures.

Any number of readings of these multivalent texts are possible. Combining Marxist, feminist, structuralist, and other critical methods could show how the ads present certain images of women, work, class, and power which serve as vehicles for certain ideological messages. Such analysis could indicate how the ads and images attempt to resolve ideological contradictions as well as contradictions between nature and culture. More systematic semiological readings could show how these ads fit into the system of contemporary advertising and exhibit certain dominant codes, models, and rules. This sort of exercise thus helps show how gender and socially approved behavior are constructed and puts in question certain dominant models and types of behavior.

Critical Literacy, Media, and Consumer Image Culture

In the previous section, I drew on several methods of interpretation to provide examples of a critical reading of contemporary image culture, mixing postmodern analysis with ideology critique and hermeneutical readings. Such mixed methods are justified, I believe, because we are now on the borderline between modernity and a new society and culture which many theorists are labeling "postmodern." Because we are still living in a capitalist and patriarchal society, however, Marxist and feminist modes of thought continue to be relevant in analyzing the contemporary social situation. Likewise, because cultural texts continue to be saturated with multi-layered social and political messages, the sort of depth-model interpretive readings associated with modernity are still relevant.

Postmodern pedagogy, however, requires obliteration of the division between "high" and "low" culture and intensified attention to reading images, to gaining critical literacy in the domain of mass-mediated culture. Advertising is merely one part of the culture industries which include radio, television, film, music, cartoons, comic books, and the other artifacts of so-called popular culture. Critical methods of reading have been developed in several of these domains and the teaching of critical media literacy should become a standard part of a progressive educational curriculum. The artifacts of the cultural industries have assumed tremendous cultural power; they are part of a cultural apparatus which has produced increased privatization, commercialization, and reification of our culture that has led to a decline of individuality, community, citizenship, and democracy (Giroux, 1988; Kellner, 1989a). Developing critical literacy helps to reverse the trends toward growing powerlessness by empowering individuals, by providing them with competencies to resist the power of the culture industry and to learn to begin remaking culture, to produce a more democratic and participatory culture and society (Giroux, 1988).

Attaining critical literacy in the domain of learning to read popular and media culture critically involves learning the skills of deconstruction, of how cultural texts work, how they signify and produce meaning, how they influence and shape their "readers." In teaching this activity, I have experienced over and over, the empowerment of students who learn to comprehend and critically evaluate taken-for-granted aspects of their culture. Invariably, they quickly take to the activity of attaining critical literacy and become adept decoders and critics of their culture. I disagree, however, with McLuhan (1964), who argued that critical media literacy is a natural asset possessed by denizens of the postmodern media culture. On the contrary, I have found that media literacy must be acquired through learning methods of reading cultural texts.

I have suggested that it is precisely "modern" methods of criticism (Marxian and feminist ideology critique, structuralism, myth-symbol criticism, etc.), in conjunction with postmodern focus on the image and popular culture, that provide important contributions to developing critical literacy. Following Freire's model of an emancipatory pedagogy, developing critical literacy should empower individuals through enabling them to learn to see through the mystifications of their environment, to see how it is constructed and operates, and to see how they can free themselves from dominating and oppressive aspects and learn to remake society as a mode of self and social activity. Dialogue is important in this process and I suggest that teaching critical media literacy is an excellent means of getting students to talk about their culture and experience, to articulate and discuss cultural oppression and domination. Students' familiarity with advertising, exposure to television, film, music, etc., enables them to engage more readily with the artifacts of their culture than more traditional book culture. Analysis of familiar cultural artifacts can demonstrate the socially and culturally constructed nature of subjectivity and values, of how society constructs some activities as valuable and beneficial while devaluing others. Studying popular culture critically can teach students to refuse and resist the imposition of certain activities (e.g., smoking, drugs, aggressive competition), of role and gender models, and of sexist and racist behavior by showing that activity and models are not natural, are not beneficial, are not even arguably "good." Such analysis requires careful use of the language of value and of discriminating between competing value systems and social valuations. Finally, study of media and consumer culture links individual experience to public policy and the language of critique to the language of public life. To illustrate this point, I conclude by how analysis of advertising can lead to concern with public policy and progressive social change.

Implications for Education and Public Policy

I indicated that in 1988, more than $102 billion, or roughly 2 % of the U.S. Gross National Product, was spent on advertising. Advertising expenditures in 1950 were about $6.5 billion a year while by 1970 $40 billion a year was squandered, and by 1980 $56 billion was wasted. Advertising expenditure almost doubled from 1980 to 1986, pointing to an alarming expansion of advertising during the 1980s. When one considers that an equal amount of money is spent on design, packaging, marketing and product display, we grasp that a prodigious amount of money is expended on advertising and marketing. For example, only eight cents of the cosmetics sales dollar goes to pay for ingredients; the rest goes to packaging, promotion, and marketing (Goldman, 1992). Consequently, consumer capitalism constitutes a tremendous waste of resources and forces consumers to pay high prices for products that they are induced to think that they need for success, popularity, self-esteem and other socially desirable qualities.

This vicious process of waste and manipulation during an age of growing scarcity of resources is a national scandal and raises the question of what can be done to combat the excesses of consumer capitalism. Such questions make advertising a public policy issue and a contested terrain subject to critique and struggle. The question of cigarette advertising immediately raises the issue of whether *all* cigarette advertising should be banned, as television cigarette advertising was banned in the 1970s. The very fact of cigarettes, a highly addictive and potentially dangerous uncontrolled substance, raises questions concerning how to deal with this public health menace. While the Surgeon General has been helping to publicize the dangers of cigarette smoking, surely stronger actions could be taken.

In the light of the massive federal deficit, heavy user taxes on cigarettes, alcohol, and other "sin" products might, in conjunction with a public health campaign, reduce the harmful effects of cigarette smoking, drinking, drug use and so on. Considering the social effects of advertising also raises the issue of whether advertising should be subject to taxation; currently, it is written off by corporations as a business expense, thus passing off advertising expenses to the taxpayer, as well as the consumer. Congress could also consider disallowing tax write-offs for advertising and could also tax advertising expenditures and advertising agencies at a higher rate, given the dubious impact of advertising on U.S. society and the massive waste of resources, talent, and human energies.[7] At the very least, television advertising could be taxed, as could print advertising for cigarettes, alcohol, and other socially undesirable products. The question of advertising also raises the question of the effects of advertising on our media system and whether a commercial media system really provides the best model.

In these ways, the language of critique can be linked to the language of struggle and change. As Giroux (1988) argues, this requires educating students to become active citizens, participants in the making and remaking of society. A critical pedagogy plays a crucial role in this process and to some extent certain postmodern political positions can be of use here in their emphasis on local, plural struggles. Radical politics needs to be redefined to encompass the politics of everyday life, ranging from developing critical literacy to achieving more equitable gender relations. While some postmodern theory promotes cynicism, pessimism, and despair, a radical pedagogy need not fall prey to these temptations, however easy it may be to succumb to despair during this period of conservative hegemony. Now is not the time to despair or give up. The linking of critical literacy with attempts to change the direction of our political system remains a challenge for a new radical politics that has yet to be produced.

Notes

1   Bibliographical citations to the key texts are found in the References which also refer to previous articles where I discuss postmodern theory in more detail; here I am supposing familiarity with postmodern positions and will concentrate on application rather than explication of postmodern theory.

2   While Postman's critique of television (1985) is often provocative and incisive, his categorical framework invites the sort of deconstruction of binary oppositions which is a central part of many postmodern epistemologies. For his book is structured around an opposition between rational, logical, discursive, and coherent print discourse ("The Age of Exposition") and an irrational, incoherent, and fragmented electronic media discourse ("The Age of Entertainment"). Print media are serious, important, contextual, and conducive to democracy and other fine values, while electronic media and the culture of the image are trivial, frivolous, and subversive of everything valuable in life (religion, education, politics, etc.). This binary absolutism covers over the more negative aspects of print culture, such as trash literature and misinformation and often rightwing political bias, while presenting a purely negative view of image and electronic culture. I offer a competing view of media culture in Kellner 1995 (2020).

3   For a further critique of postmodern cultural theory and the explication of a political hermeneutics which builds on yet goes beyond postmodern theory, see Best and Kellner (1987).

4   For attempts to link deconstructive with ideology critique, see Ryan (1982) and Spivak (1987). In the following discussion, I assume the saliency of the poststructuralist and postmodernist critiques of much "modern" epistemology and metaphysics-that is, of theoretical positions embedded in the philosophical discourses of modernity. Whether these critiques are properly "postmodern" or merely a self-reflexive version of "modern" critique is difficult to clearly answer. That is, in a sense, deconstruction is very modernist precisely in its criticisms of the discourses of modernity. In any case, it is clear that critiques of modern epistemology and the attempts to develop new methods of reading, writing, and textuality that are sometimes described as "postmodern" is a fruitful contribution to a new radical pedagogy which we might choose to call "postmodern." Or one may well be perfectly and legitimately happy to interpret such a pedagogy as a variant of "modern" pedagogy. Indeed, in this paper, I argue that a new radical pedagogy should combine positions that are deemed "modern" and "postmodern," or are claimed by both discourses.

5   The method of reading ads and interpreting advertising which follows is indebted to the work of Robert Goldman (1992). See also John Berger (1973) and Judith Williamson (1978) for excellent pedagogical introductions to reading advertisements critically.

6   The tobacco leaf is (for insects) one of the most sweet and tasty of all plants, and therefore it requires a large amount of pesticides to keep insects from devouring it. Cigarette makers use chemicals to give a distinctive smell and taste to the product and use preservatives to keep it from spoiling. Other chemicals are used to regulate the burning process and to filter out tars and nicotine. While these latter ingredients are the most publicized dangers in cigarette smoking, actually pesticides, chemicals, and preservatives may well be more deadly. Scandalously, cigarettes were long one of the most unregulated products in the U.S. consumer economy (European countries, for example, carefully regulate dye pesticides used in tobacco growing and the synthetics used in cigarette production). Government-sponsored experiments on the effects of cigarette smoking have often used generic cigarettes, which may not have the chemicals and preservatives of name brands; no truly scientifically accurate major survey on the dangers of cigarette smoking has ever been done by the U.S. government. The major media, many of which are part of conglomerates with heavy interests in the tobacco industry, or which depend on cigarette advertising for revenue, have never really undertaken to expose to the public the real dangers concerned with cigarette smoking and the scandalous neglect of this issue by government and media in the United States. Cigarette addiction is thus a useful object lesson in the unperceived dangers and destructive elements of the consumer society and the ways these dangers are covered over. Happily,

I can conclude this discussion by indicating there has been some regulation of the cigarette industry in recent years and banning of smoking in public spaces in at least 21 states; see what Uncle Google has to say about this under "Smoke regulation US" at https://www.google.com/search?q=cigarette+legislation+in+us&ei=AdubYoP2DM2ZkPIPnaOSyAs&oq=cigarette+legislation&gs (accessed June 4, 2022).

7   For an interesting revelation of how the advertising world itself is worried about forthcoming taxes on their product, see "What's Ahead?" (1988).

References

Aronowitz, S., & H. A. Giroux (1985). *Education under siege: The conservative, liberal, and radical debate over schooling.* South Hadley, MA: Bergin & Garvey.

Association of National Advertisers (1988). *The role of advertising in America.*

Barthes, R. (1972). *Mythologies.* New York: Hill and Wang.

Baudrillard, J. (1981). *Toward a critique of the political economy of the sign.* St. Louis: Telos Press.

——— (1983a). *Simulations.* New York: Semiotext(e).

——— (1983b). *In the shadow of the silent majorities.* New York: Semiotext(e).

Berger, J. (1973). *Ways of seeing.* New York: Viking Press.

Berman, Marshall (1982). *All that is solid melts into air.* New York: Simon & Schuster.

Best, S., & D. Kellner (1987). (Re)watching television: Notes toward a political criticism. *Diacritics,* Summer, 97–113.

Britton, A. (1988). The myth of postmodernism. *Cineaction* 13/14, 3–17.

Cahoone, L. E. (1988). *The dilemma of modernity.* Albany: State University of New York Press.

Derrida, J. (1976). *Of grammatology.* Baltimore: Johns Hopkins University Press.

Giroux, H. A. (1988). *Schooling and the struggle for public life.* Minneapolis: University of Minnesota Press.

Gitlin, T. (Ed.). (1987). *Watching television.* New York: Pantheon.

Goldman, R. (1992). The mortise and the frame. In *Reading ads socially,* pp. 61–85. London: Routledge.

Habermas, J. (1987). *The philosophical discourse of modernity.* Cambridge: MIT Press.

——— (1989). *On the structural transformation of the public sphere.* Cambridge: MIT Press.

Harms, J., & D. Kellner (1989). Critical reflections on recent literature on advertising and the consumer society. *Borderlines* (Winter 1989), 26–39.

Henry, J. (1963). *Culture against man.* New York: Random House.

Hirsch, E. D. (1987). *Cultural literacy.* Boston: Houghton Mifflin.

Jameson, F. (1983). Postmodernism and the consumer society. In H. Foster (Ed.), *The anti-aesthetic.* Port Townsend, WA: Bay Press.

——— (1984). Postmodernism, or the cultural logic of late capitalism. *New Left Review,* 146, 53–93.

Kellner, D. (1987). Baudrillard, semiurgy and death. *Theory, Culture & Society,* 4(1), 125–146.

——— (1988). Postmodernism as social theory: Some challenges and problems. *Theory, Culture & Society*, 5(2–3), 239–270.

——— (1989a). *Critical theory, Marxism, and modernity*. Cambridge and Baltimore: Polity Press and Johns Hopkins University Press.

——— (1989b). *Jean Baudrillard: From Marxism to postmodernism and beyond*. Cambridge and Palo Alto: Polity Press and Stanford University Press.

Kellner, D. (1984) *Herbert Marcuse and the Crisis of Marxism*. Berkeley and London: University of California Press (USA) and Macmillan Press (England).

Kellner, D., & J. Harms (1991). Critical theory and advertising. *Current Perspectives in Social Theory*, 11, 41–67.

Kroker, A., & D. Cook (1986). *The postmodern scene*. New York: Saint Martin's Press.

McLuhan, M. (1964). *Understanding media*. New York: Signet.

Postman, N. (1985). *Amusing ourselves to death*. New York: Viking.

Ryan, M. (1982). *Marxism and deconstruction*. Baltimore: Johns Hopkins University Press.

Sontag, S. (1969). *Against interpretation*. New York: Dell.

Spivak, G. (1987). *In other worlds*. New York: Methuen.

Ulmer, G. L. (1985). *Applied grammatology*. Baltimore: Johns Hopkins University Press.

Williamson, J. (1978). *Decoding advertisements*. London: Marion Boyers.

CHAPTER SEVEN

New Technologies/New Literacies: Reconstructing Education for Democracy and Social Justice

Throughout this book, I have argued that we need multiple critical media and digital literacies for our multicultural society, that we need to develop new critical literacies to meet the challenge of emergent digital technologies and social justice, and that literacies of diverse sorts—including a more fundamental importance for print literacy—are of crucial importance in restructuring education for a high tech and multicultural society and global culture. It is a burning question what sort of restructuring of education will take place in response to the turbulent technological explosion of our times, in whose interests, and for what ends. Indeed, more than ever we need philosophical reflection on the ends and purposes of education, on what we are doing and trying to achieve in our educational practices and institutions. In this situation, it may be instructive to return to Dewey and Freire and to elaborate the connections between education and democracy, the need for the reconstruction of education and society, and the value of experimental pedagogy to seek solutions to the problems of education in the present day.

Hence, a progressive reconstruction of education will require that it be done in the interests of democratization, ensuring access to emergent digital technologies and social media for all, helping to overcome the so-called digital divide and divisions of the haves and have nots, so that education is placed a la Dewey (1997 [1916]) and Freire (1972, 1998) in the service of democracy and social justice. Yet we should be more aware than Dewey of the obduracy of divisions of class, gender, and race, that we work self-consciously for multicultural democracy and educa-tion, and that we valorize difference and cultural specificity, as well as equality and shared universal Deweyean values such as freedom, equality, individualism, and participation.

Theorizing a democratic and multicultural reconstruction of education thus forces us to confront the digital divide, that there are divisions between infor-mation and technology have and have nots, just as there are class, gender, and race divisions in every sphere of the existing constellations of society and culture. Surveys of the digital divide in the U.S., however, indicate that the key indicators are class and education and not race and gender,[1] although the fact that white men control the digital technology industries, create the coding, AI, languages, and algorithms of computer culture suggest that digital technologies, search engines, and social media reflect the biases of white men and marginalize women and people of color.[2]

Rob Shields has argued that the concept of the "digital divide" serves as a marketing device for the benefit of technology disseminators and that the devel-opment of new technologies helps increase the divide between haves and have nots (2002). While no doubt high-tech corporations and affiliated government institutions have promoted the challenge of a digital divide the concept points to some serious problems and challenges. It is clear by now that providing ac-cess and computers alone without proper training and pedagogy does not advance education or social justice. Thus, more broadly conceived, the notion of a digital divide points to disparities in terms of access, training, skills, and the actual use of technologies to improve education and promote social justice.

With the proper resources, policies, pedagogies, and practices, we can, I be-lieve, work to reduce the (unfortunately growing) gap between haves and have nots, although I want to make clear that I do not believe that technology alone that will reconstruct anything in a positive way. That is, technology itself does not necessarily improve teaching and learning, and will certainly not of itself over-come acute socio-economic divisions. Indeed, without proper resources, pedagogy, and educational practices, technology might be an obstacle or burden to genuine learning and will probably increase rather than overcome existing divisions of power, cultural capital, and wealth.[3]

Studies of the implementation of technology in the schools reveal that without adequate teaching training and technology policy, the results of introducing digital and new technologies into education is highly ambiguous, and there is growing focus on teacher training.[4] During the rest of this chapter, I want to focus on the role of digital and information technology in contemporary education and the need for new pedagogies and an expanded concept of literacy to respond to the importance of digital technologies in every aspect of life. My goal will be to propose some ways that new technologies and new literacies can serve as efficacious learning tools which will contribute to producing a more democratic and egalitarian society and not just providing skills and tools to privileged individuals and groups that will improve their cultural capital and social power at the expense of others.[5]

Technology and the Restructuring of Education

To dramatize the issues at stake, we should reconsider the claim that we are now undergoing one of the most significant technological revolutions for education since the progression from oral to print and book based teaching.[6] Just as the transition to print literacy and book culture involved a dramatic transformation of education, as Marshall McLuhan (1962 and 1964), Walter Ong (1988), and others have argued, so too does the current technological revolution demand a major restructuring of education today with new curricula, pedagogy, literacies, practices, and goals. Furthermore, the technological revolution of the present era makes possible the radical reconstruction and restructuring of education and society argued for in the progressive era by Dewey and in the 1960s and 1970s by Ivan Illich, Paolo Freire, and others who sought radical educational and social reform.

Put in historical perspective, it is now possible to see modern education as preparation for industrial civilization and minimal citizenship in a passive representative democracy. The demands of the new global economy, culture, and polity require a more informed, participatory, and active citizenship, and thus increased roles and challenges for education. Modern education, in short, emphasizes submission to authority, rote memorization and what Freire called the "banking concept" of education in which learned teachers deposit knowledge into passive students, inculcating conformity, subordination, and normalization. These traits are becoming obsolete in a global postindustrial and networked society with its demands for new skills for the workplace, participation in new social and political environs, and interaction within novel forms of culture and everyday life.

In short, the technological revolution renders necessary the sort of thorough restructuring of education that radicals demanded during the last century, indeed back to the Enlightenment if one includes Rousseau (1979) and Wollstonecraft (1988) who saw the enlightened restructuring of education as the key to democracy. Today, however, intense pressures for change now come directly from technology and the economy and not ideology or educational reformist ideas, with a new global economy and new technologies demanding new skills, competencies, literacies, and practices. While this technological revolution has highly ambiguous effects, it provides educational reformers with the challenge of whether education will be restructured to promote democracy and human needs, or whether education will be transformed primarily to serve the needs of business and the global economy.

It is therefore a burning question what sort of restructuring will take place, in whose interests, and for what ends. More than ever, we need philosophical reflection on the ends and purposes of education, on what we are doing and trying to achieve in our educational practices and institutions. In this situation, it may be instructive to return to Dewey and see the connections between education and democracy, the need for the reconstruction of education and society, and the value of experimental pedagogy to seek solutions to the problems of education in the present day. A progressive reconstruction of education will urge that it be done in the interests of democratization and social justice, ensuring access to new technologies for all, helping to overcome the so-called digital divide and divisions of the haves and have nots, so that education is placed a la Dewey (1997 [1916]) and Freire (1972, 1998) in the service of democracy and progressive social change.

Yet we should be more aware than Dewey of the obduracy of divisions of class, gender, and race, and work self-consciously for multicultural democracy and education. This task suggests that we valorize difference and cultural specificity, as well as equality and shared universal Deweyean values such as freedom, equality, individualism, and participation. Further, studies of the implementation of technology in the schools reveal that without adequate teaching training and technology policy, the results of introducing computers and digital technologies into education are highly ambiguous.[7] In this study, I focus on the role of computers and information technology in contemporary education and the need for new pedagogies and an expanded concept of literacy to respond to the importance of new technologies in every aspect of life. I propose some ways that new technologies and new literacies can serve as efficacious learning tools which will contribute to producing a more democratic and egalitarian society, and not just providing skills and tools to privileged individuals and groups that will improve their cultural capital and social power at the expense of others. How, indeed, are we going to restructure education to provide individuals and groups with the tools, the competencies, the literacies to overcome the class, gender, and racial divides that bifurcate our society and at least in terms of economic indicators seem to be growing rather than diminishing?

First, however, I wish to address the technophobic argument against new technologies per se. I have been developing a critical theory of technology that call attention to uses or types of technology as tools of domination, and that rejects the hype and pretensions of new technologies. A critical theory of technology sees the limitations of pedagogy and educational proposals based primarily on technology without adequate emphasis on pedagogy, on teacher and student empowerment. It insists on developing educational reform and restructuring to promote multicultural democracy and calls for appropriate restructuring of technology to democratic education and society. Yet a critical theory also sees how technology can be used, and perhaps redesigned and restructured, for positive purposes such as enhancing education, democracy and overcoming the divide between haves and have nots, while enabling individuals to democratically and creatively participate in a new economy, society, and culture.[8]

A critical theory of technology avoids both technophobia and technophilia. It rejects technological determinism, is critical of the limitations, biases, and downsides of digital technologies and social media, but wants to use and redesign technologies for education for democracy and for social reconstruction in the interests of social justice. It is also, in the Deweyean spirit, pragmatic and experimental, recognizing that there is no agreed upon way to deploy new technologies for enhancing education and democratization. We must be prepared to accept that some of the attempts to use technology for education may well fail, as have no doubt many of our own attempts to use new technologies for education. A critical theory of technology is aware that technologies have unforeseen consequences, and that good intentions and seemingly good projects may have results that were not desired or positive—it is now a time to be daring and innovative and not conservative and stodgy in our rethinking of education and the use of new technologies in educational practices and pedagogies.

We need to overcome the dichotomies of technophilia with its attendant optimism that technological revolution is necessarily producing beneficial results, contrasted to a technophobia that deplores the impact of new technologies on social and individual life. I am occasionally attacked for "optimism" when I make proposals advocating the use of media and information technologies for democratization and social reconstruction. I would argue, however, that we need to go beyond the dichotomies of optimism and pessimism, that a gloomy pessimism gets us nowhere, that while there are plenty of troubling phenomena to criticize, Gramsci's "pessimism of the intellect, optimism of the will" (1971) is the most productive way to engage the problems and dangers of the contemporary era, rather than pessimistic "critique" that is devoid of positive proposals for reconstruction and change. I am aware that there are serious challenges to democracy and causes for grave concern in regard to the development of the global economy and technological revolution, but in these studies, I am concentrating on a positive reconstructive agenda.

Consequently, the question is not whether computers are good or bad in the classroom or more broadly for education. Rather, it is a question of what to do with them: what useful purposes can computers serve, what sort of skills do students and teachers need to effectively deploy computers and digital information technology, what sort of effects might computers and digital technologies have on learning, and what new literacies, views of education and social relations do we need to democratize and improve education today?

Education and Literacy

Both traditionalists and reformists would probably agree that education and literacy are intimately connected. "Literacy" comprises gaining competencies involved in effectively using socially-constructed forms of communication and representation. Learning literacies involves attaining competencies in practices in contexts that are governed by rules and conventions. Literacies are socially constructed in educational and cultural practices involved in various institutional discourses and practices. Literacies evolve and shift in response to social and cultural change and the interests of elites who control hegemonic institutions.

Literary involves gaining the skills and knowledge to read and interpret the text of the world and to successfully navigate and negotiate its challenges, conflicts, and crises. Literacy is thus a necessary condition to equip people to participate in the local, national, and global economy, culture, and polity. As Dewey argued (1997), education is essential to enable people to participate in democracy, for without an educated, informed, and literate citizenry, a robust democracy is impossible. Moreover, there are crucial links between literacy, democracy, empowerment, and participation, and without developing adequate critical literacies, differences between haves and have nots cannot be overcome, and individuals and groups will be left out of the contemporary economy, networked society, and culture.

To reading, writing, and traditional print literacies, one could argue that in an era of technological revolution and evolving digital technologies and social media, we need to develop new forms of critical media literacy, digital literacies, and multimedia literacies that I and others call by the covering concept of "multiliteracies" or "multiple literacies."[9] Emergent technologies and cultural forms demand novel skills and competencies and if education is to be relevant to the problems and challenges of contemporary life it must expand the concept of literacy and develop new curricula and pedagogies.

I would resist, however, extreme claims that the era of the book and print literacy are over. Although there are discontinuities and novelties in the current constellation, there are also important continuities. Indeed, in the new information-communication technology environment, traditional print literacy takes on increasing importance in the computer-mediated cyberworld as people need to critically scrutinize and scroll tremendous amounts of information, putting new emphasis on developing reading and writing abilities. For instance, Internet discussion groups, chat rooms, e-mail, and various forums require writing skills in which a new emphasis on the importance of clarity and precision is emerging as communications proliferate. In this context of information saturation, it becomes an ethical imperative not to contribute to cultural and information overload, and to concisely communicate one's thoughts and feelings.

Critical Media Literacy: An Unfulfilled Challenge

In the new multimedia environment, critical media literacy is arguably more important than ever (Kellner and Share, 2019). Cultural studies and critical pedagogy have been teaching us to recognize the ubiquity of media culture in contemporary society, the growing trends toward multicultural education, and the need for critical media literacy that addresses the issue of multicultural and social difference.[10] There is expanding recognition that media representations help construct our images and understanding of the world and that education must meet the dual challenges of teaching critical media literacy in a multicultural society and sensitizing students and publics to the inequities and injustices of a society based on gender, race, and class inequalities and discrimination. Recent critical studies see the role of mainstream media in exacerbating or diminishing these inequalities and the ways that media education and the production of alternative media can help create a healthy multiculturalism of diversity and more robust democracy. They confront some of the most serious difficulties and problems that currently face us as educators and citizens.

Yet despite the ubiquity of media culture in contemporary society and everyday life, and the recognition that the media themselves are a form of pedagogy, and despite criticisms of the distorted values, ideals, and representations of the world in media culture, media education in K-12 schooling has never really been established and developed. The current technological revolution, however, brings to the fore more than ever the role of media like television, popular music, film, and advertising, as the Internet rapidly absorbs these cultural forms and creates new cyberspaces and forms of culture and pedagogy. It is highly irresponsible in the face of saturation by digital and media culture to ignore these forms of socialization and education; consequently, a critical reconstruction of education should produce pedagogies that provide critical media and digital literacies and that enable students, teachers, and citizens to discern the nature and effects of media and digital culture.

Media culture has long taught proper and improper behavior, gender roles, values, and knowledge of the world (Kellner, 1995 [2020]). Individuals are often not aware that they are being educated and indoctrinated by media culture, as its pedagogy is frequently invisible and subliminal. This situation calls for critical approaches that make us aware of how media construct meanings, influence and educate audiences, and impose their messages and values. A media literate person is skillful in analyzing media codes and conventions, able to criticize stereotypes, values, and ideologies, and competent to interpret the multiple meanings and messages generated by media texts. Media literacy helps people to use media intelligently, to discriminate and evaluate media content, to critically dissect media forms, and to investigate media effects and uses (see Kellner, 1995 [2020]; Kellner and Share, 2019).

Within educational circles, however, a debate persists over what constitutes the field of media pedagogy, with different agendas and programs. A traditionalist "protectionist" approach would attempt to "inoculate" young people against the effects of media addiction and manipulation by cultivating a taste for book literacy, high culture, and the values of truth, beauty, and justice, and by denigrating all forms of media and computer culture. Neil Postman in his books *Amusing Ourselves to Death* (1985) and *Technopolis* (1992) exemplifies this approach. A "media literacy" movement, by contrast, attempts to teach students to read, analyze, and decode media texts, in a fashion parallel to the advancement of print literacy. Media arts education in turn teaches students to appreciate the aesthetic qualities of media and to use various media technologies as instruments of self-expression and creation. Critical media literacy, as conceived by Kellner and Share (2019), builds on these approaches, analyzing media culture as products of social production and struggle, and teaches students to be critical of media representations and discourses, but also stresses the importance of learning to use the media as modes of self-expression and social activism.

Developing critical media literacy and pedagogy also involves perceiving how media like film or video can also be used positively to teach a wide range of topics, like multicultural understanding and education. If, for example, multicultural education is to champion genuine diversity and expand the curriculum, it is important both for groups excluded from mainstream education to learn about their own heritage and for dominant groups to explore the experiences and voices of minority and excluded groups. Media literacy can promote multicultural literacy, conceived as understanding and engaging the heterogeneity of cultures and subcultures that constitute an increasingly global and multicultural world.[11]

Critical media literacy not only teaches students to learn from media, to resist media manipulation, and to use media materials in constructive ways, but is also concerned with developing skills that will help create good citizens and that will make them more motivated and competent participants in social life. Critical media literacy is tied to the project of radical democracy and concerned to develop skills that will enhance democratization and participation. Critical media literacy takes a comprehensive approach that would teach critical skills and how to use media as instruments of social communication and change. The technologies of communication are becoming more and more accessible to young people and ordinary citizens, and can be used to promote education, democratic self-expression, and social progress. Technologies that could help produce the end of participatory democracy, by transforming politics into media spectacles and the battle of images, and by turning spectators into cultural zombies, could also be used to help invigorate democratic debate and participation (Kellner, 1990, 1998, 2000; Kellner-Share, 2019).

Indeed, teaching critical media literacy could be a participatory, collaborative project. Watching television shows or films together could promote productive discussions between teachers and students (or parents and children), with emphasis on eliciting student views, producing a variety of interpretations of media texts and teaching basic principles of hermeneutics and criticism. Students and youth are often more media savvy, knowledgeable, and immersed in media and digital culture than their teachers and can contribute to the educational process through sharing their ideas, perceptions, and insights. On the other hand, critical discussion, debate, and analysis ought to be encouraged with teachers bringing to bear their critical perspectives on student readings of media material. Since media culture is often part and parcel of students' identity and most powerful cultural experience, teachers must be sensitive in criticizing artifacts and perceptions that students hold dear, yet an atmosphere of critical respect for difference *and* inquiry into the nature and effects of media culture should be promoted.

Critical media literacy thus involves developing conceptions of interpretation and criticism. Engaging in assessment and evaluation of media texts is particularly challenging and entails careful discussion of specific moral, pedagogical, political, or aesthetic criteria of critique. That is, one can, a la British cultural studies, engage the politics of representation discussing the specific images of gender, class, race, ethnicity, sexual preference, or other identity categories in media texts (Kellner, 1995 [2020]). Or one could discuss the moral values and behavior represented, what specific messages or representations of social experience are presented, how they are interpreted by audiences, and potential pedagogical effects. One can also attempt to determine criteria for aesthetic evaluation, discussing what constitutes a good or bad media text.

In developing critical media literacies, we need to develop sensitivity to visual imagery, sound, and discourse, as well as narrative structure and textual meaning and effects. Thus, we can draw upon the aesthetics developed in literary, film and video, and art studies, combining such material in addressing the specificities of the text or artifact in question. Media studies is exciting and challenging in that it can embrace artifacts ranging from familiar film and television programs to popular music, to cultural practices and creation.

A major challenge in developing critical media literacies, however, results from the fact that it is not a pedagogy in the traditional sense with firmly-established principles, a canon of texts, and tried-and-true teaching procedures. Critical media pedagogy is in its infancy; it is just beginning to produce results and is more open and experimental than established print-oriented pedagogy. Moreover, the material of media and digital culture is so polymorphous, multivalent, and polysemic, that it necessitates sensitivity to different readings, interpretations, perceptions of the complex images, scenes, narratives, meanings, and messages of media and digital culture which in its own ways is as complex and challenging to critically decipher as book culture.

It is also highly instructive to teach students at all levels to critically explore popular media materials, including the most familiar film, television, music, and other forms of media culture. Here one needs to avoid an uncritical media populism, of the sort that is emerging within certain sectors of British and North American cultural studies. In a review of *Rethinking Media Literacy* (McLaren, Hammer, Sholle, and Reilly, 1995), for instance, Jon Lewis attacked what he saw as the overly critical postures of the contributors to this volume, arguing: "If the point of a critical media literacy is to meet students halfway—to begin to take seriously what *they* take seriously, to read what *they* read, to watch what *they* watch—teachers *must* learn to love pop culture" (1996: 26). Note the authoritarian injunction that "teachers *must* learn to love popular culture" (italics are Lewis'), followed by an attack on more critical approaches to media literacy.

Teaching critical media literacy, however, involves occupation of a site above the dichotomy of fandom and censor. One can teach how media and digital culture provides significant statements or insights about the social world, empowering visions of gender, race, and class, or complex aesthetic structures and practices, thereby putting a positive spin on how it can provide significant contributions to education. Yet we ought to indicate also how media culture can advance sexism, racism, ethnocentrism, homophobia, and other forms of prejudice, as well as misinformation, problematic ideologies, and questionable values, promoting a dialectical approach to the media.

Critical media literacy teaching should engage students' interests and concerns and involve a collaborative approach between teachers and students since students are deeply absorbed in media culture and may know more about some of its artifacts and domains than their teachers. Consequently, students should be encouraged to speak, discuss, and intervene in the teaching/learning process. This is not to say that critical media literacy training should romanticize student views, however, that may be superficial, mistaken, uniformed, and full of various problematical biases. Yet exercises in critical media literacy can often productively involve intense student participation in a mutual learning process where both teachers and students together learn critical media and digital literacy skills and competencies.

It is also probably a mistake to attempt to institute a top-down program of critical media literacy imposed from above on teachers, with fixed texts, curricula, and prescribed materials. Diverse teachers and students will have unique interests and concerns and will naturally emphasize varying subject matter and choose examples relevant to their own and their student interests. Courses in critical media literacy could thus be flexible enough to enable teachers and students to constitute their own curricula to address material and topics of current concern, and to engage their own interests. Crucially, educators should discern that we are in the midst of one of the most intense technological revolutions in history and must learn to adapt emerging digital technologies to education and to develop new critical digital and multimedia literacies.

Critical Digital and Multimedia Literacies

In an earlier era, with the widespread introduction of home computer technology (PCs) in the 1980s, users needed to learn new forms of computer literacy which quickly expanded from using your home computer to produce texts to communicating through email to accessing computer data bases to engaging on the internet and always expanding domains of cyberculture. Soon it was necessary to develop conceptions of computer literacy that went far beyond standard technical notions. Critical computer literacies involved learning how to use computer technologies to do research and gather information, as well as to perceive computer culture as a terrain containing texts, spectacles, games, and interactive multimedia which call for cultivating multiple literacies. Further, computer culture became a discursive and political location in which students, teachers, and citizens could all intervene, engaging in discussion groups and collaborative research

projects, creating web sites, producing innovative multimedia for cultural dissemination, and engaging in novel modes of social interaction and learning. Computer
and multimedia culture enabled individuals to actively participate in the production of culture, ranging from discussion of public issues to creation of their own
cultural forms. However, to take part in this culture required not only accelerated
skills of print literacy, which are often restricted to the growing elite of students
who are privileged to attend adequate and superior public and private schools, but
also demanded new forms of computer and multimedia literacies.

It has been a defining fact of post-1990s and 21st century culture that the
contemporary era is one in which digital technologies and social media have been
proliferating and transforming every dimension of life from work to education.
To respond intelligently to the dramatic technological revolution of our time, it
was necessary to begin teaching computer and digital literacies from an early age.
Computer and digital literacy, however, itself needs to be theorized. Often the
term is synonymous with technical ability to use computers, to become proficient
in the use of existing programs, and maybe undertake some programming. I suggest expanding the conception of digital literacy from using computer programs
and digital devices to a broader concept of information and multimedia literacy.
This necessitates promoting more sophisticated abilities in traditional reading and
writing, as well as the capability to critically dissect cultural forms taught as part of
critical media and digital literacy and multimedia pedagogy, as well as becoming
proficient in information literacy.

Computer and digital literacies thus initially involved learning how to use
computers, access information and educational material, use e-mail and list-serves,
and construct websites. Computer and digital literacy comprised the accessing and
processing of diverse sorts of information proliferating in the so-called "information society" (for critiques of this concept see Webster, 1995). It encompassed
learning to find sources of information ranging from traditional sites like libraries
and print media to Internet websites, data bases, and search engines. Computer-
information literacy involved learning where information is found, how to access
it, and how to organize, interpret, and evaluate the information that one seeks.

One exciting development in the technological revolution of the past decades
is that library materials and information have become accessible from the entire
world. To some extent, the Internet is potentially the all-encompassing library,
imperfectly constructed in Alexander, Egypt, that would contain the great books
of the world. Yet while a mind-boggling amount of the classics are found on the
Internet, we still need the local library to access and engage books, journals, and
print material not found on the Internet, as well as the essential texts of various
disciplines and culture as a whole. Information literacy, however, and the new tasks

for librarians, also involve knowing what one can and cannot find on the Internet and digital sources, how to access it, and where the most reliable and useful information is at hand for specific tasks and projects.

Critical computer and information literacies also involve learning how to read hypertexts, traverse the ever-changing fields of cyberculture, and to participate in a digital and interactive multimedia culture that encompasses work, education, politics, culture, and everyday life. There are two major modes and concepts of hypertext, one that is primarily literary, that involves new avant-garde literary/ writing strategies and practices (see Joyce, 1995), contrasted to one that is more multimedia, multisemiotic, multimodal, and that mushroomed into the World Wide Web. Hypertext was initially seen as an innovative and exciting new mode of writing which increased potentials for writers to explore novel modes of textuality and expression (Joyce; Landow, 1992, 1997). As multimedia hypertext developed on the Internet, it was soon theorized as a multisemiotic and multimodal form of culture. This mode is now increasingly seen as the dominant form of a new hyperlinked, interactive, and multimedia cyberculture (see Burbles and Callister, 1996, 2000; Snyder, 1997).[12]

Genuine critical computer digital literacy, however, involves not just technical knowledge and skills, but refined reading, writing, research, and communicating ability. It involves heightened capacities for critically accessing, analyzing, interpreting, processing, and storing both print-based and multimedia material. In the now dominant information/entertainment society, entertainment and knowledge and information come not merely in the form of print and words, but through images, sounds, and multimedia material as well. Critical computer and multimedia literacies thus involve the ability to discover and access information and intensified abilities to read, to scan texts and computer data bases and websites, and to access information and images in a variety of forms, ranging from graphics to visual images, to audio and video materials, to good old print media. The creation of new multimedia websites, data bases, and texts requires accessing, downloading, and organizing digitized verbal, imagistic, and audio and video material that are the new building blocks of multimedia culture.

Within multimedia digital culture, visual literacy takes on increased importance. Computer screens are more graphic, visual, and interactive than conventional print fields that disconcerted many of us when first confronted with the new environments. Icons, windows, digital devices, and the various clicking, linking, and interaction involved in computer-mediated hypertext dictate new competencies and a dramatic expansion of literacy. Visuality is obviously crucial, compelling users to quickly scan visual fields, perceive and interact with icons and graphics, and use technical devices to access the desired material and field. Yet tactility is also important, as individuals must learn navigational skills of how to proceed from one field and screen to another, how to negotiate hypertexts and links, and how to move from one program to another if one operates, as most now do, in a window-based multi-media digital environment.

In my expanded conception, critical digital and multimedia literacies involve technical abilities concerning developing basic typing skills, mastering digital technology and media programs, accessing information, and using digital and multimedia technologies for a variety of purposes ranging from interpersonal communication to artistic expression to political debate. There are ever more hybrid implosions between media and computer culture as audio and video material became part of the Internet, as CD-ROM and multimedia developed, and as emergent digital and multimedia technologies become part and parcel of the home, school, and workplace. Therefore, the skills of encoding and decoding images, sounds, and spectacle learned in critical media literacy training can also be valuable as part of critical digital literacies, and key skills for living and surviving in a high-tech society.

Multiple Critical Literacies

The emergent digital and multimedia environments thus necessitate a diversity of types of multisemiotic and multimodal interaction, involving interfacing with words and print material and often images, graphics, and audio and video material. As technological convergence develops apace, individuals need to combine the skills of critical media and digital literacy with traditional print literacy and new forms of multiple literacies to access and navigate the new multimedia hypertext environments. Literacy in this conception involves the abilities to engage effectively in socially-constructed forms of communication and representation. Reading and interpreting print was the appropriate mode of literacy for books, while critical media literacy entails reading and interpreting discourse, images, spectacle, narratives, and the forms and genres of media culture. Forms of multimedia communication involve print information, speech, visuality, and audio, in a hybrid field which combines these forms, all of which involve skills of interpreting and critique.

The term "multiple critical literacies" points to the different kinds of literacies needed to access, interpret, criticize, and participate in the emergent new forms of culture and society.[13] The key root here is the multiple, the proliferation of media and forms that demand a multiplicity of competencies and skills and abilities to access, interact, and help construct a new semiotic terrain. Multiple literacies involve reading across varied and hybrid semiotic fields and being able to critically and hermeneutically process print, graphics, moving images and sounds. The term "hybridity" suggests the combination and interaction of diverse media and the need to synthesize the various forms in an active process of the construction of meaning. Reading a music video, for instance, involves processing images, music, spectacle, and sometimes narrative in a multisemiotic activity that simultaneously draws on diverse aesthetic forms. Interacting with a website or CD-ROM often involves scanning text, graphics, moving images, and clicking onto the fields that one seeks to peruse and explore, looking for appropriate material. This might lead individuals to draw upon a multiplicity of materials in emergent and expanding interactive learning or entertainment environments, whereby they must simultaneously read and interpret images, graphics, animation, and text.

While traditional literacies concern practices in contexts that are governed by rules and conventions, conventions and rules of multiliteracies are currently evolving so that their pedagogies comprise a bustling and evolving field. Multimedia sites are not entirely new, however. Multisemiotic textuality was first evident in newspapers (consider the difference between *The New York Times* and *U.S.A. Today* in terms of image, text, color graphics, design, and content). and is now evident in textbooks that are much more visual, graphic, and multimodal than the previously linear and discursive texts of old. Yet it is web sites, digital data bases and archives, and multimedia that are the most distinctively multimodal and multisemiotic forms. Critical educators need to theorize the literacies necessary to interact in these emergent multimedia environments and to gain the skills that will enable individuals to learn, work, and create in emergent cultural spaces and domains.

Cultivating critical media and digital literacies and reconstructing education for democratization will also involve constructing new critical pedagogies and social relations between teachers and student. Digital and multimedia technologies enable group projects for students and more of a problem-solving pedagogy in the spirit of Dewey and Freire than traditional transmission top-down teaching models (1972, 1998).[14] To enable students to access information, engage in cultural communication and production, and to gain the skills necessary to succeed in the evolving digital high-tech economy and culture, students need to acquire enhanced literacies, abilities to work cooperatively with others, and to navigate emergent digital cultural and social terrains. Such group activity may generate more egalitarian relations between teachers and students and more democratic and cooperative social relations. Of course, it also demands reconsideration of grading and testing procedures, rethinking the roles of teacher and student, and constructing projects and pedagogies appropriate to the digital and multimedia cultural and social environments.

Moreover, we are soon going to have to rethink standard achievement tests in relation to the media and digital technologies and multimedia; having the literacy and skills to successfully access, communicate, work, and create within digital and multimedia culture is quite different from reading and writing in the mode of print literacy. While traditional skills of reading and writing continue to be of utmost importance in cyberculture, they are sublated within multiliteracy, so eventually an entirely different sort of test is going to need to be devised to register individuals' multiliteracy competencies and to predict success in a new technological and educational environment. In this new environment, it becomes increasingly irrational to focus education on producing higher test scores on exams that themselves are becoming obsolete and outdated by the changes in the economy, society, and culture.[15]

Critical pedagogies must also confront the problem of on-line education, of how the cultural terrain of cyberspace produces new sites of information, education, and culture, as well as novel on-line forms of interaction between students and teacher. In addition, possibilities of students developing their own spaces, cultural forms, and modes of interaction and communication should be promoted. The challenge will also arise of how to balance classroom instruction with on-line instruction, as well as sorting out the strengths and limitations of print versus on-line multimedia material.[16] Indeed, the digital technologies and cultural spaces require us to rethink education in its entirety, ranging from the role of the teacher, teacher-student relations, classroom instruction, grading and testing, the value and limitations of books, multimedia, and other teaching material, and the goals of education itself.

The COVID-19 pandemic of 2020 and 2021 closed down schools and entire cities for months on end forced education to go on-line with mixed results. While many teachers and students were challenged by on-line education and did not have the pedagogical or digital skills to do crash-course teaching on-line, those with digital technology skills were able to develop engaging courses.

Indeed, the COVID-19 pandemic itself became a teachable moment. In using critical media literacy to teach students about the COVID-19 pandemic, it is important, first, to teach about how the pandemic was originally misrepresented by the state and sectors of the media. As deaths and panic from the virus expanded in the U.S. by March 2020, Trump renamed the COVID-19 virus "the China virus," and used the crisis to deflect blame on China, the World Health Organization, and other global entities, as he tried to deny the intensity of the crisis. Indeed, the virus was global in scope, illustrating the dark side of globalization that could transmit deadly viruses as well as goods, democracy, and interpersonal communication (see Kellner 2021). Scientific experts believed that the COVID-19 virus arose in Wuhan animal markets which trafficked in illegal animals, like bats, which have previously conveyed deadly viruses to humans, as well as exhibiting dangerous interactions between humans and animals in what are called "wet markets."[17] This brought attention to the dangers of production of mass animal harvesting in animal breeding/feeding operations in factory farms in China which contributes to a global environmental crisis, as well as the slaughter of many species of animals and dangers of viruses being transmitted from animals to humans.

The COVID-19 crisis thus illustrates what the Frankfurt School called "the revenge of nature" (Alford, 1985), as the human project of the domination of nature produces destruction of animals, plant life, and the earth itself. Through this project, nature is subjected to exploitation and ravages as human beings colonize animals, plant life, and the earth for human use and profit. Since the mass production of animals takes place throughout the world, it intensifies species extinction, global eco-crisis, and the spread of diseases from one country to anywhere in the world in an era of global commerce, trade, and population movement.

The COVID-19 virus quickly spread through Asia, Europe and the United States. Following the Wuhan, China outbreak in December 2019, The World Health Organization declared the outbreak a Public Health Emergency of International Concern on January 30, 2020 and a pandemic on March 11, as the COVID-19 original virus spread through Italy, Iran, South Korea, Japan, and other countries from Asia to Europe. At the same time, the Secretary General of the United Nations, António Guterres, Tweeted, "Our common enemy is #COVID19, but our enemy is also an 'infodemic' of misinformation" (March 27, 2020). This was followed by an attempt to combat the "disinfodemic" in two policy briefs from UNESCO. They reported that "COVID-19 has led to a parallel pandemic of disinformation that directly impacts lives and livelihoods around the world. Falsehoods and misinformation have proven deadly and sowed confusion about life-saving personal and policy choices" (Posetti and Bontcheva, 2020).

In the face of disinfodemic reports, students should be taught how media can convey false information that concerns life and death issues and how important it is to critically question all media and information. The pandemic also creates opportunities for students to learn about globalization and global pandemics as the example above indicates concerning the WHO analysis of the origins of the pandemic. Students should learn that while all information is biased, there are some sources of information that are more reliable than others and they should develop the skills to investigate, question, and critically assess the messages and the medium.

Another teachable moment in the pandemic concerns vaccinations as an important part of the solution to pandemics. Students should learn the historical context about smallpox, polio, and other deadly diseases that took millions of victims and how they were eradicated or greatly alleviated through mass vaccinations. Critical thinkers can make better informed decisions when they explore multiple sources of information and question the context, the text, and the medium through which the information travels. We see that critical media literacy is an important resource in battling global health pandemics as well as international disinfodemics.

Finally, on-line education and virtual learning also confronts us with novel problems such as copyright and ownership of educational materials; collaborations between computer programmers, artists and designers, and teachers and students in the construction of teaching material and sites; and the respective role of federal and local government, the community, corporations, and private organizations in financing education and providing the skills and tools necessary for a new world economy and global culture. Furthermore, the technological revolution forces a rethinking of philosophical problems of knowledge, truth, identity, and reality in virtual environments. Both philosophy and philosophy of education must be reconstructed to meet the challenges of democracy and a new high-tech economy.

The technological revolution thus forces us to radically rethink and reconstruct education. The terrain and goals of education must be reconsidered along with the conception of literacy expanded. Questions of the digital divide must be confronted and the ways that education can promote democratization and social justice should be discussed and developed. While there are certainly dangers that the technological revolution will increase divisions between haves and have nots, it is possible that old gender, race, and class divisions can be overcome in a society that rewards new critical literacies and provides opportunities for those who have developed competencies in the digital technologies and culture. In this context, it is especially important that appropriate resources, training, and pedagogies be attained to help those groups and communities who were disadvantaged and marginalized during the past epoch of industrialization and modernity.

In addition, individuals should be given the capacities to understand, critique, and transform the social and cultural conditions in which they live, gaining capacities to be creative and transformative subjects and not just objects of domination and manipulation. This necessitates developing abilities for critical thinking, reflection, and the ability to engage in discourse, cultural creation, and political action and movements. Active and engaged subjects are produced in social interaction with others, as well as with tools and techniques, so social skills and individual capacities for communication, creativity, and action must be part of the multiple literacies that a radical reconstruction of education seeks and cultivates.

Crucially, multiliteracies and critical pedagogies must become reflective and self-critical, aware of the educational, social, and political assumptions involved in the restructuring of education and society that we are now undergoing. In response to the excessive hype concerning digital technologies and education, it is necessary to maintain the critical dimension and to reflect upon the nature and effects of digital and multimedia technologies and the pedagogies developed as a response to their challenge. Many advocates of emergent technologies, however, eschew critique for a purely affirmative agenda. For instance, after an excellent discussion of new modes of literacy and the need to rethink education, Gunther Kress argues that we must move from critique to design, beyond a negative deconstruction to more positive construction (1997). Yet rather than following such modern logic of either/or, we need to pursue the logic of both/and, perceiving design and critique, deconstruction, and reconstruction, as complementary and supplementary rather than as antithetical choices. Certainly, we need to design alternative technologies, pedagogies, and curricula for the future, and should attempt to design new social and pedagogical relations as well, but we need to criticize misuse, inappropriate use, overinflated claims, and exclusions and oppressions involved in the introduction of digital technologies and multimedia into education. The critical dimension is needed more than ever as we attempt to develop improved teaching strategies and pedagogy, and design new curricula. In this process, we must be constantly critical, practicing critique and self-criticism, putting in question our assumptions, discourses, and practices, as we experimentally develop novel and alternative literacies and pedagogy.

In all educational and other experiments, critique is indeed of fundamental importance. From the Deweyean perspective, progressive education involves trial and error, design, and criticism. The experimental method itself comprises critique of limitations, failures, and flawed design. In discussing new technologies and multiple literacies, we also need to constantly raise the questions: Whose interests are these new technologies and pedagogies serving? Are they helping all social groups and individuals? Who is being excluded and why? We need to raise the question both of the extent to which new technologies and literacies are preparing students and citizens for the present and future and producing conditions for a more vibrant democratic society, or simply reproducing existing inequalities and inequity.

Further, creating multiple critical literacies must be contextual, engaging the lifeworld of the students and teachers participating in the new adventures of education. Learning involves developing abilities to interact intelligently with the environment and other people and calls for vibrant social and conversational environments. Education requires doing and can be gained from practice and social interaction. One can obviously spend too much time with technologies and fail to develop basic social skills and competencies. As Rousseau, Wollstonecraft, and Dewey argued, education involves developing proficiencies that enable individuals to successfully develop within their concrete environments, to learn from practice, and to be able to interact, work, and create in their own societies and cultures. In the dynamically evolving and turbulent global culture, multiple literacies necessitate multicultural literacies, being able to understand and work with a heterogeneity of cultural groups and forms, acquiring literacies in a multiplicity of media, and gaining the competencies to participate in a democratic culture and society (see Courts, 1998; Weil, 1998).

Moreover, as Freire reminds us (1972, 1998), critical pedagogy comprises the skills of both reading the word and reading the world. Hence, multiple critical literacies include not only multimedia and digital literacies, but a diverse range of social and cultural literacies, ranging from ecoliteracy (e.g., understanding the body and environment), to economic and financial literacy to a variety of other competencies that enable us to live well in our social worlds. Education, at its best, provides the symbolic and cultural capital that empowers people to survive and prosper in an increasingly complex and changing world and the resources to produce a more cooperative, democratic, egalitarian, and just society. Thus, with Plato, Rousseau, Wollstonecraft, Dewey, Freire, and others I see philosophy of education as reflecting on the good life and the good society and the ways that education can contribute to creating a better world. But as the world changes, so too must education that will be part of the problem or part of the solution as we enter a new millennium.

The project of transforming education will take different forms in different contexts. In the overdeveloped countries, individuals must be empowered to work and act in a high-tech information economy and must learn skills of media and computer literacy to survive in the new social environment. Traditional skills of knowledge and critique must also be enhanced, so that individuals can name the system, describe, and grasp the changes occurring and the defining features of the new global order, and can learn to engage in critical and oppositional practice in the interests of democratization and progressive transformation. This process challenges us to gain vision of how life can be, of alternatives to the present order, and of the necessity of struggle and organization to realize progressive goals. Languages of knowledge and critique must be supplemented by the discourse of hope and praxis.

The global struggle for daily existence is paramount and meeting unmet human and social needs is a high priority. Yet everywhere education can provide the competencies and skills to improve one's life, to create a better society, and a more civilized and developed world. Moreover, as the entire world becomes part of a global and networked society, gaining the multiple critical literacies discussed in this chapter becomes important everywhere as media and cyberculture become more ubiquitous and the world economy demands ever more sophisticated technical skills.

This is a time of challenge and a time for experiment. It is time to put existing pedagogies, practices, and educational philosophies in question and to construct new ones. It is a time for new pedagogical experiments to see what works and what doesn't work. It is a time to reflect on our goals and to discern what we want to achieve with education and how we can achieve it. Ironically, it is a time to return to classical philosophy of education which situates reflections on education in reflections on the good life and society at the same time that we reflect on how we can transform education to become relevant to a high-tech society. It is time to return to John Dewey to rethink that intimate connection between education and democracy at the same time we address the multicultural challenges that Dewey (in the midst of a still vital melting pot ideology and liberal progressivist optimism) did not address.

Most saliently, it is time to take up the Deweyean attitude of pragmatic experimentation to see what it is that the emergent digital technologies and social media can and cannot do, in order to see how they can enhance education. Yet we should also resist the hype, maintain a critical attitude and pedagogy, and continue to combine print literacy and progressive classroom pedagogies with emergent digital literacies, data bases, and always-expanding digital materials. It is a mistake to advance an either/or logic of print literacy versus computer literacy, or to privilege books over digital technologies, for both can enhance education and life and require different literacies. In the current turbulent situation of the global restructuring of capitalism and worldwide struggles for democratization, I believe that we have for the first time in decades a chance to reconstruct education and society. In this conjuncture, technology is a revolutionizing force, whereby all political parties and candidates pay lip-service to education, to overcoming the digital divide, and to expanding literacy. Hence, the time is ripe to take up the challenge and to move to reconstruct education and society so that groups and individuals excluded from the benefits of the economy, culture, and society may more fully participate and receive opportunities not possible in earlier social constellations.

In the concluding chapter, co-authored with Steve Gennaro, we shall engage "Digital Culture, Media, and the Challenges of Contemporary Cyborg Youth." We discuss the implosion of youth with their digital technologies and the multiple uses that youth and teachers are making of digital technologies and social media to reconstruct education and society. Youth and people of all generations today are challenged to use their technologies to create desired identities and lives and to resist identities that they find oppressive and constricting. Of course, gender, race, class, and sexuality remain highly contested fields of identity, exclusion, and oppression, and today's cyborg youth face the challenges of using their technologies and creating lives and identities opposed to sexism, racism, classism, homophobia, and the biases of the past. While we fully recognize the dangers of immersion in cyberspace and the new to engage in one's social environment and socio-political world, we applaud "fighting cyborg youth" who are using their digital technologies and social media to mobilize and struggle for a better and freer world with oppressions and alienations of the past seen as social conditions and problems to be overcome in a non-racist, non-sexist and homophobic, non-classist, society, aiming at a freer, happier and more egalitarian future. We find evidence of fighting cyborg youth in the Occupy Movement, Black Lives Matter, Dreamers, #MeToo, Bernie Youth, and gay and lesbian movements, as well as environmental and peace movements, and the other efforts to create a freer and happy world, with liberty, education, and justice for all in a future full of hope and challenges.

Notes

1   The "digital divide" emerged as the buzzword for perceived divisions between information technology have and have nots in the current economy and society. A U.S. Department of Commerce report released in July 1999 claimed that digital divide in relation to race is dramatically escalating and the Clinton administration and media picked up on this theme (See the report "Americans in the Information Age: Falling Through the Net" at http://www.ntia.doc.gov/ntiahome/digitaldivide/). A critique of the data involved in the report emerged, claiming that it was outdated; more recent studies by Stanford University, Cheskin Research, ACNielson, and the Forester Institute claim that education and class are more significant factors than race in constructing the divide (see http:cyberatlas.internet.com/big-picture/demographics for a collection of reports and statistics on the divide).

In any case, it is clear that there is a gaping division between information technology haves and have nots, that this is a major challenge to developing an egalitarian and democratic society, and that something needs to be done about the problem. See the section on the digital divide during the 2020 pandemic in the PEW Research site at https://www.pewresearch.org/topics/digital-divide/ (accessed March 24, 2021). The site includes an article by Emily A. Vogels, "59 % of U.S. parents with lower incomes say their child may face digital obstacles in schoolwork." September 10, 2020 at https://www.pewresearch.org/fact-tank/2020/09/10/59-of-u-s-parents-with-lower-incomes-say-their-child-may-face-digital-obstacles-in-schoolwork/ (accessed March 24, 2021). My contribution involves the argument that empowering the have nots requires the providing of digital devices and dissemination of critical media and digital literacies to empower groups and individuals previously excluded from economic opportunities and socio-political participation.

2 Stephen Cave and Kanta Dihal, "The Whiteness of AI," *Philosophy & Technology*, Volume 33, August 6, 2020, pp. 685–703 at https://link.springer.com/article/10.1007/s13347-020-00415-6 (accessed April 15, 2021. See also Shields, 2002 Noble, 2018 and Burbules and Thomas Callister 2000.

3 In the first decade of the Internet, it was perceived that although an increasing amount of money was being spent by schools, not enough was spent on teaching training. See Bernard Warner, "Digitals for Youth: Spreading the Net," *The Standard*, March 27, 2000 which reports: "A study conducted recently by Denver-based Quality Education Data showed school districts across the country spent $6.7 billion on technology in the 1998–1999 school year, up almost 25 percent from the previous year. But the same study revealed that an equally crucial funding component—digital training for teachers—was startlingly low, rising just 5.2 percent over the same period." In June 2000, however, President Bill Clinton argued for increased funding for teaching training to use new technologies so it appears that there was growing recognition of the problem. Indeed, there is now a U.S. Government Department for "Funding Digital Learning" including remote learning, connectivity, providing technology resources and teacher training; see "Office for Educational Technology" at https://tech.ed.gov/funding/ (accessed April 5, 2021).

4 See "Digital technologies, teacher training and teaching practices" at https://www.scielo.br/scielo.php?pid=S1517-97022019000100515&script=sci_arttext&tlng=en (accessed April 5, 2021). See also the discussion of these issues in the Ph.D. dissertations by two of my UCLA students, Jennifer Janofsky Rawls, *The Role of Micropolitics in School-Site Technology Efforts: A Case Study of the Relationship Between Teachers and the Technology Movement at their School*. Ph. Dissertation, UCLA, 2000; and Roy Zimmermann, *The Intersection of Technology and Teachers: Challenges and Problems*. Ph. Dissertation, UCLA, 2000.

5 See Kellner and Share 2019.

6 There are by now a tremendous amount of books and articles on the new digital economy, technological revolution, new cultural spaces, and the implications for every aspect of life from education to war. See, for example, the monumental studies by Castells (1996, 1997, 1998) and the analyses of the restructuring of capital, technological revolution, and the postmodern turn in Best and Kellner (1997 and 2001) and the more recent critiques by Gleick (2011).

7 See also Bernard Warner, "Computers for Youth: Spreading the Net," *The Standard*, March 27, 2000 which reports: "A study conducted recently by Denver-based Quality Education Data showed school districts across the country spent $6.7 billion on technology in the 1998–1999 school year, up almost 25 percent from the previous year. Yet the same study revealed that an equally crucial funding component—computer training for teachers—was startlingly low, rising just 5.2 percent over the same period." In June 2000, however, President Bill Clinton argued for increased funding for teaching training to use new technologies so it appears that there is growing recognition of the problem. For the level of computer funding for teachers and the classroom in the 2020s, see the site of the Office of Educational Technology at https://tech.ed.gov/funding/ (accessed March 24, 2021).

8 For arguments on the need to reconstruct technology to meet the needs of democratization, see Feenberg (1991, 1995, 1999).

9 The New London Group has produced the concept of "multiliteracy" to describe the types of literacy required to engage new multimedia technology, while Semali and Watts Pailliotet and their collaborators (1999) propose the concept "Intermediality" to call attention to the need to generate literacies that allow interaction between various media and new multimedia, and that promote interdisciplinary and interactive education in an attempt to create education that

facilitates democratic social change. I develop a concept of multiple critical literacies in the pages that follow.

10   For an earlier and expanded discussion of media literacy, see Kellner (1998). Carson and Friedman (1995) contain earlier studies dealing with the use of media to deal with multicultural education. Examples of teaching media literacy which I draw on include Masterman (1985), Kellner and Ryan (1988), Schwoch, White and Reilly (1992), Fleming (1993), Giroux (1992, 1993, 1994, 1996), Giroux and McLaren (1994), Sholle and Densky (1994), McLaren, Hammer, Sholle, and Reilly (1995), Kellner (1995a, 1995b), Luke (1996, 1997a, 1997b), Giroux and Shannon (1997), and Semali and Watts Pailliotet (1999). This work was drawn on and updated in Kellner and Share (2019) who introduce the notion of "critical media literacy" (CML) that I use in this chapter. It is a scandal that there are not more efforts to promote critical media literacy throughout the school system from K-12 and into the University. Perhaps the always-expanding ubiquity of digital and multimedia culture will finally awaken educators and citizens to the importance of developing critical media literacies to create individuals empowered to intelligently access, read, interpret, and criticize contemporary media and cyberculture.

11   On multicultural literacy, see Courts (1997) and Weil (1998).

12   Yet some early advocates of hypertext attacked the emergence of the World Wide Web as a de-based medium which brought back into play the field of earlier media, like television, forcing the word to renegotiate its power against the image and spectacles of sight and sound, once again decentering the written word (see, for instance, Joyce, 1997 and the discussion in Landow, 1992, 1997). As the Internet evolved into a multimedia hypertext, however, it is clear that contemporary education must teach reading and engaging multimodal hypertexts as a basic skill and mode of literacy.

13   For other conceptions of multimedia literacy that I draw upon here, see the discussions of literacies needed for reading hypertext in Burbules and Callister (1996, 2000); the concept of multiliteracy in the New London Group (1996) and Luke (1997); and the papers in Snyder (1997), Semali and Watts Pailliotet (1999), and Semali (2017).

14   Since some people associated with critical pedagogy are technophobes, it is interesting that Freire was positive toward media and new technologies, seeing technologies as potential tools for empowering citizens, as well as instruments of domination in the hands of ruling elites. Freire wrote that: "Technical and scientific training need not be inimical to humanistic education as long as science and technology in the revolutionary society are at the service of permanent liberation, of humanization" (1972: 157). Freire also stated that: "It is not the media themselves which I criticize, but the way they are used" (1972: 136). Moreover, he argued for the importance of teaching media literacy to empower individuals against manipulation and oppression, and using the most appropriate media to help teach the subject matter in question (114–116).

15   On the centrality of preparation for exams in contemporary education and the role of standardized tests in the U.S. educational and social system, see Lemann 1999. Most critiques of SAT tests and their biases focus on how they are skewed against poorer schools in working class and communities of color, yet I would also highlight the obsolescence of many standardized tests in the emergent digital technology and social media environment, and the need to come up with new testing procedures based on the new cultural and social fields that we are increasingly immersed in. I would predict that proposals for devising such tests will emerge and that this issue will be hotly debated and contested in the future. It is significant to note that during the 2020–22 COVID-19 pandemic the University of California system suspended SAT tests until Fall 2024, and that the COVID-19 pandemic required new modes of teaching and learning for

which the standardized SAT tests were inappropriate and becoming obsolete. See Sarah Moon, "University of California will suspend SAT and ACT testing admission requirement until 2024" *CNN News*, May 22, 2020 at https://www.cnn.com/2020/05/22/us/uc-suspends-sat-act-for-admissions-until-2024/index.html (accessed January 23, 2021).

16 For sensible critiques on on-line education see Feenberg (1999).

17 "Wildlife Markets and COVID-19," Humane Society International, April 19, 2020 at https://www.hsi.org/wp-content/uploads/2020/04/Wildlife-Markets-and-COVID-19-White-Paper.pdf (accessed on August 11, 2020). For background on pandemics, viruses and human animal markets, see Quammen (2013). Multiple theories continue to spread about the origin of the COVID-19 virus highlighting the need for critical and digital literacies to appraise information sources.

References

Best, Steven, and Douglas Kellner (1991) *Postmodern Theory: Critical Interrogations*. London and New York: Macmillan and Guilford Press.

Burbules, Nicholas C. and Thomas Callister (1996) "Knowledge at the Crossroads: Some Alternative Futures of Hypertext Learning Environments," *Educational Theory* 46(1) (Winter): 23–50.

———— (2000) *Watch IT. The Risks and Promises of Information Technology*. Boulder, CO: Westview Press.

Castells, Manuel (1996) *The Information Age: Economy, Society and Culture*. Volume I: *The Rise of the Network Society*. Cambridge, MA: Blackwell Publishers.

———— (1997) *The Power of Identity*. Oxford: Blackwell.

———— (1998) *End of Millennium*. Oxford: Blackwell.

Courts, Patrick L. (1998) *Multicultural Literacies: Dialect, Discourses, and Diversity*. New York: Peter Lang.

Dewey, John (1997 [1916]) *Democracy and Education*. New York: Free Press.

Feenberg, Andrew (1991) *Critical Theory of Technology*. New York: Oxford University Press.

———— (1995) *Alternative Modernity*. Berkeley: University of California Press.

———— (1999) *Questioning Technology*. New York and London, Routledge.

Fleming, Dan (1993) *Media Teaching*. Oxford: Basil Blackwell.

Freire, Paulo (1972) *Pedagogy of the Oppressed*. New York: Herder and Herder.

———— (1998) *A Paulo Freire Reader*. New York: Herder and Herder.

Giroux, Henry (1992) *Border Crossing*. New York: Routledge.

———— (1993) *Living Dangerously. Multiculturalism and the Politics of Difference*. New York: Peter Lang.

———— (1994) *Disturbing Pleasures*. New York: Routledge.

Giroux, Henry and Peter McLaren (editors) (1994) *Between Borders. Pedagogy and the Politics of Cultural Studies*. New York: Routledge.

Gleick, James (2011) *The Information: A History, a Theory, a Flood*. New York: Pantheon.

Gramsci, Antonio (1971) *Prison Notebooks*. New York: International Publishers.

Joyce, Michael (1995) *Of Two Minds: Hypertext Pedagogy and Politics*. Ann Arbor: University of Michigan Press.

Kellner, Douglas (1995a and 2020) *Media Culture*. London and New York: Routledge.

—— (1998) "Multiple Literacies and Critical Pedagogy in a Multicultural Society," *Educational Theory*, 48(1): 103–122.

—— (1998 "Multiple Literacies and Critical Pedagogy in a Multicultural Society," in *The Promise of Multiculturalism*, edited by George Katsiaficas and Teodros Kiros (pp. 211–236). New York and London: Routledge.

—— (in press) "Trump, Authoritarian Populism, Covid-19, and Technopolitics," in *The Trump Presidency, Journalism, and Democracy*, edited by Ted Gutsche. New York and London: Routledge.

Kellner, Douglas and Jeff Share (2019) *The Critical Media Literacy Guide: Engaging Media and Transforming Education*. Rotterdam, The Netherlands: Brill-Sense Publishers.

Landow, George (1992) *Hypertext. The Convergence of Contemporary Critical Theory and Technology*. Baltimore and London: Johns Hopkins University Press; second edition, *Hypertext 2.0* (1997).

Luke, Carmen (1996) "Reading Gender and Culture in Media Discourses and Texts," in *The Literacy Lexicon*, edited by G. Bull and M. Anstey. New York and Sydney: Prentice-Hall.

Masterman, Len (1985) *Teaching the Media*. London and New York: Routledge.

McLaren, Peter, Rhonda Hammer, David Sholle and Susan Reilly (1995) *Rethinking Media Literacy. A Critical Pedagogy of Representation*. New York: Peter Lang.

McLuhan, Marshall (1962) *The Gutenberg Galaxy*. New York: Signet Books.

—— (1964) *Understanding Media: The Extensions of Man*. New York: Signet Books.

New London Book Group (1996) "A Pedagogy of Multiliteracies: Designing Social Futures," *Harvard Educational Review*, 66: 60–92.

Ong, Walter (1988) *Orality and Literacy: The Technologizing of the Word*. London and New York: Routledge.

Quammen, David (2013) *Spillover: Animal Infections and the Next Human Pandemic*. New York: W.W. Norton & Company, Inc.

Semali, Ladislau and Ann Watts Pailliotet (1999) *Intermediality*. Boulder: Westview.

Shields, Rob (2002) *The Virtual*. London and New York: Routledge.

Webster, Frank (1995) *Theories of the Information Society*. London and New York: Routledge.

Weil, Danny K. (1998) *Toward a Critical Multicultural Literacy*. New York: Peter Lang.

Wollstonecraft, Mary (1988) *A Vindication of the Rights of Woman*. New York: Norton.

CHAPTER EIGHT

Digital Culture, Media, and the Challenges of Contemporary Cyborg Youth

Steve Gennaro and Doug Kellner

We revisit the philosophical concept of the cyborg developed by Donna Haraway and the ways that youth and others are shaped today by technology and digital cultures. As a description of the relationship between contemporary youth and their technologies, the project requires a particular focus on the role that technological forms play in understanding media and the lives of cyborg youth. For Haraway 'the cyborg is a matter of fiction and lived experience that changes what counts as women's experience in the late 20th century', and this is precisely what we are seeking to understand for contemporary youth, giving further credence to Haraway's claims of cyborg as a 'hybrid of machine and organism, a creature of social reality as well as a creature of fiction' (1985/2006: 117).

We argue that primary differences between the current transformations in media and their interactions with human beings and earlier historical media technologies include the *primacy*, *intimacy*, and *expediency* of the mediums themselves in today's high-tech worlds across which the media travels. Unlike earlier advancements in technology, in the current digital media environment, the actual mediums themselves, which transport media content, are no longer merely an extension of the individual, but also involve an entangled embodiment of technologies, capitalism and selves. This matrix constitutes a hybrid of *poiesis* and *technē*, and is deployed by a centaur of human and machine, which Haraway describes as a "cyborg." And while a political economy of technology of media would suggest an exploration of the objects, apparatuses, and physical spaces that translate and transpose their images, messages, and ideologies, the necessity to emphasize and expose the uses and power relations of the objects and hardware themselves is central to the current moment because of the primacy, intimacy, and expediency of the technology apparatuses, encompassing an ever-expanding range of media.

Haraway and Cyborgs: An Introduction

Donna Haraway's 1985 essay 'A Cyborg Manifesto' evokes the spirit of Marx and Engels and their 'Communist Manifesto' (1848/1976) to envision the metaphor of a cyborg as a path to engage politics of identity concerned with intersectional feminism. The manifesto is part ironic, part prophetic, part a call to arms and part revolutionary theoretical action. As Haraway notes, it is important to recognize technologies as 'crucial tools recrafting our bodies', and how the tools not only recraft human bodies, but social relations too, marking them 'as frozen moments of the fluid social interactions constituting them, [and therefore] they should also be viewed as instruments for enforcing meaning' (Haraway, 1985/2006: 130).

The *informatics of domination* are contentious and oppressive, but they are not fixed or static, since Haraway reminds us that the boundary between tool and myth is permeable, and that all moments of oppression, power, and marginalization, can also be seen as a locus for hope and change. If technology as oppressor exists, then its binary opposite, technology as liberator must also exist too![1]

What then, do we make of today's teenagers, who conduct themselves live like cyborgs, whose connection to their tools has become so profound and so seamless that it's difficult to tell where the tool ends, and their bodies begin? And what, then, does this mean for the informatics of domination in the lives of young people, whose identities are heavily mediated by the technology of social media platforms? Do they live separate mediated identities in digital spaces—different from their physical existence—or are they instead cyborgs in both the physical and the digital realm, occupying neither fully?[2] And how do they construct and live features of their identities such as gender, race, class, and sexuality in their virtual digital lives?

In our media-saturated environment, the content of the media—be it friends' lists, tweets, snapchats, TikTok, likes, or wall posts—all require critical media and digital literacies for decoding and understanding emergent digital media and cyborg youth. However, the same could be said about earlier advancements in communications technology from print to radio, or radio to TV.[3] Primary differences between the current transformations in media and their interactions with human beings and earlier historical media technologies include the *primacy*, *intimacy*, and *expediency* of the mediums themselves in today's high-tech worlds across which the media travels. Unlike earlier advancements in technology, in the current digital media environment, the actual mediums themselves, which transport media content, are no longer merely an extension of the individual, but also involve an entangled embodiment of technologies, capitalism and selves. This matrix constitutes a hybrid of *poiesis* and *technē*, and is deployed by a centaur of human and machine.[4] And while a political economy of technology of media would suggest an exploration of the objects, apparatuses, and physical spaces that translate and transpose their images, messages, and ideologies, the necessity to emphasize and expose the uses and power relations of the objects and hardware themselves is central to the current moment because of the primacy, intimacy, and expediency of the technology apparatuses, encompassing an ever-expanding range of media.

While many of our recent works (see Kellner and Share, 2019; Kellner, 2020; Gennaro and Miller, 2021) examined the content of media and its importance to understanding changing social landscapes and the critical importance of critical media literacy (CML) involving the politics of representation and its significant dimensions of gender, race, and class, our project in this study revisits the philosophical concept of the cyborg and the ways that youth and others are shaped by technology and digital cultures. As a description of the relationship between contemporary youth and their technologies, the project requires a particular focus on the role that technological forms play in understanding media and the lives of cyborg youth. For Haraway 'the cyborg is a matter of fiction and lived experience that changes what counts as women's experience in the late 20th century', and this is precisely what we are seeking to understand for contemporary youth, giving further credence to Haraway's claims of cyborg as a 'hybrid of machine and organism, a creature of social reality as well as a creature of fiction' (1985/2006: 117).

Engaging and Theorizing Cyborgs and Cyberspace

IF contemporary youth are cyborgs, THEN it is their physical selves that are now the containers for their digital identities. More on this unpacking of objectivity and subjectivity of digital selves will follow later. Let us first examine the containers or mediums that house specific media. If new media require new literacies, it is not only the ability to decode the letters and symbols, but the ability to decode the forms or containers, that acts as conduits of media messages (and ideologies inherent in all media content) that is essential to developing new critical media and digital literacies for cyborg youth. This process will help to gain an understanding of what is at stake politically if the container moves from outside the individual into the individual themselves.

One of the real challenges facing the ongoing analysis of literacies in the digital environment is the focus on the Internet as an object for study and exploring transformations and permutations of Internet culture in the lives of cyborg youth. Questions abound in ethnographic research and quantitative data analysis surrounding how the Internet has created a digital landscape that has transformed the social relations and lives of individuals. In line with this type of analysis is the discussion of the potential and pitfalls of the Internet as a space for activism, for political participation, and the dynamics of subversion or marginalization (Kellner, 2021). However, the 'Internet', as it has been theorized for the last two decades, does not exist, primarily because the Internet itself, is in fact not an object open for analysis, that we can remove from social context, or the intricacies of its coding, for exploration. The Internet is neither hardware or software, form or filler, content, or container. The Internet is not only a space we can visit, activate, engage with, or take part in, but an environment in which we live on-line identities.

Certainly, at one point, early in the development of online technologies, going 'online' meant using the world wide web via the Internet. However, these terms (online, World Wide Web, and Internet) are not interchangeable. For example, most businesses who use online spaces for the transportation of email or other encrypted data do NOT house their email servers or business databases on the World Wide Web. This is true for the Universities where both Kellner and Gennaro teach. York University, where Gennaro teaches, housed its student, staff, and faculty email prior to 2020 on a private server where students, faculty, and staff accessed their email by typing https://mymail.yorku.ca/ into the address tool bar of their web browser. What was absent from this web address was the "www" because the server was not on the World Wide Web. In fact, if one were to type https://www.mymail.yorku.ca into the tool bar it would not more to the personal email since a webpage by that name did not exist. The same experience is true for private messaging, which happens between two handheld devices using BBMs, WhatsApp, or a private messaging function of a social media platform. The majority of digital interpersonal (person to person) communication in digital spaces in the 2020s does not exist on the internet or the world wide web. Instead, it exists through social media channels, via mobile phone to mobile phone text messaging, or through products such as Apple's Facetime or Facebook's WhatsApp or Facebook Messenger; none of which require the opening of a web browser, the use of the World Wide Web, or even access to the Internet. Think about it, when you sign up for a mobile plan with an access provider you pay not for Internet access, but for a data plan!

The Internet as a concept is now an outdated model for exploring and under-standing social relations in digital environments. After all, the Internet is not just a home for information, an entrepot for business, or a den of thieves and demons, but is many other things as well. The 'Internet' is an empty word we have assigned as a cover-all that is supposed to encase all intersecting players in digital environ-ment, such as media outlets, service providers, hardware and software builders, advertisers, game players, emailers, bloggers, social media influencers, and other online participants.

Indeed, how can one word possibly describe with any accuracy or speak for the many interesting players and activities online? The answer: that it can't! And when we try to create digital theories built around exploring the Internet, what gets overlooked or left out is the fact that in the digital world there are many active participants who are part of an ongoing process in the creation of meaning simul-taneously, instantaneously, and continuously in many domains. Using a phrase as simple as 'the Internet' to explain a series of processes as complex as those found in digital environments, not only hides the power relations and inequality of re-sources (and inequality in access to those resources), but it also simplifies the processes of being online to the lowest common denominator to suggest that it is only an exploration of content and content provider that is required to be digitally literate—and this is simply false!

Instead of viewing the Internet as a space for unpacking digital landscapes, a more concrete focus is required on the mediums themselves that allow for on-line access. Certainly, there is a benefit to exploring the media outlets, service providers, and content generators online, but of equal importance is a discussion of the mediums that access the endless streams of digital content. In addressing cyborg youth in the following analyses, we carry out an exploration of the mobili-zation of the technologies through which individuals access media. In this space, media and medium take on separate roles. In basic grammar, medium is the plural of media, but for a more in-depth analysis, the two terms need to be separated so that medium provides for a description of the container that houses the content and media takes on the definition of the content itself. In separating media and medium into two distinct terms we see a new and vital reconceptualization of Marshall McLuhan's (1964) argument that the medium in is the message. It is about form as much as function. It is about container as much as content. Nowhere is this media/medium entanglement more obvious and at the same time in greater need of decoding then when discussing the notion of cyborg youth whom them-selves occupy both sides of this coin.

Since the handheld smartphone or tablet is often the first point of media contact for many individuals in today's high-tech world in the overdeveloped countries, in that the news or information to be accessed is first received by the user via their handheld devices, understanding the *primacy* of the medium is a key requirement for critical media and digital literacies. Furthermore, an apparatus like a smartphone or tablet are both handheld and mobile, and are generally kept close to one's personal body.[5] In addition to their close physical proximity to users, the type of applications downloaded to the device and used multiple times daily by users such as email, Facebook updates, tweets, and calendar, news updates, and weather information, all allow the apparatus to perform many of the social roles previously occupied by friends, partners, assistants, and so on, and highlights the importance of understanding how the *intimacy* of the medium requires a further unpacking and explication for critical media and digital literacies.

Lastly, media messages are sent and received instantaneously and often without censor by the sender and without sorting by the receiver and without an active participation from the individual to access diverse opinions and to take part in active discourse. As has become apparent over the last two U.S. Presidential Elections (2016, 2020), exploring the dissemination of news via social networking sites like Twitter, the *expediency* of travel of information becomes a core arena for further research for critical media and digital literacies.

Information functioning in politics is often described by particular biases, and bias can best be defined as a lack of diversity in representation. This lack of diversity refers to all three prongs of Douglas Kellner's (1995/2020) three-pronged approach to critical media and cultural studies: political economy, textual analysis, and audience reception. On this model, one analyzes the production of broadcasting news and entertainment, or on-line communication; textual analysis of the ideology and messages; and audience reception study of how different audiences receive media messages (Kellner, 1995/2020, 2009). For instance, one could analyze how different U.S. cable news network analyze a particular political event in the Trump or Biden era as presented by the major U.S. cable networks like CNN which generally has a centrist optic, contrasted to Fox which has a conservative/ pro-Republican/pro-Trump bias, while MSNBC has a liberal and pro-Democratic Party bias (see Kellner, 2010). Or one could analyze the on-line campaign in the 2016 U.S. presidential election in which the Russians used Facebook and other social media to spread, often by bots, pro-Trump messages and anti-Clinton disinformation (Jamieson, 2018).

For Michael Bugeja in *Living Ethics: Across Media Platforms* (2007: 215), an irony exists in our technological age: while the world is getting more global, the world view of news professionals is not necessarily doing the same, and 24/7 globalization allows audiences to feel they are exposed to a 'sense of diversity' without ever actually experiencing it. This lack of lived diversity refers to not only the news we see on the television or read in daily newspapers, but also to the education of journalists, the hiring process of the media companies, how the stories are told to the public and then how those stories are then lived out by the public themselves. And this is what makes representation such an important issue, because how a society talks about its citizens can tell us a lot about that society's values, culture, priorities, and inherent power structure. Think simply about who gets represented and who is left voiceless. Media discourse in spaces such as news or search engine results are important spaces for analysis and critical media and digital literacy, because discourses are symbols, which reflect both the desires and the fears of a particular society, often through the misrepresentation and essentializing that represents one as many and cultural myth as reality.

When news is sent to our phones directly, the personification of that news immediately suggest to us that its content is real, legitimate, trustworthy, unbiased and that it fully represents the world locally and globally it purports to cover. However, in news media, too often bias appears as stereotypes, racial inappropriateness, and cultural exclusion. Further, this bias appears through symbols, which get encoded by news agencies, but require a more active decoding from viewers. When the news arrives in one-lined tweets, if the reader does not click to read the entire story or spend some time unpacking who the source is and what the context of the story is, then the news itself gets swallowed and digested without being chewed and transmitted without consciousness of its message and potential effects. The expediency of media and the sensationalized one-liner headline that was written to lure the reader to the news corporations home site, instead becomes naturalized as the news itself and then takes on the perception of truth—even when the perception is an empty and hallow symbol, or an outright lie.

For Bugeja, there is a gap between the representation (how the media portrays people) and reality (who those people really are). The expediency of digital media extends this issue on the professional practice of media professionals in that 'technology promised a global village and delivered an indoor simulated one instead' (Bugeja, 2007: 215). Yet what becomes of the relationship between the subject and object when the object no longer exists as an extension of the self, but can be argued to replace the self entirely? The *primacy*, *intimacy*, and *expediency* of the technology apparatus (aka the mediums) now pose greater ontological questions which we take up in the following section.

The Objectivity and Subjectivity of Cyborg Youth

Following Haraway, deconstructing the politics of the cyborg requires a feminist political economy of both the objectivity and subjectivity of youth, where communication technology and human biology are both crucial tools for unpacking how young people recraft their bodies in each technological moment. In her work, 'Intersections and New Directions on Feminism and Political Economy', Ellen Riordan (2002) notes that:

> Feminism seeks to understand and theorize power as it pertains not only to women, but also to other groups marginalized on the basis of their race, class, sexuality, religious background, ethnicity, age, disability, etc. A feminist political economy ... seeks to understand these interconnections and how different groups of people are politically, economically, and socially disenfranchised. (Riordan 2002: 13)

It is true, as Haraway states, that technologies 'are frozen moments of the fluid social interactions constituting them', but they are also 'instruments for enforcing meaning' (Haraway, 1985/2006: 119). These tools, new technologies, and digital devices embody and enforce social relations—and in doing so, impact young people disproportionately—and this marginalization is then multiplied across intersectional lines of race, class, gender, sexuality, ability, and more. However, despite this crystallization of unequal power dynamics in the technology, Haraway is also quick to point out that the inequities of the tool are not fixed or static, since the boundary is permeable between tool and myth; and as story-telling creatures we possess the possibility to use the tools to speak back and tell different stories.

Another way of putting this point is that although the objectivity of cyborg youth is partially constituted through their interaction with media and digital technologies, they can resist the dominant meanings and create their own subjectivities. That is, women can submit to or resist patriarchal images of women, while people of color can resist racist constructions of race and ethnicity and create their own identities, and deconstruct hierarchies between white and Black, with slogans in the 1960s like 'Black is Beautiful!', or by asserting in the contemporary moment that 'Black Lives Matter!' Further, all individuals can question the politics of representations in media narratives and depictions of gender, race, class, sexuality, and the other constituents of identity, calling out and critiquing sexism, racism, classism, or homophobia in the media. Yet this critical decoding of media requires the cultivation of critical media and digital literacies so that individuals can be the subjects of their own creation, rather than the objects of domination.

Critical media and digital literacies are distinguished from many varieties of media and digital literacies through the engaging of the politics of representation and the dynamics of gender, race, class, sexuality, and identity (Kellner and Share, 2019), with active decoding and in some cases contesting dominant representations and, for instance, sexist, racist, or homophobic media representations presented as objective norms. The media provide role models for right and wrong behavior, style and fashion, social role models and professions, and show how institutions function from the world place to law to policing and to business and politics that are dominant social forces in state capitalist societies. The task of the creation of cyborg youth who resist sexism, racism, homophobia, and other biases thus requires critical media and digital literacies that we will further discuss in the next section.

Critical Digital Literacies for Cyborg Youth

What are the Critical Digital Literacies necessary for Cyborg Youth to negotiate the high-tech future and deal with a myriad of questions concerning schooling, jobs, family, media, and the future? In one sense, the situation of contemporary youth encompasses the betwixt-and-between period negotiating from childhood to adulthood that has been the perpetual adventure of youth through the ages. Youth must negotiate its relations in the family, with their cohorts, with schools, and institutions like the law, the police, jobs, and business, as well as the demands and challenges of society at a point in time in history. As explained by adolescent psychologists, such as Hall or Freud, or even Erikson and Piaget, this stage of development involves finding one's position in the world, navigating social and cultural expectations, defining and redefining social relations to institutions, and developing physiologically as an individual human being (see Gennaro, 2010).

Like the previous generation that grew up with broadcast media and plunged into social media at an early age, today's digital youth are 'early adopters' of new technologies who have grown up with a cornucopia of digital devices, depending on their economic class, region, and circumstances. They spend more time on social media and with their digital devices than did previous generation of youth with their media.

In fact, the change in media use is so stark, that if we compare American teenagers in just a five-year period, from 2014 to 2018, we see a significant uptick in social media engagement. According to PEW Research data, in the United States of America, teen access to smartphones rose from 73 % of teens surveyed in 2014–2015 to 95 in 2018 and usage rates spiked to almost half of all teens claiming to use the Internet 'almost constantly', including social media visits 'several times per day' (Anderson and Jiang, 2018). This engagement, according to PEW Research, is not just about conversations or socializing with friends. The engagement and practices of young people online occupies several key roles in youth identity formation and development: there is play, there is socializing with peers, there is social-self presentation, there is the exchange and gathering of news and ideas, and even (in large part as a response to Covid-19) these spaces currently are occupying primary spaces for education.

Hence, Critical Media Literacy is a necessary component of Critical Digital Literacies (CDL), which are necessary for survival in the high-tech world of the present and future. Print and Broadcasting Media are still major forces in the economy, polity, social life, and a diversity of contemporary cultures, even if they are accessed through digital devices and circulated further through digital circuits of communication. There was once concern that the Internet would replace previous forms of news and information delivery. Questions were asked, such as, if *The New York Times* goes online, will this be the death of newspapers? Recognizing now that Jay David Bolter's claims of *remediation* as a valuable path for understanding how new technologies builds on previous ones, not to replace, but instead to remediate and incorporate, we see that remediation now perhaps best describes the current technological moment for young people (see Bolter and Grusin, 1999). It may also best describe the process of 'cyborgization' that is occurring to young people themselves too. Cyborg youth have not replaced contemporary youth or contemporary youth experiences, but instead represent for us a remediated version of the self and the processes of youth exploring the world in the digital age.

Critical Digital Literacies necessarily involve becoming literate in high-tech environments and being proficient in the use of social media, digital devices and access to the digital worlds of information, entertainment, games, social connections, and the far corners of the digital world. CDL requires engaging multiple subcultures which involve youth in special interests (not always legal or socially approved) involving sex, exchange of music and video materials, pranks and hacks, secret societies, and spaces not known to their parents, teachers, or even digital culture researchers. Instead, youth themselves are remediating their experiences of *Sturm und Drang* revolts that were once only to occur outside of the home, outside of school, and outside of adult supervision. These 'third spaces' of youth experiences are where a youth's *Bildungsroman* happen, and youth seek their own life paths and experiences are now existing for public display on social media channels.[6]

Critical Digital Literacies necessarily involve becoming literate in all dimensions of high-tech environments including the construction of new spaces and environments. Digital Youth learn coding at an early age and how to make their own environments or to subvert or reconstruct existing spaces. Harry Braverman (1974) discussed how capitalism, Taylorism, and the assembly line deskilled labor and created worker bees subject to the domination of monopoly capital. Haraway argued how the end of the 20th century witnessed a new capitalist structure 'the homework economy', made possible by the new technology and which did not result in just a deskilling of labor, but instead a re-organization of labor where 'the factory, home, and market are integrated on a new scale' and a redefinition of who are the working class (1995: 130). A homework economy for Haraway is about a feminization of labor, a deskilling of labor, a dehumanization of labor, and a merger between the factory, home, and marketplace.

Haraway's analysis raises significant issues around areas of gender, race, sexuality, and ability. For example, if we draw on Haraway's discussion of the homework economy and the 'feminization of poverty' we see that there are real consequences in the everyday lives of women and a concrete example of this at the turn of the millennium can be seen from a quick glance at the lives of single working moms in Canada. According to 2006 Census data, 31.6 million people lived in Canada and reported an average family income of $82,325. Lone parent families earned an average of $42,000 per year, and female parents accounted for 75 % of lone parent families. On average, women in lone parent families reported earning $13,000 a year less than male lone parented families and accounted for almost all of the 2.2 million families who (or one-quarter of all Canadian families) who reported a family income under 40,000 annually (Statistics Canada, 2021).

Furthermore, today's youth face a gig economy where they do not have the security of their parents who may have had corporate jobs with life-time security and benefits, or unionized working-class jobs that at least provided some security and the possibility of trappings of a middle class life, before deskilling or the homework economy took root. Labor in a gig economy, by contrast, is mediated by the demands of an ever-evolving labor market with no security against economic downturns, recessions, or the whims of one's employer. Even the high-tech industry is subject to high turnover and often provides exceptionally high stress workdays (and sometimes nights and weekends). The 2008 market collapse, or the 2020 economic shut down due to Covid-19, serve as clear examples of how volatile the marketplace can be and how those in service-based work in the gig economy disproportionately bear the economic burden without the safeguards and protections of the corporations they service. Thus, today's youth face an increasing unstable labor force and future where it is hard to chart out a career and follow the script of previous generations as they enter adulthood.

Yet this precarious situation forces youth to be able to take on a multiplicity of projects, gigs, and positions that provide ever new digital and interpersonal skills and proficiencies. Thus, critical digital literacies are not only a job requirement for cyborg youth, but they constitute a set of survival skills and life-time proficiencies that are ever evolving, expanding, and mutating, as the high-tech economy and global culture mutates, providing new opportunities and possibilities, as well as new crises to mediate and survive. In the current global pandemic, youth service industry jobs abound in the pandemic gig economy, but they are dangerous and precarious as they will disappear when life returns to quasi-normal (if it ever does).

This situation demonstrates, once more, the dualism of both the appreciation and lack of regard for the health and well-being of our youth.

In this precarious situation, gender roles mutate, as young women as much as young men participate in the gig economy, delivering essential goods, working for Amazon or Walmart or local grocery stores, to provide goods, as well as working on-line to help provide infrastructure for the gig economy and participating in the further digitization of workplaces. Thus, like Haraway's original cyborg, strict gender lines are mutated, and feminism is faced with new issues as cyborg youth mix gender lines and identities and young women take on new challenges, as well as dealing with older ones. For Haraway, in the original Manifesto, changing roles in the economy or capitalism are directly and dialectically related to changing notions of the family. The displacement of the self in the light of advancements in information and communication technologies, creates not only a technological diaspora, but an altered set of gender roles and expectations (Haraway, 1985/2006: 136). In many ways, the reframing of the self in light of new technologies appears to be a larger goal of white capitalist patriarchy, or what has since morphed into the informatics of domination, to reduce all human life into code, into a simple set of binary numbers of 1s and 0s to organize, to categorize, and control.

Conclusion: Cyborg Youth in the Contemporary Moment

Haraway's 'Cyborg Manifesto' is thus still a call to arms against traditional western categories of knowledge binaries. And youth are up to the task. Ultimately the same globalization that exploits, can also unite. For example, look at the ability of activist Greta Thunberg and young people to unite for School Strikes for Climate on September 20, 2019, using social media to co-ordinate student walkouts in 150 countries. The same technology that excludes also unites. While youth in the developing world were typically behind the over-developed world in technology adaptation, the Arab Spring was initiated, and mass upheavals followed, by youth and citizens mobilized through social media (Kellner, 2012). Likewise, throughout the world in 2011, the Occupy and other movements mobilized youth through social media to demand fundamental political change and dramatized an intolerable situation in which the 1 % dominate the 99 %.

Many youth have lived the pandemic year online and have made new connections, projects, and taken on multiple gigs, some of which may propel them into new and unanticipated futures. Life in the digital fast lane is always going to be unpredictable, there will always be crashes and wrecks, but some will cross the finish line and score rewards and bonuses while others will profit from the wreckage. Capitalism is always a risky business and the high-tech environment intensifies the risks, potential crises, and even possible collapse. Life under capitalism for cyborg youth is always a question of what's happening? What next? Where are we going? WTF is going on? Yet possibilities and connections emerge in the most likely and unlikely of places, as Haraway notes, 'if we learn to read these webs of power and social life, we might learn new couplings, new coalitions' (Haraway, 1985/2006: 136).

The cyborg is about challenging the categorization of knowledge, the construction of knowledge, the coding of knowledge and the dissemination of that knowledge as 'fact', demystifying the bias, ideologies, and social construction of knowledge. To critique this mystification, we must recognize how privilege and exclusion work. This process requires a further exploration of binaries such as self and other, or the one who is dominated vs. the forces of domination. The cyborg does not privilege binaries, but challenges dualisms. The cyborg challenges some of the most powerful binaries of Western civilization: mind vs body, human vs machine, nature vs nurture. For with each of these binaries that are challenged by their dualistic nature, the synergy of the cyborg, such that it is not clear who makes up what part or where the division begins or ends between one and the other.

Furthermore, for Haraway, 'our bodies are the maps of power and identity' (Haraway, 1985/2006: 146). Indeed, for today's youth, relations of power and domination and possibilities for self-development and social change are a constitutive part of everyday life. Cyborgs are not innocent but are socially constructed and can be reconstructed. People are not innocent, and of course as already explained to us by Jean Baudrillard, maps are not innocent either. Maps are the original simulacrum, and work to divide, to categorize and to separate us. Maps works to classify, to code, and to construct our perceptions of life, liberty, power, and identity, around arbitrary constructs of citizenship, nationhood, and identities as facts (see Gennaro and Miller, 2020).

Cyborgs, by their very nature, challenge these traditional structures of knowledge creation, construction, and dissemination. Youth as cyborg challenge this too, and are constructing their own maps, projects, and classifications. Perhaps this is why today's cyborg youth, led by activists like Greta Thunberg, force us to rethink our relationship to each and every component of this planet. Perhaps this is why Haraway's concluding thoughts resonate so profoundly decades after the text was written and well into a technological universe where the cyborgs of the last centuries' science fiction novels now roam the streets in earbuds with iPhones, while demonstrating against racism, sexism, or destruction of the earth.

As Haraway reminds us, and we give the last word to her: "The machine is not an *it* to be animated, worshipped, and dominated. The machine is us, our processes, an aspect of our embodiment. We can be responsible for machines; *they* do not dominate or threaten us. We are responsible for boundaries; we are they." (Haraway, 1985/2006: 146)

Notes

1 Informatics of domination is a Haraway term that she equates to the technological social equivalent of white, capitalist, patriarchy (Haraway, 1985/2006: 128), and later goes as far as to say: 'The only way to characterize the informatics of domination is as a massive intensification of insecurity and cultural impoverishment, with common failure of subsistence networks for the most vulnerable.' (1985/2006: 134).

2 Whereas we are writing on contemporary youth and technology, we are aware that the cyborgization of human beings today crosses all dimensions of age, including ourselves and our generations, as well as those before us.

3 Older generations have always attacked the latest forms of youth culture and from film to radio and television to rock and roll and succeeding youth cultures, there have been a succession of moral panics around media and youth—a theme emphasized by British cultural studies in the 1970s and beyond (see Hebdige, 1979; Kellner, 1995/2020).

4 The Greek words *poiesis* signifies aesthetic creation while *technē* signifies technique and technologies. Heidegger argued that *poiesis* and *technē* could inscribe a world, as he and Nietzsche argued Greek tragedy did for the Greeks and Heidegger claimed Holderlin's poetry did for the Germans at a point in history (On Heidegger and poiesis, see Di Pippo, 2000). We will argue that today's cyberyouth find themselves in a new aesthetic and technological world constituted by their digital devices and culture that are aesthetic-technical creations that inscribe their bodies, selves, and relations to the world.

5 It is important to note that this primacy, intimacy, and immediacy are not unique features for the developed world. In fact, in many of the thirty-seven sub–Saharan African nations, the primary access point for online access is via mobile broadband. According to the GSMA, in 2019, sub-Saharan Africa had 816 million SIM connections, accounting for a penetration rate of 77 % of the population. Furthermore, while there were 272 million users mobile Internet users in 2019 GSMA projects that number to almost double to 475 million users accounting for 40 % of the population by 2025 (GSMA, 2020).

6 *Sturm und Drang* are German terms describing the "storm and stress" of German youth struggling into maturity and where the focus of The German *Bildungsroman* (i.e. the novel of experience). These novels described epics of youth gaining experience of the world by writers like Goethe and Schiller through Thomas Mann that documented the adventures of youth forming themselves as individuals and creating their identities and fortunes in the world. Herbert Marcuse wrote his doctoral dissertation on the German *Bildungsroman* which is interesting since Marcuse became a revolutionary role-model and guru for youth himself in the 1960s (see Kellner, 1984).

References

Anderson, M., & Jingjing, J. (2018). Teens Social Media and Technology 2018. PEW Research Centre, 31 May. https://www.pewresearch.org/Internet/2018/05/31/teens-social-media-technology-2018/. Accessed March 29, 2021.

Bolter, J., & Grusin, R. (1999). *Remediation: Understanding New Media*. Cambridge, MA: MIT Press.

Braverman, H. (1974). *Labor and Monopoly Capital: The Degradation of Work in the Twentieth Century*. New York: Monthly Review Press.

Bugeja, M. J. (2007). *Living Ethics: Across Media Platforms*. New York: Oxford University Press.

Di Pippo, A. F. (2000). The Concept of Poiesis in Heidegger's an Introduction to Metaphysics. In *Thinking Fundamentals, IWM Junior Visiting Fellows Conferences, Vol. 9*. Vienna: Institut für die Wissenschaften vom Menschen. https://www.iwm.at/wp-content/uploads/jc-09-03.pdf. Accessed March 16, 2021.

Gennaro, S. (2010). *Selling Youth: How Market Research at the J. Walter Thompson Company Framed What It Meant to Be a Child (and an Adult) in 20th Century America*. Saarbrücken: VDM Verlag Dr. Müller.

GSMA (2020). The Mobile Economy Sub-Saharan Africa. https://www.gsma.com/mobileeconomy/sub-saharan-africa/. Accessed March 16, 2021.

Haraway, D. (1985/2006). A Cyborg Manifesto: Science, Technology, and Socialist-Feminism in the Late 20th Century. In J. Weiss, J. Nolan, J. Hunsinger, & P. Trifonas (Eds.), *The International Handbook of Virtual Learning Environments* (pp. 117–158). Dordrecht: Springer. https://doi.org/10.1007/978-1-4020-3803-7_4.

Hebdige, D. (1979). *Subculture: The Meaning of Style*. Routledge.

Jamieson, K. H. (2018). *Cyberwar: How Russian Hackers and Trolls Helped Elect a President: What We Don't, Can't, and Do Know*. New York: Oxford University Press.

Kellner, D. (1984). *Herbert Marcuse and the Crisis of Marxism*. Berkeley and London: University of California Press and Macmillan Press.

——— (1995/2020). *Media Culture*. Second Edition. New York and London: Routledge.

——— (2009). Towards a Critical Media/Cultural Studies. In R. Hammer & D. Kellner (Eds.), *Media/cultural Studies: Critical Approaches* (pp. 5–24). New York: Peter Lang.

——— (2010). Media Spectacle, Presidential Politics, and the Transformation of Journalism. In S. Allen (Ed.), *The Routledge Companion to News and Journalism* (pp. 116–126). London: Routledge.

——— (2012). *Media Spectacle and Insurrection, 2011: From the Arab Uprisings to Occupy Everywhere*. London and New York: Continuum/Bloomsbury.

——— (2021). *Technology and Democracy: Toward a Critical Theory of Digital Technologies, Technopolitics, and Technocapitalism*. New York: Springer.

Marx, K., & Engels, F. (1975). The Communist Manifesto. In *Marx-Engels-Collected-Works (MECW), Volume 6*. https://www.marxists.org/archive/marx/works/1848/communist-manifesto/index.htm. Accessed March 20, 2021.

McLuhan, M. (1964). *Understanding Media: The Extensions of Man*. New York: McGraw-Hill.

Riordan, E. (2002). Intersections and New Directions on Feminism and Political Economy. In E. R. Meehan & E. Riordan (Eds.), *Sex and Money: Feminism and Political Economy in the Media* (pp. 3–15). Minneapolis, MN: University of Minnesota Press.

<COVNTERPOINTS>

Studies in Criticality

General Editor
Shirley R. Steinberg

Counterpoints publishes the most compelling and imaginative books being written in education today. Grounded on the theoretical advances in criticalism, feminism, and postmodernism in the last two decades of the twentieth century, Counterpoints engages the meaning of these innovations in various forms of educational expression. Committed to the proposition that theoretical literature should be accessible to a variety of audiences, the series insists that its authors avoid esoteric and jargonistic languages that transform educational scholarship into an elite discourse for the initiated. Scholarly work matters only to the degree it affects consciousness and practice at multiple sites. Counterpoints' editorial policy is based on these principles and the ability of scholars to break new ground, to open new conversations, to go where educators have never gone before.

For additional information about this series or for the submission of manuscripts, please contact:

> Shirley R. Steinberg
> c/o Peter Lang Publishing, Inc.
> 80 Broad Street, 5th floor
> New York, New York 10004

To order other books in this series, please contact our Customer Service Department:

> peterlang@presswarehouse.com (within the U.S.)
> orders@peterlang.com (outside the U.S.)

Or browse online by series:

> www.peterlang.com

www.ingramcontent.com/pod-product-compliance
Lightning Source LLC
Chambersburg PA
CBHW050651280326
41932CB00015B/2869